Oregon Shakespeare Festival Actors

Telling the Story

Oregon Shakespeare Festival Actors
Telling the Story

Mary Z. Maher
Alan Armstrong

WELLSTONE PRESS
Ashland, Oregon

Printed in the United States of America

ISBN 978-1-930835-15-3

Library of Congress Control Number: 2014942893

Cover photography: *Jenny Graham, Oregon Shakespeare Festival*
Interior photographs: *Jenny Graham, David Cooper, T. Charles Erickson*
Cover and interior design: *JGB Book Design*

Authors: *Mary Z. Maher and Alan Armstrong*

For copies and information, contact
Jonah Bornstein, Wellstone Press
@ www.wellstonepress.com | 541.488.3831

WELLSTONE PRESS
Ashland, Oregon
www.wellstonepress.com
541.488.3831

DEDICATION

For our actors, all of you,
with many thanks and much appreciation.

Table of Contents

Introduction

I N THE SUMMER OF 2012, Alan Armstrong and I had coffee at the Starbucks near the Southern Oregon University (SOU) campus. We'd chatted over a period of a couple of years about a project that interested us both, which was to interview some of the fine actors we'd admired over the years at the Oregon Shakespeare Festival (OSF) in Ashland, Oregon, and to put their stories into a book. We all wish that more evidence of Shakespeare and his fellow actors had survived—how they rehearsed, how they thought about their roles, how they talked with their fellow actors about their art, how they worked together as a company. A single funeral poem contains most of what we know about the work of Richard Burbage, the company's lead actor. We believe that OSF actors, four centuries later, also have a legacy that needs to be recorded.

Alan had a long acquaintance with the Oregon Shakespeare Festival as the founding Director of SOU's Center for Shakespeare Studies. For twenty-three years there, he created an extensive and fruitful town-and-gown relationship between the

University and the Festival, with symposia, NEH institutes, and other programs that brought teachers and scholars together with OSF actors and directors. He also had interviewed Dan Donohue and Robin Nordli for Michael Shurgot's *North American Players of Shakespeare*, and he was the production dramaturg for seven of OSF's Shakespeare productions from 2006 to 2012.

I had written three books on the performance of Shakespeare, based on actor interviews: *Modern Hamlets and Their Soliloquies*; *Actors Talk about Shakespeare*; and a biography, *Nicholas Pennell: Risking Enchantment*. All of these involved extensive travel to interview hallmark American, Canadian, and British actors such as Kevin Kline, Ben Kingsley, Kenneth Branagh, Derek Jacobi, our own OSF alumnus Stacy Keach, and many others. Before retiring to Ashland, I had directed and was dramaturg at my home base, the University of Arizona.

Both of us had extensive play-watching experience as well, especially of Shakespeare productions, in the U.S., Canada and Britain. We knew that too few good actors are recognized for their talent and their skills. We wanted to remedy that situation by focusing on the Oregon Shakespeare Festival, one of North America's largest theater companies, which stages eleven plays in repertory over a ten-month season to a total audience of 400,000 in its three theaters. The season's several Shakespeare productions are still the cherry that tops the OSF season.

We had a vision. We knew that we wanted to write not for an academic audience but for the playgoers who faithfully return to the Festival each year: locals from Ashland and the Rogue Valley, visitors from the Western states (OSF playgoers travel an average of 125 miles to see the plays), and a growing national and international audience. They include first-time playgoers, seasoned theater-lovers, families who want their kids to see Shakespeare, the grown-ups who have been coming since those parents first brought them thirty years ago, students, teachers, and aspiring theater professionals. We wanted to create a different kind of book made of personal interviews that captured each actor's voice, glimpsed the person behind the artist, explored each actor's particular process, and also sketched the larger collaborative process of a busy repertory company.

The next job was to sit down and make a list. *Who* should be in this particular book? There are around 100 actors in the Festival's company, from young novices to experienced veterans—an embarrassment of riches. Some live in Ashland, send their kids to the local schools, and even buy the proverbial lawnmower (see Mark Murphey's chapter). Others work both in and out of the company over a span of many years. Some come for a few short seasons only and then go their way. We were very lucky that day over coffee. We had each brought in a separate list of our candidates, and they coincided—not exactly one for one, but within negotiating distance of determining the dozen or so we wanted for our endeavor.

We wanted actors who consistently present onstage characters who seem *real* to us. We wanted actors skilled in delivering their lines understandably and meaningfully. We wanted actors versatile enough to excel in new plays as well as in Shakespeare and other classical drama, actors who transport and inspire us. Our choices included both relative newcomers and seasoned OSF veterans. In the following list, however, and in our book of interviews, we have ordered our actors alphabetically, as professional companies' cast lists sometimes do. They are: Mark Bedard, Danforth Comins, Michael Elich, Nell Geisslinger, Jonathan Haugen, Anthony Heald, Richard Howard, David Kelly, Kevin Kenerly, Mark Murphey, Vilma Silva, and John Tufts. After dividing the list between us, Alan and I recorded interviews of our actors. We questioned them about a range of topics: their theater training and early mentors; their preparation to perform a role; their relationships with directors, designers, lighting and sound artists in the collaborative endeavor of theater; their approach to the variety of performance spaces at OSF.

Finally, each actor chose a few specific roles to discuss in more detail. We began with the over-arching idea of discovering each actor's *process*, the art that begins in an actor's training and grows exponentially with experience earned by performing in several dramatic genres on different stages: mastering ways of using the body in movement and dance and stage combat, using the voice with strength and clarity, dissecting a long speech, searching out meaning in the script, memorizing lines. Every actor develops his or her own way of analyzing a character, drawing carefully from what is called *text*, the playwright's written words on the page. Additionally, savvy actors watch other colleagues at work and chat with them about acting. A special result of the interviews was discovering how much invaluable mentoring happens within the OSF company, how open, interactive, and generous these artists are with one another. Our actors shed light on the shorthand in a repertory company, using phrases like "in the moment" or "telling the story," which are understood by each performer in the context of rehearsal and performance, but might not be easily described outside of it. Process is not isolated; it happens inside all of the preparatory steps to performance, and continues throughout the actual performance, the long run of each OSF show.

Because OSF is a *Shakespeare* Festival, the interviews supply abundant information about that specialized genre, but their insights and stories also embrace the other work performed by the company: classics from Marlowe to Moliere to Chekhov, touchstones of American drama from Tennessee Williams to August Wilson, and new plays like Bill Cain's *Equivocation*, Mary Zimmerman's *The White Snake*, and Robert Schenkkan's *All the Way*, which OSF audiences are lucky enough to enjoy and critique the first time around.

The pages here are a snapshot in time, documenting the immediate past, especially the 2009-2014 seasons. Our rich and varied range of actors includes some who have a long history with the company, and some who are just beginning to write their own career stories. Veteran actors talk about working with former OSF Artistic Directors Jerry Turner and Henry Woronicz, and Mark Murphey talks about OSF founder Angus Bowmer, providing us a sense of the Festival's genealogy. Other actors tell how their careers were nurtured by Libby Appel, artistic director from 1995-2007. Iconic names familiar to OSF audiences—Jim Edmondson, Ed Brubaker, Barry Kraft, Bill Patton, and many more—weave in and out of the actors' personal histories.

It was exciting to glean stories from actors on both ends of the spectrum. We hope that you enjoy the fresh voices and vibrant energy of the relative "newbies," which is how I think of Mark Bedard, Danforth Comins, Nell Geisslinger, and John Tufts, still mapping out a future career and establishing a way of working: Mark Bedard zipping through *commedia dell'arte* to Groucho's comic genius; Danforth Comins striding forth as Coriolanus and then cresting Tennessee Williams' heroes; Nell Geisslinger compassing Kate and Stella as a virtual comet of a newcomer; and John Tufts traveling the royal road from bad-boy Prince Hal into that "star of England," Henry V.

We set these stories against those of the masters, some in their consummate stride, others mapping out the twilight of richly satisfying careers. Michael Elich is the high achiever of delicious roles; he bites them off, then offers them up to us in a burst of panache. The wise and witty Anthony Heald, once a director and now an actor on stage, screen, and television, marries together the fruits of all his careers. Richard Howard brings the same calm and magisterial focus he earned in classical drama to OSF world premieres of new work. David Kelly doles out his unmatchable and exuberant comic gift, both instinctive and trained. Mark Murphey remembers early days at OSF with wisdom and balance couched in rock-solid honesty. Vilma Silva details her creative sleuthing into the motives of her many fascinating and multi-faceted characters. And that's not all. Kevin Kenerly heats up Hotspur with the same energy that he brings to a long line of August Wilson protagonists. And you'll find out why Jonathan Haugen can handle Faustus in one breath and then deliver Henry Higgins in glorious operatic bursts of song. Listening to them weave their stories, we were continually inspired by the concentration and focus of these actors as they worked to find their groove.

Now, some nuts and bolts, because there is a way to read this book. Early on, Alan said to me, "You just turn on the tape recorder, and it flows." So, after the interviews were completed, we decided to jettison the traditional Q&A format, with its stop-and-start interruptions. We eliminated our voices completely from the final text. This left the actors *telling the story*. The actors' interviews naturally gravitated toward oral history and personal memoir, as they stuck to the topic of the actor's process, beginning with their training, then moving on to the challenges and insights born of their experience onstage and in the rehearsal room. All the chapters contain related kinds of information, yet each one sings its own tune. Transmitting each actor's distinctive voice was an imperative of our work, because it is a large component of "personality," a quality that feeds directly into acting roles.

You will note that a variety of alternative, even contradictory ways to prepare a role are disclosed in these interviews. Inevitably, even preferably, there are differences among actors. Does this mean that one of these methods is absolutely correct and another dead wrong? Do Van Gogh's painting techniques trump Picasso's? Of course not. The creative process not only permits but *encourages* individuality and innovation. The actor's process is something that deserves wonder and respect rather than a critique. Work habits that evolve within the acting profession are shared, copied, and refined. Analyzing, reflecting, and exploring these, each artist finds an individual journey to the end result. These work practices can change over time as well. Readers of this book have the luxury of seeing and comparing a treasure-trove of ideas about acting offered by artists whose work has won applause for a number of seasons. The interviews, however, confirm a premise of our project: *there is no single, correct way to approach performance.* Whatever the script, no artist works exactly like any other.

The chapters following are not, and could not be, minutely accurate transcripts of the three to four hours of interviews that we conducted with each actor. Spoken discourse is full of extra connectors, indefinite pronouns, false starts, interruptions, redundancies, and in-house actor talk. Inevitably, it took some gentle editing, some winnowing and compression of the transcribed interviews, to clearly capture what our actors had to say about their process, while still preserving faithfully each actor's singular and authentic voice.

We've reduced the longer résumés of each actor to introductory blurbs at the head of each chapter, listing recent and memorable roles played by the interviewees at OSF, because it is the Festival story we are focusing on. Each year in July, actors are offered a one-year contract—never longer—to perform here. Contracts are offered to performers currently in residence, to former company members returning from work elsewhere, and to new actors from outside the company who have earned a place by auditioning. There is a constant flux in and out of the acting company of people at all levels of skill and experience. None of our actors has worked *only* at OSF. Most have considerable professional achievements in a number of theaters nationwide, as well as in film and television. You can access that fuller list in any OSF playbill from the current season.

A brief word about "Words, words, words." Occasionally, the Thomas Theatre is referred to as "the Thomas," or remembered by its earlier name as the "New Theatre." The Allen Elizabethan

Theatre is sometimes called "the Lizzie." Notable OSF figures like Turner, Edmondson, Appel, and Rauch are just plain Jerry, Jimmy, Libby, and Bill when actors talk. Technical rehearsals (involving lighting and costumes and sound effects, and running tediously from one lighting and/or sound cue to another) come near the end of the rehearsal process. These are followed by dress rehearsals, usually full run-throughs of the play in full costume and with all props. Actors always refer to these merely as "tech" and "dress." We've generally left widely used actor jargon intact, in keeping with the informal style of actual conversation. Rather than pepper the chapters with footnotes, we have, where necessary, silently inserted surnames, work titles, dates, or other information. This will help you track who "Bill" (Bill Rauch, OSF Artistic Director) or "G. Val" (G. Valmont Thomas, actor) is, and tell which of OSF's many productions of *The Taming of the Shrew* is being referred to.

A few final words to put our actors in context. The Oregon Shakespeare Festival is a "destination Shakespeare" site. Roughly translated, that means that tourists are charmed by Ashland, Oregon, the town, with its fine restaurants, alluring shopping, outdoor recreation, and general laid-back ambience. Like Celia in the Forest of Arden, they like this place, and willingly could spend their time in it. But most of them really come for the theater. After all, OSF is a top-notch, Tony Award-winning company, not only for its talented actors but for its varied repertory, directorial excellence, and the superb technical support provided by costumers and lighting, scenic, and sound designers. As the director of an East Coast Shakespeare company said to Alan, "OSF is our gold standard."

During the two years we worked on this project, lines from that first and greatest of modern plays, *Hamlet*, often crossed our minds—from Hamlet's instructions to the traveling actors visiting Elsinore ("Speak the speech, I pray you, as I pronounced it to you, trippingly on the tongue. . . .") to his instructions to Polonius about them ("Let them be well used; for they are the abstract and brief chronicles of the time."). The lines that resonated most with us come in a moment when the prince is angry at those pests, Rosencrantz and Guildenstern: "You would play upon me, you would seem to know my stops, you would pluck out the heart of my mystery. . . ." At times, Alan and I felt we were doing just that as we worked on this book. Yet, we discovered that the secret of being natural and believable onstage—that apparently simple achievement that characterizes all of our actors here—may be ultimately elusive, always a bit shrouded in mystery. We trust that whatever light these chapters cast on the actors' process will make their achievement shine even brighter for you, as it has for us.

—*Mary Z. Maher*
Alan Armstrong

Mark Bedard as Groucho in *Animal Crackers*. Photo: Jenny Graham, OSF.

Mark Bedard

In 7 seasons at OSF, Mark Bedard has played, among other roles, Mr. Hammer (Groucho) in *The Cocoanuts*, which he also adapted, and Jeffrey T. Spaulding (Groucho) in *Animal Crackers*; Truffaldino in *The Servant of Two Masters*; King Ferdinand in *Love's Labor's Lost*; Launcelot Gobbo in *The Merchant of Venice*; Balthasar in *Much Ado About Nothing*; Moth and 1st Fairy in *A Midsummer Night's Dream*; Antipholus of Ephesus in *The Comedy of Errors*; and Biondello in *The Taming of the Shrew*.

EVERYONE IN MY FAMILY SINGS, especially on my mother's side, so I just took that for granted as a kid. She was a big influence even though she was a bit shy. She got us all the right movies, *Pirates of Penzance*, the Disney films. She loved that stuff. Anytime there was a family gathering, my uncles and my aunt would pull out guitars and sing pretty much everything—from barbershop songs to Peter, Paul and Mary. People would join in and harmonize on popular songs. There were Christmas carols at my Dad's family, and though he was more business-minded, he encouraged singing. An aunt on my father's side sang on cruise ships—she was the only one I knew from show business. I didn't tell the family that I'd declared drama as a major in college, but once they came to OSF and saw what I was doing, they came along with it.

Growing up, there was a school pageant or a talent show, but I never thought I would go into stage acting. I would dabble in this or that, play in a band, play football. At my all-boys' prep school, I did a ton of homework. We also performed plays with our sister school, and so I auditioned for *Guys and Dolls*. They cast me as Sky Masterson in my first role. It was *so* much easier than football, where I got beat up all the time—suddenly I thought I should have done drama all along. In college, I auditioned for *Jesus Christ Superstar*, and then *Oklahoma!* came along and I got cast in both. I did these plays *for fun*, never realizing that this could be what I wanted to do with my life. When I went to a professional theater performance, I always thought it was special and that you had to be really great, so I guess I didn't consider myself worthy.

A girlfriend knew a director at the community college, Tom Amon, who sat me down and sort of smacked me around and said, "Hello! Wake up! You can do this!" It was the first time anyone had talked to me like that. He said I could make it as an actor and suggested I get a theater degree. It was the first time I ever had any clarity in college or in my school life, and that totally turned it around for me. Now I began looking for parts for a serious actor. I did John Proctor in *The Crucible* and I thought— American classics, I can see me doing that; it felt special.

When I made an educated decision to become a theater major, I understood how competitive and unstable that was professionally. I'll never forget this period, because I hit the books and became a straight-A student for the first time. I knew I had to make up for lost time because my classmates had been doing theater from age six—they were "theater kids" and I was a jock. I wanted to work my way toward playing Clifford Odets and Tennessee Williams (I did play a gangster in *Paradise Lost* in my third season at OSF).

I went to a community college and then transferred to UC Irvine in my junior year. This was a graduate-focused theater program, and grad students would get all the roles—the rest of us could audition for what was left. So I went back to my community college to try out for big roles there, and it worked: I played Hamlet and got more stage experience. At UC Irvine, I had begun acting training and found really good educational offerings. I decided to audition as a spear carrier there. I'd forgotten that I was older than all the undergrads and had far more theater credentials and stage experience. I was super-prepared, knew what to select for audition materials, and UCI cast me in two lead roles there my final year.

The undergrad acting classes were not as satisfying as the ones I wanted to take on the graduate level. However, Eli Simon taught an amazing class on clowning, Richard Brestoff taught film, and Tony Kubiak was very good on playwrighting, so I'd talk to them and pick their brains. I was determined to get my money's worth out of college. I took Bill Rauch's directing class because I thought it would make me a better actor. He was contracted to teach for three years at Irvine. I knew he was the director for Cornerstone Theater, but I didn't really know what that meant. He liked my work in one scene from *Doll's House*, so I acted in other folks' scenes in class as well. He told me he was a guest director at the Oregon Shakespeare Festival—I didn't confess that I'd never heard of it, although I had heard of Utah Shakespeare Festival. He arranged for me to audition at OSF.

A month after that, Bill was announced as the new artistic director there. I had gotten a callback from Penny Metropulos and Tim Bond, but I didn't get an offer, and Bill thought they hadn't taken me. Mid-December came, I had $2000 in the bank, and I was packing up to go to New York to find an apartment. I got a call from David Dreyfoos at OSF. Someone had dropped out of his contract at the last minute, and he said, "Can you be here in two weeks?" I said yes, cancelled my New York trip, and drove to Ashland.

I've been fortunate in my career, ready for the lucky breaks when they come—I try hard to live up to that. The whole game is about contacts and networking.

In Rauch's directing course, Bill emphasized that a great director discusses with the actor what happens within a scene and *why*. Then he leaves the *how* up to the actor. Regarding the how, I knew I should not be so rigid. I don't need to nail it every time. There will come times when you nail it Tuesday, Wednesday, Thursday, and then you don't on Friday. Failure is a necessary component of process and performance. That part is hard to come to terms with and to be *okay* with that.

Every role I prepare is different from the one before, and I am relearning my process for each one, but there are also some things I do the same each time that continue to work for me. I'm still young, and my process will keep evolving. I read *The Audition* by Michael Shurtleff, a great book about both acting and preparing an audition. It is the starting point for my process. You can take the principles in that book and apply them to acting a part. The author states that technique is there for you when inspiration fails: when the magic is not happening, you fall back on technique. Another book, *Backwards and Forwards* by David Ball, covers script analysis, structure, and plot analysis.

So I have these techniques I use where I scrutinize the journey of the character, looking at where he ends up, and then try to discover how I can make the beginning as opposite to that as possible—how I can start the play in a different place from where my character finishes? Sometimes the character has a very small or a subtle journey; sometimes the character is a clown and has a huge journey.

Much of the work is similar to college prep, and I'd had really good private schooling when I was a kid. I do as much research as possible for each character—about the part, what the part means to me, and how I play it. A lot of my process is about structure. What is the structure of the play, what is my character's function in the play, how do I fit within that, and how can I highlight that information? If there are deficiencies in the play, how can I try to fill those? *Can I* fill those—often requires a talk with the director.

Every script is different and every role is different, so my process may shift and develop. As soon as I am cast, I analyze all those structural issues because once I feel I have it all under my belt, *then* I can start living in it and breathing in it and figuring out where the truth and the humanity lie in the role. I am a very Type A personality, so I have to get that structure into place. That's it in a nutshell. I have certain guideposts, a checklist that I use to do the research—the more I do, the freer I feel in playing the role. I go back to my books and read over them again, taking lots of notes on the play. A point comes when I can't think about it anymore. It's just time to get up and do it.

I started self-teaching in community college. We had a Shakespeare unit where we were doing scenes, and a couple performed the balcony scene. The professor coached Romeo in saying, "But soft, what light through yonder window breaks . . ." telling the actor to speak right to the audience and to be delighted. All of a sudden, I was *riveted.* I'd totally written off Shakespeare, because I'd never seen it done live at that point. So I dove in, reading the balcony scene, and decided I would have to hit *that certain* word more, to emphasize it so that the line would make sense: I began to engage.

My process now is to imagine that the audience has people like the former me in it (as I was at the beginning of my language study), and I decide how to say the Shakespearean line so that it will make sense to that kind of person. How can I make this soliloquy inspire *them,* especially to see more Shakespeare? I do not perform it for people who already know Shakespeare well or who know this particular play very well.

When I approach a Shakespeare play, the first thing I do is read it, and if I don't understand something, *I do not look things up.* I am someone imagining the whole play as I read, and I say to myself—I think that line means this or those images mean such and such. As I go back and check myself on text, I find I am getting more and more correct about those spots as I do more and more Shakespeare. I go back and work with those not-so-sure-of lines because I want to make certain when I perform them that I can make them clear to an audience. Then I start looking at *why*—looking up words and deciding how I can make each word specific for the listeners. That's my whole approach to language: how can I deliver the maximum clarity to an audience? Once I have those words defined and under my belt, I can work on making the line come alive and be real for an audience.

I tend to be irreverent with Shakespeare. It's already poetry, so I don't have to work to make it sound like poetry. My job is to tell the story of it, to deliver the message and the sense of it, to figure out the action of it, and to perform those things clearly. If the character needs to actually sound like the meter is important, that's a role decision. Most often, I don't want it to sound rhythmic or rhyme-y—I can't stand that. As an audience member, I don't understand it when it is too versified, so why would I want to speak it that way as an actor? Also, I like to model after someone I've enjoyed in a Shakespeare role who speaks the language naturally. That's my aesthetic.

I found working in the schools tour for OSF to be hugely informative. I've participated in those four times. Through OSF, we do Shakespeare for middle school through high school students, and if I am going to reach them on that day, I've got to have it make sense for that audience. That experience is more immediate because the kids are *not polite*. They are not going to sit there and say, "Yes, yes. Bravo." They can get totally distracted, and they let you know if you are not clear.

My process in playing King Ferdinand of Navarre used a number of these ideas. I try to rent versions of the play on film and TV, to get my ideas swimming and percolating. I read critiques of performances of *Love's Labor's Lost*, and the main thing I agreed with (I don't always agree with critics' essays) was that the show does not have a lot of plot. Barely anything happens, and there is a lot of fluff. I love doing comedies, but my favorites actually have substance and something solid to say.

Having the structure of the scenes and the possible issues within the play in my mind, I started looking at what my character's function really was. I began to notice that any bit of foolishness got established by King Ferdinand. He's the one who created the oath about the men not being able to see women. He's the one, in a sense, who made Berowne renege on the oath so that the men *can* woo the women. As I approached this role and moved into it, my main thrust in rehearsal was, "Okay, whatever fun we inject into this play, *my function* is to make sure we all take this oath seriously. Because there is not much plot. What little bit is there, we're gonna milk it for what it's worth and we're gonna hang onto that." So, I am going to be really a hard-nosed king. I wanted to set it up seriously but keep to a sense of childish fun in the balancing act, bringing together what we do within the performance and what I see as my function in the play.

In the second scene, we meet the women in the play, Maria, Katharine, Rosaline, and, of course, my match, the Princess of France. I'd seen other versions where the king goes gaga over her, but I felt that is not my job here. Other characters may do that, but not me. So a lot of that production was about my wire-balancing act about how much I can maneuver within this fragile plot. Once I have a good sense of that in place, I can live it and make the king a real person, trying to figure out why he would make particular decisions, what in his life makes him find importance in the things he does. You start to think—well, where are his parents and why are they not mentioned in the play? The princess' father has just died, but my father must have, too, because clearly I am the king. Have I been messing about all my life and suddenly I have to stop all that and go cold turkey, forswear all those excesses? There is this young and impulsive quality within the play—a bit like "This is our fort and no girls allowed." Kids take those kinds of things very seriously. So that was my function—it's my kingdom and I say we don't want any women here.

The only times the story moves forward often happen when Ferdinand is speaking. Rosaline and Berowne are bantering and cracking jokes and one-upping one another—the king's language is much more straightforward. I took great comfort in that, even in the first speech. When I begin a Shakespeare play, I feel the weight of "Can I get the audience on board, tuning their ears to the language, so that we can move this story along?" The whole first speech sets up the plot: he's trying to convince the young men that they will be famous if they all keep the vow. I highlighted that by delivering it directly to the audience, the weight and importance of that first plot stroke. Actually, I had an easier job than Berowne, who is a super-brainy fellow, very intellectual, and uses all sorts of metaphors and other rhetorical devices, expounding and taking time to elaborate. (I played that role later on at Shakespeare and Company in Massachusetts.)

I loved Kenneth Branagh's movie version of *Love's Labor's Lost* because the text was so clear. However, it was best when they *weren't* singing. The songs felt forced and weren't that related to the language in the play—like "I'd Rather Charleston than Follow the Oaths." They were trying to appeal to a non-Shakespearean viewing audience to get them involved in Shakespeare. Good sets and costumes, and solid work on that speech about how Berowne can't believe that he's in love. (The earlier BBC version did not have a sense of fun, and it was more about how deliciously smart they all think they are.)

In our production, Michael Winters as Holofernes, the pedantic schoolteacher, was brilliant with the language. He is one of the people I really like to watch as an actor. Anyone I admire (I picked this up in college), I know I have to soak up that information, and where else could I get it? This is an important part of being self-taught. So, books and interviews are part of my groundwork, and when I run into a great teacher, I watch and listen. The actors I most admire never stop learning or trying new things. I want to stay humble and not act like I know everything. If a guy like Winters has a certain take on a scene, I want to hear that. What is his process? How did he learn what he knows? Sometimes I sit in the vom [vomitorium] and watch certain actors do things over and over again.

David Kelly is another actor I watch. I notice he never does the same scene the same way twice, no matter what the play is. I've only recently started doing that in *Servant of Two Masters* and *Animal Crackers*. I'm not comfortable with it normally because Type A people like to find the perfect way to do the scene and do that over and over again, but David is always toying with the scene. I'm trying to tune into that idea more. I'll watch him do a scene and wonder, "How does he do that?" I am always observing so I can pick up on what other actors are doing.

I also like working with Vilma Silva and Robin Nordli. How do they come up with those right choices? How did they know the moment was going to be that good? So, I observe and I get advice from people like Robynn Rodriguez and Christopher Liam Moore. The great thing about OSF is that there are people who take you under their wing. There are great resources and it's such an open company, many of whom I consider both friends and mentors. Although it's still important to go out and experience doing plays in other theaters and to see what the rest of the country is doing, there are so many talented people and so many support systems right here.

We have a program at OSF, started twenty years ago, called SHARES. It stands for Shakespearean Actors Requiring Employment Soon. It was established and funded by actors, and we fly in directors from all over the country. We get them housing and tickets to shows, and they audition us. Since we find out whether we are returning for the next season every July, SHARES helps us find work for the next season before this one ends. This is good information to have and aids our careers immensely. I've helped run the organization, and I know how valuable it is: you meet new people when you work for OSF. After director Jason Minidakis saw me here in *Servant*, I got cast to play Didi in his Marin Theatre production of Beckett's *Godot*.

Now, Posthumus in *Cymbeline*—whom I performed at the

Shakespeare Theater Company in Washington, D.C.—you take Romeo and Othello and put them together and make them a little more dislikeable, maybe throw in some Bertram, and you've got Posthumus. That was a really hard role. I look at the structure first, right? Posthumus makes a mistake in accepting a wager with Iachimo about his wife, an unforgiveable move in the eyes of a modern audience. However, there has to be something redeemable about him, otherwise Imogen, who takes him back at the end of the story, is a complete fool, which we know she is not. But his better side is not terribly visible within the scenes we get to watch, nor within the text. We never get to see what happened before the play began or the back story, or any of that. He has a lot of speeches, three scenes at the beginning of the play, where he makes more bad decisions, and then he disappears until Act V, where he has three or four soliloquies when he goes to battle. Figuring out his character arc took some juggling.

Dan Molina played him here in 2013. The director was very smart to have an actor play him who looks very young, because it helps the audience see that he can be impulsive and easily led. The good thing about the character is that, with misinformation, he impulsively orders Imogen's death, and the next time we see him, three acts later, he regrets what he's done. It was obviously a heat-of-the-moment stupid response and he realizes it. I like Dan's acting a lot.

Launcelot Gobbo in *Merchant of Venice* is another difficult part. I'd never played an anti-Semitic clown before. In his first entrance, he comes out and says, "Ah well, the Jew over here . . ." and he's trying get laughs at Shylock's expense. The comedy is uncomfortable at times. The thing I noticed about structure is that Launcelot has a definite role to play: he leaves Shylock's house, he helps Lorenzo and Jessica get together by passing information along, and he helps them elope from Shylock's house. As the play goes along, Lorenzo and Jessica and Launcelot often get left at Portia's house in Belmont, while the main plot, Shylock's trial, continues. The time in Belmont becomes a secondary plot with those three characters hanging out at her place. What does that mean? Why does the audience care about them there? The beginning of the play is relatively easy but the latter part is much more difficult to figure out.

Launcelot starts out as an endearing clown, and despite his shortcomings, he can make an audience laugh. There are a couple of ways to go. Do we want him to turn into a jerk at the end of the play? *Merchant* is classified as a comedy, where everyone comes together and marriages happen at the end, but there are so many different directions possible. I'm the kind of actor who needs to know where my character winds up because I can't plan the beginning until I know that. Not knowing the end throws me up in the air, because my job is to know his journey.

So it's a tricky play. There is that ring plot going on, with Nerissa and Portia testing Bassanio and Gratiano. The original play ends up happily but it is also somewhat anti-climactic. *Merchant* has always been a challenging play to do, and nowadays we do it with community involvement to tone down the anti-Semitism. Yet, it would be a tragedy not to perform the play at all, because we never want to forget our history—then indeed we are destined to repeat it.

I've also performed my first Samuel Beckett now. I'd only ever read *Endgame,* so performing *Waiting for Godot* at the Marin Theater was a huge introduction to that playwright. Beckett modeled the characters on the comedy team of Laurel and Hardy, and I played the clown-like tramp named Vladimir/ Didi. The material is deep and bleak, and it questions whether there is any hope in the relationship between Didi and Gogo. I fell in love with this meaty and relevant play. However, reading Beckett off the page is impossible—you wonder what the characters are talking about. Once you get on your feet in rehearsal, you start making the connections and you hear why the character said each line. That process is similar to playing Shakespeare.

People kept telling me how lucky I was to have a Beckett

under my belt, and that I'd appreciate working on that play, and I did. In the student matinee, the kids enjoyed it. They were much freer, and the lines didn't have to make complete sense for them because they were there to have fun. The adult audiences did not laugh, so you got to see how different generations reacted to the play. One evening, the movie actor Robin Williams came backstage—he told us about his playing Gogo in New York in 1988, with Steve Martin playing Didi, and F. Murray Abraham playing Pozzo.

Servant of Two Masters in 2009 was my first big event here. I'd had two seasons as a non-union actor, and now I was getting a big part that would get me into the Actors' Equity union. At OSF, those who are cast in the major roles carry the show and lead by example, and the ensemble follows. I was a new member, I'd read that the play was very funny, and that there was a famous banquet scene, and I wanted to really nail that. I hadn't had any training in *commedia dell'arte* style nor in improvisation. I needed to study up and work the hardest, no matter how hard anyone else worked. God bless this cast. I was surrounded by veteran comedians, but *I* had to bring it. I went in with that energy, and I felt the pressure. Dan Donohue was a mentor, so I often picked his brain because he's done lots of research and loaned me books about *commedia*.

This new adaptation was really funny on the first day when we all read it together. Tracy Young, the director, and her writing partner Oded Gross, created a truly hysterical script. Now all I had to do was not mess it up. The big challenge was that the script specifically said "Truffaldino enters here and picks out people in the audience and talks to them." *I was terrified of that.* The rest of the play I can talk about really fondly because it was all structure, all comic bits, all about timing. I watched a lot of *Looney Tunes* when I was a kid, and I loved math (which is odd for an actor)—so comic timing somehow I intrinsically get.

Tracy Young was a great director. She trusted me. Sometimes we'd stay after rehearsal and have arguments about certain scenes. She would collaborate and let me change a line at certain moments—we were both building this part. I loved working with her, that cast, and that choreographer. Tracy really understands the rigor and structure of comedy but also the freedom that has to be in it. She knows that comedy doesn't have to be all silliness and laughter, that you can deliver great heart.

So many things could have gone wrong in that fast-moving script. Any one person could have messed it up, but we had an amazing team. The choreographer was flexible: "Do you think you can catch the prop if you run this way?" "Yeah, let's try it." We were constantly moving into different rehearsal rooms, staging the blocking in one room, in another a music rehearsal, in another the dance routines, shifting them every half hour, working so diligently to get the show up that all the structured parts of the play felt really good—that only the improvisational and ad-libbed parts I had not done quite yet....

Tracy wisely set up the idea that the other characters held the plot together and were the base, but that I, Truffaldino, had permission to bump into that at any moment. It is such a temptation to interrupt if it is your prerogative to do so, because you can mess with people and do these crazy antics. It could turn into mayhem. Tracy understood that *commedia* was like Dean Martin and Jerry Lewis, because every clown needs a straight man, so she delineated a function to each group. If a comic bit was initiated, my character would do it. I loved that structure. Otherwise, everyone would be deviating and we'd never get to the end of the play.

There were planned ad-lib sections, such as asking the audience for a sandwich, or I could start an extended joke if I wanted to. If a cell phone rang, someone sneezed in the middle of a scene, or a sound cue was late, I'd look up at the crew and react to that—I was taking stimuli from everywhere, and anything was fair game. I was "on" for two and a half hours—great training for our *Animal Crackers* in 2012.

One of the things you experience as an actor is that you can get so nervous you feel like you have to throw up. That usually goes away after the opening night jitters—it never went away for *Servant*. That scene where I was trying to wheedle sandwiches out of the audience was my third entrance in the play. Right before, I'd be sitting in the vom thinking I *was going* to *vom*! I kept thinking about never having done this kind of work before and learning it on the fly. Kyle, my stagehand and my prop man, would try to distract me and tell a joke. I'd think, I gotta *focus*: in the last show we did, one lady said such and such and I did not have a good response and what am I going to do if that happens again?

In every show, I was learning things and putting new ideas into my tool belt. What if someone really hands me a sandwich? Or something *in*edible. During the whole show, people said to me, "You made it look so easy, like you really enjoyed it." But I didn't. Right from the get-go. People handed strange things to me from the audience—cake, leftover steak, piece of homemade pie, Polish sausage. I told the whole cast that if they saw me get handed a piece of food, find a way to steal it from me, because that was what drove the plot, my being hungry. I riffed off of these offerings. If I started a comic bit, it was more interesting if my fellow actors interacted and acknowledged what I'd just done. We had to find that balance, of my starting an ad lib, and their countering with an ad-lib, and then we'd get back into the plot afterwards with a cast member steering us back. I was more comfortable with Truffaldino toward the end of the run because I had more material. In rehearsal, we had assumed no one would have food to give us. The script dictated, "He doesn't eat." So for the first several shows, I'd get food and I wouldn't know how to respond to that. As time went on, I came up with good excuses not to eat, ones I could use twelve shows later. Then, I started to move the goal post and eat some of the food they gave me—if it was only a candy bar, I could still be hungry. I had more options at my disposal.

When I performed Hamlet at school, I did directly address

the audience at times, so I used that technique in *Servant*. The biggest help was the clown class at UCI, where we learned a style of direct address where you never broke with the audience, a *key* piece of training, really. Basically, you never look away. You learn how to connect with an audience. You never lose eye contact with them, and if you drop a prop or something, you have to find it without actually looking for it. So *they* see, and you learn what *they* want to do, and they *guide* you, and they *laugh* when you get it. When you do the right thing, they reward you. It is the most immediate audience connection, so liberating when you stop trying to control how you want them to respond. I loved working in the Thomas Theater, because I felt so close to the audience and the intimacy is perfect for comedy.

In the traditional *commedia* script, there is only the barebones one-page plot, filled with *lazzi*. Cast members developed their own individual comic specialties that could be set into motion. There was the "blackout *lazzi*" which everyone knew how to perform once it was initiated, where we literally shut off all the lights (as opposed to actors pretending they couldn't see anything and fumbling around in the dark). We would blame it on the recession and OSF budget cuts. Jokes and unseen events were described—"Hey, I'm juggling all these deadly objects perfectly!" When the lights came on, silly new props or the discovery of a murder might be revealed.

Kate Mulligan, dressed as a man for this show, was one of the masters—she would always play. When I messed with her head, I could get her to break up pretty often. If I went one way, she would go along, and I loved improvising with her because she was so open. (Sometimes, actors will literally shut off and cease to be in the moment so that they won't break.)

One of my *lazzi* was the famous letter-sealing bit, shared with Kate: I open a letter and talk to the audience as I chew up some bread and make it paste-y and then reseal the envelope with it, while the audience groans, "Eeeuuuw!" In one particular performance, I began to have a bloody nose, which went drip, drip, drip. Soon, it was really gushing and falling onto the letter. An usher handed me Kleenex and I shoved it up my nose, chewing madly all the time and hoping I could finish the *lazzi*—I soaked through *that* tissue! Kate Mulligan came on, not quite knowing the situation, and she said, "It looks like this letter has been resealed with bread. *And with blood!*" I began to sweat because there was a lot of the play left to go before I could leave the stage.

Eventually, the backstage crews gave entering cast members more tissues to wipe my hands on. This came to a head when David Kelly came onstage and pulled an entire box of Kleenex from his coat. The audience totally loved all of this, and finally Elijah Alexander (Florindo) said to me, "Come on Truffaldino. Let's get you out of here and find a doctor." I got a tampon backstage, cut it in half, stuffed that in each nostril, and went back onstage to finish the act. Somehow we made it through the whole show. I came out for the first bow, and the rest of the cast came out behind me as usual. There was a blackout, and when the lights came back up, the entire cast was taking bows with wads of Kleenex sticking out of their noses!

Many people said to me afterwards, with a hint of pride, "I was in the audience during the Bloody Nose Performance."

Groucho Marx was a whole new experience. I was just about to leave Ashland for New York again, to check out the theater world there, and I told Bill Rauch my plans. He countered with, "What if we were about to offer you Groucho Marx?" I wanted to tell Bill I didn't even like the Marx Brothers when I was a kid because I didn't understand them, because they were about anarchy and social comment and not about story. So, the first thing I did was figure out a way to like them and also to admire their ringleader. Even if you are playing a villain, you have to love your character and understand what that person does and why.

I watched one documentary and totally flipped my opinion about the life of the Marx Brothers. They did vaudeville to pay their mortgage, and they found out how to entertain and work with the worst audiences, to hold their attention and make them laugh using any means necessary. Those were the seeds of all that craziness. I read biographies of both Groucho and Harpo. I watched their movies, and I fell in love with them very quickly as I continued my research. I went onto YouTube and looked up other peoples' interpretations of Groucho. I actually thought, "Oh, god, that's terrible" about many of them. Then I remembered that was going to happen to *me*, performing him for 125 times this season. You can't go into a toy shop without buying his face. He's had a huge influence in this country, on comedy, in the world, and I had to play him!

I'd never done impersonation before, but using the books and films, I had to learn how to *be* him and to make it good. I took extensive notes about his movements, the famous "shrugs," the wiggling eyebrows, the cigar, the ad-libs—to get all those characteristics into my toolbox in order to give Groucho-like audience responses during the show. I got his vocal inflections down, listening to his voice over and over again so that I could have the whole impersonation under control. I wanted to be thinking of comebacks without worrying about "am I in his style?" I spent months researching and practicing the rhythms and intonations of his jokes. In rehearsal, Scott Kaiser, the voice coach, helped me with the final bits of the accent, like saying "goils" instead of "girls." I found that Groucho tends to move away from the plot—he reacts to whatever happens around him. Groucho, Chico, and Harpo have free rein to do whatever they want. There wasn't just me—we were a team. Nice.

Groucho's jokes are groaners, all about quantity, not quality. When you look at his dialogue, you see this series of filler jokes until you get to The Good One. None of this makes any sense until you learn about Groucho's process. George S. Kaufman wrote the script for *Animal Crackers*, and then the brothers would come in and add in a joke here and another there, and after awhile it was a monologue of joke heaped on joke. There is a to-hell-with-you attitude about the Marx Brothers that is just delightful.

There was another trial by fire: Groucho would make it a point to add a *new* joke in *every* successive show. He'd always wanted to be a writer, and the way he could write as an actor was by ad-libbing, so, he made every performance different. There was no separation between the brothers in the movies and the brothers in life: we had to capture that anarchy somehow in a live experience, which was super-scary. I was doing more than I was in *Servant* because I was constantly testing the limits of what was I was "allowed" to do—with stage management, with administration, with the audience—exactly what the Marx Brothers would have done. (There are even these stories of them going naked.)

Groucho himself created the makeup I wore. In vaudeville, he'd played Napoleon because he loved making fun of historical characters. He created the famous moustache, and he was always gluing it on, going out to eat, taking it off, putting it back on. One day, he ran into the theater a little late, and he slathered on black grease paint very quickly—the audience laughed just as much at that alteration if not *more* than at the original fake moustache. The theater manager was mad at him, and Groucho said, "What's the difference?" He added bigger eyebrows and waggled them even more. Such a cool story, and it came from a mistake. I'm just trying to look like him when I put on that tattoo paint.

The cast was so flexible. Eddie Lopez was a pretty good target for me to mess with, but then he got clever about stopping me from breaking him up. We changed out our Chico's—actor John Tufts rehearsed and opened the show, and actor Daisuke Tsuji moved into his place when John went out of our cast to perform Henry in *Henry V,* then John came back into the show later. This was a transition, and we weren't sure what the switching off would create: both fit perfectly into the show, almost like Groucho adding jokes to each show. The different change-outs actually helped to keep things fresh and different. Both actors were so good and so versatile. Interesting that Daisuke was an Asian presenting a Jew presenting an Italian—Chico.

Brent Hinkley was more Harpo than Harpo himself. He'd add things in each performance, which was glorious. In rehearsal, we ran into the moat in front of the forestage and then ran right back up on stage. When we ran out into the audience in the second act, that move was created in a performance. Next time, we went up a few rows, and finally we went all the way to the back of the house. By the end of the run, Harpo would stay out in the audience and hijack the whole play! The rest of us just sat down onstage and waited for him. It was brilliant (not to mention he never had to think of making up actual lines).

Near the end of the run, we got really crazy because we could. I knew I had to do something special for Halloween—audience members would be coming in costume. I went to the Renaissance Rose shop and found a weird outfit, basically a Jewish woman with a baby sitting on her back. I felt everyone would expect it to happen in the second act, so I decided to do it in the first act in one of the early "lovers" numbers when the fountain came out and those two began to sing. I started crossing with my face upstage, which looked oddly like Groucho smoking a cigar while he had a woman on his back holding a baby. One of the singers, Eddie Lopez, was keeping it all together, but his partner Laura Griffith lost it completely. Behind the scenes, they heard her stop singing. The whole show stalled, and I yelled, "Get out of the way—I need to go to the pharmacy!" That matinee on Halloween went overtime seventeen minutes, which made it a little tough for the changeover crew to prepare the stage for the evening performance of *Romeo and Juliet*.

For the last two shows, we had Tufts and Tsuji, the two Chicos, coming on together. We pelted them with fake vegetables from the 99-cent store at curtain call. The audience loved it. It's important to remember that actors *like it* when the audience laughs. There is an exchange of energy—they give, and you give back, and they give more.

Our 2014 project is *Cocoanuts,* the name of the hotel in the play owned by Groucho on Cocoanut Beach. He sells dicey real estate in Florida to unsuspecting tourists. He's after a rich society matron, who wants a certain marriage for her daughter, who is in love with the hotel clerk. Of course, the quirky brothers roll onto the scene and complications arise. This was the Marx Brothers' second Broadway show, and their first movie.

For the OSF production, I've adapted *The Cocoanuts* to be less like a vaudeville musical and more like a book musical based on their two highest grossing films, *A Day at the Races,* and *A Night at the Opera,* keeping in as many Marx Brothers' and George S. Kaufman's jokes as possible.

Cocoanuts has a sweet love story once you rearrange the plot, and that makes it a better theater piece. I've put the songs back in, wonderful tunes like Irving Berlin's *Always,* an American standard, as well as other songs that haven't been heard. There is a small orchestra. I gave Zeppo the character development he'd never had before—thinking, "What would a fully-realized fourth Marx brother really be *like?*" In rounding out the quartet, I complemented the hijinks of the three devil-take-all brothers by creating a highly strung Marx brother who in a sense cares *too much* about everything. Additionally, I've collapsed the roles of the bellhops and hotel clerks into one role for Zeppo, played by Eduardo Placer. This puts him at the heart of the love story.

The cast will continue to go crazy with improvisations and horseplay and comic bits, particularly doable with the kind of repertory theater that we have at OSF. Good improvisation comes out of the actors knowing each others' work, and that helps all of us in creating loony stage business and *schtick,* feeding into the kind of jokes Groucho loved—plays on words. Our director David Ivers tells people, "Be careful where you

sit," because this cast (which includes many of the "usual sus-
pects" from *Animal Crackers*) loves audience interaction and involvement.

There is something magical about creating a character. No
matter how concrete you try to be, there is always that mystery
and the unknown quality about how it happens. Your character
is joining with your own personality, so of course it will be fresh
and original. In college I learned that the character is the bones,
but you lay your flesh on it. The structure is set, but you get
to create from there. Every time I get the opportunity to play
a character I've never done before, or to do something in an
entirely different style, I grow more as an actor. And that stays
with you.

Danforth Comins as Mark Antony in *Julius Caesar* (with Vilma Silva as Julius Caesar).
Photo: Jenny Graham, OSF.

Danforth Comins

In 11 seasons at OSF, Danforth Comins has played, among other roles, Stanley Kowalski in *A Streetcar Named Desire*; Mark Antony in *Julius Caesar*; Brick in *Cat on a Hot Tin Roof*; Bassanio in *The Merchant of Venice*; Bertram in *All's Well That Ends Well*; Coriolanus in *Coriolanus*; Cassio in *Othello*; Orlando in *As You Like It*; Lucentio in *The Taming of the Shrew*; Bo in *Bus Stop*; the Dauphin in *King John*; Richmond in *Richard III*; and Benvolio in *Romeo and Juliet*.

FOR ME THERE'S A BIG correlation between athletics and acting. What I learned from playing soccer and basketball and football and baseball was team dynamics, which translated perfectly to working with a cast. Like a team, the show truly is as strong as its weakest link, and you work better when you're challenged by your peers, your collaborators. I went to college on a soccer scholarship, intending to be an electrical engineer, but I got an injury in training camp that first year and my scholarship went away. I felt lost without it. Here I was, twenty years old, and I'd played soccer since I was four. It was all I knew. I stumbled into an acting class to fulfill a general university requirement. I really loved it, partly because I got that same high octane drive, that rush, that endorphin kick when I finished a play as I did when I finished a game. My competitive athletic days dovetailed right into my training as a theater artist.

Bill Becvar, Bill Parker, and Jeff Clapp were big mentors early on for me, at Pacific Lutheran University. It was a small theater program, but I learned a holistic appreciation for the craft. I had to help light the sets, build them and paint them, as well as act on them and stage manage them. Because it wasn't a huge program, Becvar and Parker focused on the art of truth-telling, as opposed to, say, Restoration comedy technique. Just "What is the playwright trying to say? How as a human can you embody that naturally and realistically, to tell the truth?" I will be in their debt forever because they instilled a sense of honesty that I try to approach all of my roles with. If the audience doesn't believe it, then why would they care to watch it?

Because I got into theater late, I realized that I also needed more technique—to understand all the different genres of theater better, how to change your physicality from a contemporary play to a classical play, the difference between acting for a camera and acting for a 1200-seat theater. So grad school was the route for me. The University of Illinois, when I got there, was going through a huge faculty changeover, so I didn't have a continued presence throughout my entire education there— with the exception of the man who did movement for us, Robin McFarquhar. He taught me as much about acting as anyone ever has. I had come from a program that stressed inside-out work, and he really opened my eyes to outside-in work, starting with the physicality of a character. How does that affect the internal life? If you can carry yourself in a certain position, how does that resonate through your knees and your ankles; how does that change your outlook?

My first acting paycheck was in a little summer stock theater on the campus at Illinois. They offered three Equity contracts, and grad students would play the rest of the roles. Every summer I would work in a regional theater, like the Wisconsin Shakespeare Festival in Platteville. My wife Shannon and I both decided when we finished grad school that we wanted to head back out West. So we moved to Seattle, where my mentor at PLU, Bill Parker, had retired and they were looking for someone temporarily to cover his teaching. It was wonderful to have a job right out of grad school, but I knew it wasn't where I wanted to be. I needed to do my own work before I felt like I could teach others.

That's when I got my first big job, at the Utah Shakespeare Festival. Through my Utah work I got the opportunity to come to OSF, initially in 2002 as a non-Equity actor. After a couple of years here, I was not hired back, and went off for a year before coming back to OSF in 2005 as an Equity actor. Richmond, who takes over at the end of *Richard III,* was my first meaty OSF role. Two years prior, my last year of non-Equity, I had a great contract, playing Benvolio in Loretta Greco's *Romeo and Juliet,* with Kevin Kenerly and Nancy Rodriguez in the title roles. I also played all of the messenger roles in Penny Metropulos' production of *Antony and Cleopatra*—quite a lot of dialogue, when you're *the* messenger between Egypt and Rome. But Richmond was the role that established me here, that enabled Libby Appel to hire me as Bo in *Bus Stop* the next year, my first big splash in a lead. I'm forever indebted for that opportunity to play Richmond and for her seeing enough from me in that production to cast me as Bo in *Bus Stop.*

So that was my path from grad school—a smattering of other regional theaters in there, but that was the trajectory: Illinois, Seattle, Ashland. We've been here for the last ten years. Every few years, I take a little break, go do *Timon of Athens* at Chicago Shakespeare or *Hamlet* at the Utah Shakespeare Festival.

I love what we have here in Ashland and OSF, being a part of a company. To sleep in the comfort of your own bed most of the year—which is usually not the case for actors—is a remarkable thing. To be able to experience things that actors often aren't allowed to experience, settling down or having some semblance of roots. While it's important to continue to work elsewhere, to go away every few years to get new inspiration, to meet new collaborators, it's also wonderful to come back and to work in a company where you have a shorthand, where you've had a relationship with someone for ten or fifteen years. You don't have to start out on page zero and say "Hi, I'm Danforth Comins. Is it okay if I touch you on the shoulder here in this scene?" I know that I can grab hold of Dan Donohue as hard as I want to, and he'll be okay with that. I know that I can whirl Miriam Laube or Vilma Silva around and that they'll respond. We don't have to do that delicate dance of meet-and-greet. Which is wonderful and important, vastly important to an artist.

Nine times out of ten when you're doing a play you don't know who you're going to meet. When you don't know anyone, you have even more doubt about how the play is going to turn out, because you don't know the ability level of all the players involved. At OSF you can look at a pre-season cast list and think "Oh, wow! This should be great!" Just on the page, you have high expectations. That doesn't exist when you go off to do a play, walking in blind—which is exhilarating and freeing in its own right. Ultimately I think that the greatest theater has come out of company settings.

With the Utah *Hamlet*, none of the cast knew me. Nor I them, except for the Claudius, Phil Hubbard, who I had worked with in Cedar City in 2000-2001. The first couple of weeks were touch-and-go, discovering how our energies were all going to intertwine. I had been cast before anyone else. Waiting to see how the chips were going to fall, I asked them to consider casting a Gertrude who was physically in her own body, willing to push the boundaries. It might even get abusive in the moment, because that scene with Mom where Polonius is stabbed is harrowing, the climax of the play. Everything in the play falls away from that scene, and I wanted to explore all possibilities.

Fortunately, the director, Marco Barricelli, and I had known each other for ten years. We'd been in the same company but never worked together. Marco wanted my input in the cutting. After we got through Shakespeare's first act, up through Hamlet's meeting the Ghost, I said, "So far I agree with everything you've cut. You know the play, just take it and run with it." So Marco took over and edited the whole play. That was a relief, because I could just lay out all the side-by-side texts with the cut version that Marco gave me and see if there was anything I wanted to insert back, anything that had been missed. All actors need good direction and good administrative help in that area, in particular early on. We'll fall in love with everything, and want to have every line, but especially with *Hamlet*, you need to prune, because most theaters these days are not going to do a production longer than three hours.

My first Hamlet was eight years ago. They say that every seven years every cell in your body changes over. So in that respect, it was a whole new me approaching this amazing, complex, soul-excavating script. That's exciting, to know that I'm a completely different person. And I felt that, because some of those lines were not coming back as easily as I thought they would. Other lines were "Oh, right, I remember how this flows"—which is tricky because I found myself in spots reverting to the way I did it the first time. I had to be conscious of not discarding a great choice but also not hanging on to one because that's the way I did it before. It's a delicate balance. Eight years older, with more life experience, I am a different person. People ask whether working on these amazingly provocative and deep scripts enriches your life. And of course they do. But the quality of the life I live affects my work in these plays as much as the plays affect me. One of the things I find important about Ashland is that growing tomato plants on my back deck plays as much of a part in my art as sitting in my chair and doing that text work.

Morning is my work time. I'll get up, make coffee, sit on my favorite chair. Usually the cat joins me, sits on my lap, and I read and write and cross-reference. So with *Hamlet*, for instance, I'll have my text on 8-1/2 x 11 size paper. On the other side, which is blank, I make columns. For *Hamlet* Marco turned me on to *The Heart of Hamlet*, by Bernard Grebanier, an academic who said "Hogwash!" to Eliot and Freud and all the other literary critics. He said, "Let's just look at the play line by line and we'll see what actually happens in *Hamlet*." Hamlet's not a procrastinator. In fact, he's one of the busiest protagonists you could ask for. He's got to make sure that what that Ghost has said is accurate, because if not, his soul is damned. So Grebanier is one column. I go through line by line, cross-referencing his notes or comments for each scene. The column next to that, this time, is the Arden *Hamlet*. I find the Arden to be very actor-unfriendly, much more scholarly—but you never know where inspiration will come from. So occasionally there'll be one little phrase that I really love in that over-annotated Arden. And next to that will be the *Lexicon* (Alexander Schmidt's *Shakespeare Lexicon and Quotation Dictionary*), the bible that I always go back to, just to gloss each and every word. And then I'll throw in a random couple of editions of the play—the Norton and the Oxford, for *Hamlet*—so I've got four or five columns on the opposite side of the page. Some pages are pretty blank and other pages are completely filled up with my writing.

Take, for example, the nunnery sequence. You could probably play that scene, one of the hardest in the canon, a million different ways. It's so quick, such a shotgun blast, so layered with innuendo. Every line has two or three or five meanings, depending on which editor you believe. I just like to have all that information out there, and know it, so I can choose my own path, in terms of which gloss resonates more strongly. Sometimes none of them will, and it'll just be my own thoughts on the matter. That sometimes can be perilous, other times triumphant, to play in the moment.

After annotating my script, I try to familiarize myself with the text, which is to say memorize—but I don't approach it with the *goal* of memorizing. I just hope that's the byproduct of this intense script analysis. I'll read forward a few pages, then back a few pages, and move through the whole script, going back from where I left off the day before, and then pushing forward a few pages each day. After a month of doing that, a lot of the memorization work is done, because the language has worked its way into the subconscious, and I've thought about every word in every line. I've scanned it, of course, for meter. I know that a line starts with a trochee, or could possibly have a spondee in the middle of it. I know where all those metered feet pop, and then it just sinks in. I find this process far easier than the donkey work of saying a line a hundred times until you get it. You end up having to do that a lot anyway, because there are certain lines that don't get in any other way: "Aye, truly, for the power of beauty will sooner transform itself from what it is to a bawd than the force of honesty can translate beauty into his likeness." Lines like that are such massive brain and tongue twisters that you have to drill them over and over and over again until you get it right. I remind myself to read aloud because I tend to read in my head. While I can glean a huge amount of inspiration and information from reading silently, the sounds of the words are so important—the way they fit in the mouth, the way it feels when too many syllables are crammed into a line or another is made out of only monosyllables.

So as I'm sitting there in the morning, reading out loud, I'll think, "Oh, gosh, that thought makes me jump back," and I'll flip back thirty pages to read another line out loud, because that one resonates. Look how often Hamlet talks about hell gaping open. So I'll look back and I'll try to recall "Where's that other one? Oh, wait, it's in Act III, Scene 4, with Mom," or wherever it is. The best way to describe that early process for me is intense immersion. Now I have what I call my "dirty" script—the script that I've worked on. On the first day of rehearsals I ask for a clean script, which then becomes my working stage script. I can go back and look at my notes, but I can also—because I find this to be a really important part of the process—come to a place where I'm okay to set aside all those months of work and study, and pick up the blank slate again. I don't have to drag that preparatory work around with me, but I trust that it's in there.

In my clean script, I can write down thoughts and blocking and moments of frustration or moments I want to come back to, to get more clarity on. I can write in that script, "still unsure what this line means," and then I'll pull up the old one to help me sort through it. Take, for example, "The insolence of office, and the spurns / That patient merit of the unworthy takes." "And the spurns"—what is that? After I go back and look at it again, I realize, "Oh, right, three different editors had three different versions of what that line means." So free yourself of worrying about this one, and know that the line may wash over to the audience as one of these other three glosses. That's the thing with Shakespeare. You know the audience isn't going to get 100 percent of what's written because even scholars disagree on 100 percent of what's written. Anyhow, the dirty script/clean script is definitely part of my process. Talking about it is like trying to scoop up a handful of sand and not let any of the grains fall. It's different each time out. It has to be, because every character and every role is different. I have learned to embrace and enjoy that.

I try to give myself months to research a role. I like to familiarize myself with any available material that's out there—reading as many editions of the script as I can, or watching a film performance of the piece. I try to do a lot of that work early so that I can then forget it. Everything is borrowed, everything is recycled in some fashion or form, so that enables me to borrow from the greats without having to remember that I'm borrowing from them eight months later when I actually get on stage. Shakespeare requires much more research and much more analytical study. For *Coriolanus*, *The Art of War* was a real inspiration that got me in a martial mindset, and I also studied Plutarch's *Life of Coriolanus*, Shakespeare's source. The research that I did for *Cat on a Hot Tin Roof* was more visceral, just trying to inhabit Brick, trying to put myself completely in his shoes. It wasn't as academic, as cerebral an endeavor. I didn't need to watch more documentaries or movies about alcoholism. So I just jumped in and tried to live in the language, imagine what it would be like to be that guy, have all those things happen to you and your family on one day, in one non-stop three-hour period.

Building a character physically sometimes comes early, sometimes comes late. Brick is a great example. I had to maintain three things about his physicality at all times. One, he's got a cast on his foot; two, he's got a crutch in one hand; thirdly, he's got a crutch in the other hand. That third crutch is a highball of bourbon. This guy is an athlete, at that point just before his body begins to fall apart. He still looks great, still has an athlete's frame and carries himself well, but alcoholism is going to change that soon. If Brick lives another year or two, that potbelly pops out and those muscles deteriorate.

It's also important that he's a caged animal. Maggie's a cat on a hot tin roof, but in some ways Brick is that wounded animal who's trapped in a cage. They're poking him with a stick to get him out of his depression, out of his alcoholism, but they're poking him. So that was about researching how you move if your right foot is in a cast. He only uses one crutch, because he wants that drink in his hand. We decided that as Brick got drunker, the correct way to hold the crutch—on the side opposite the injury— would give way to a more dangerous, precarious way, with the crutch in the right hand, so he could move faster. I eventually developed tendinitis in both wrists.

In the rehearsal hall I noticed that constantly holding on

made my hands tense and taut. Big Daddy has that wonderful speech in Act II: "All of my life I been like a doubled up fist —poundin', smashin', drivin'! Now I'm going to loosen these doubled up hands and touch things *easy* with them. . . ." I remember watching Mike Winters—one of the most generous actors you'll ever work with—opening up that clenched fist and then running his hands down an imaginary soft body below him. Then I thought about all the tension I was holding in my fists, and what grew out of that was a way to end the play at "Wouldn't it be funny if that were true?"

We wanted to have Maggie and Brick collapse back onto the bed. There's a lot of different ways you could play that last moment, whether she pushes him down, or she climbs on top. Stephanie Beatriz and I and Christopher Liam Moore, the director, felt strongly that it wasn't Maggie taking advantage of him, but that he did remember in that last moment that he loved her, and that he was trying to work his way towards forgiving her and himself for what he had allowed himself to do with Skipper. Because Maggie throws the crutch away, I'm just holding on to the bedpost, with that foot lifted up. As I started to lower myself onto Stephanie, the last thing to let go was the hand on the bed railing. When my hand recoiled back—and it kind of happened by accident one day—my hand just naturally went back into a closed fist because I had been clenching it the whole three hours. So the last thirty seconds of the play was not dialogue but physical: I'm clenching that fist and putting my hand on her body and caressing it, echoing that Big Daddy moment. All of that was found because of the physicality of that role—something that Brick learns from Big Daddy, how to unclench those hands that are so bound, so tight, so anger-filled and to allow himself to feel something soft and good again.

That was an outside-in moment. You have to remember that the physical can inform the emotional. We are bodies. You can learn as much from feeling as from seeing, from touching as from listening. Michael Chekhov (*To the Actor*) does work with psychological gesture that always resonated with me, finding a physical gesture that encapsulates the essence of that person in that place and time going through those emotions. When I tear up over that damn AT&T or Hallmark commercial, I think, "Stop, okay, you're tearing up, what is your breath doing right now, what is your chest doing, are you concave, are you folding in on yourself?" I'll have these little schizophrenic moments where I'm really emotional over something. I don't do it in real life moments, say, if my wife and I have an argument. I don't think, "Okay, check in with your breathing." But when I have those moments of conscious schizophrenia, I try to stop and pay attention, because you can take that information and recreate it on stage. When I start to get emotional, my nose starts to get a little drippy first, I can feel my breathing get shallow, I feel a knot in my chest. Can I then physically recreate those symptoms to get back to that emotional state? Often you can, and then the emotion will kick in and produce the desired tear or the desired rage.

If I'm playing a character who's supposed to be winded when he comes in, I'll do fifty pushups right before that entrance. Why fake it? And what do I learn when I'm winded entering that scene? Last year during *Julius Caesar*, as Mark Antony I had that famous re-entrance into the Capitol after Caesar has been murdered. I can't imagine anything less than a sprint from Mark Antony, at least into the outer chamber, before he cautiously walked into the inner chamber. Given the circumstance—a god has just been assassinated—where would that put his breath? He would be panting, and I tried to do a lot of pushups to get my heart rate up, so that when I entered my body was buzzing the way it would if the situation were real. Occasionally I will physically recreate the circumstance that the actor has to be in. I try not to go overboard, I try to remember that it is make-believe, but I also try seriously to put myself in that physical state as well as the emotional state. Ultimately they inform each other. I've found that the one cannot exist without the other; they're the two sides of a coin.

I try to be as much off book as humanly possible when I start rehearsal, because the real work begins once the memorization is done. It's hard to craft a moment with somebody when one eye is on the person and the other eye is on the page. The old unwritten rule is that you hold your script for first blocking and then when you come back to that scene the second time, you shouldn't have a script in your hands. I try to hold true to that. I don't want to get to the fifth act of *Hamlet* and be thinking about lines.

In the beginning of my career, I remember people saying, "Oh, don't learn beforehand, you'll lock yourself in." That may be true for some, but not for me. The better I know the line, the more I can play with it. I was looking over a *Hamlet* line the other day: "For me to put him to his purgation would perhaps plunge him into far more choler." Just playing around with that line in my head, I came up with three different readings that I really liked, because I knew the line well. We'll see which of those three, if any, make it into the final performance. But I may get to that moment in rehearsal and be given something totally different by my partner, and I have to be ready to react to that. Acting is 90 percent listening.

When I'm in the rehearsal room, I try to give 100 percent of my attention. I turn off my cell phone when I walk into the room. I get there early—not walking in at one minute and setting down your bag, but actually getting there early, having your bag open and your script out. You're warmed up and you've checked out the props for the day, you've walked the space and seen what's different. When the bell rings, you're ready to go and to work hard. A late actor is an unemployed actor.

I might be considered a hard-ass in rehearsal. I believe that

we're there to work. To be a violinist in the London Philhar-
monic Orchestra, you have to play for hours a day every day,
all year. The majority of actors don't practice their craft four to
eight hours a day every day all year. When they're not working on a play, how many actors are taking apart monologues,
trying to practice their dialect for Mississippi, or working on
stichomythic banter? Acting is an organic, living art form that
you inhabit with your own person and your own body. Your instrument is yourself. We have a tendency to be—lazy is not the
right word, we just have to check our work ethic. It's too easy to
figure, "Oh, in real life I pick up a glass like this. I know how to
do that, let's move on." But on stage, you're under a microscope,
so you may need to rehearse—"Let's figure out what this moment is where I pick up the glass and you grab my hand." So I
have a strong work ethic in the rehearsal hall.

I'm a firm believer that the world's greatest actor needs a good
director. Just as one can be limited by the script and the material, one can also be limited by the director. It's actually easier to
find a great actor than a great director. To be able to work with
all of those egos and to maintain a vision and to keep the entire
production on track takes a skill that few have, though many
try. A great director for me may not make a great director for
someone else. I don't like having to come up with everything.
I hate it when a director says, "Okay, just get up there and do
it. Let's see what happens." A lot of time can be wasted when
we just start wandering around. If the director actually has an
idea of where he wants this scene to start, by all means tell me,
because I've got a lot of other things in my head. I don't need to
keep in mind where Ophelia's going to enter from. That can be
the director's job.

I like directors that will give me a rough idea of how they
want the scene to flow and where they want it to go on the
stage. That can mean blocking, or where we want the arc of the

scene to go emotionally, and that sets a nice foundation to build that house on. The director helps pour that foundation for all those rooms early. There's flexibility in those floor plans, so that you can put a master suite on towards the end if you feel like it, but those footers are poured, so you can start stacking lumber on it and start building that house. The best directors will give you a nudge in the direction that they want, but they will allow you to take ownership and feel like you've discovered that nudge yourself. The best directors are masters of "You know, why don't you just try going in this direction a little bit more." Then you go that direction, and you discover something that chances are they wanted you to discover in the first place. They had a gut instinct that that nudge was the right direction to move in. So: confidence in the storytelling and in what they want to say with the story, but not heavy enough hands to make every moment micromanaged, because that can paralyze an actor. I've worked with directors who are on you for everything you do, until you're too self-conscious to reach across a table and pick up your sunglasses. I can count the number of great directors I've worked with on my two hands. Laird Williamson, Christopher Liam Moore, Amanda Dehnert, Jimmy Edmondson, Marco Barricelli, Bill Rauch; I've recognized moments of greatness from them as directors.

These days, like a lot of professions, ours is becoming so specialized. The world of directing is no different. If you don't have a directing MFA from one of the pedigree schools, you don't get looked at. What I see in a lot of young directors is an inability to talk to actors, an inexperience of what the craft of acting is actually about. They're just looking for end results and for pictures; they're directing for film on stage. Some of the best directors I've ever worked with in my career have been actors. You have to slay some demons when you're doing big roles, whether it's just stage fright or a prior life experience blocking you emotionally. A good director who has trod the boards, who knows the inside of the craft, can really help actors break through those roadblocks. I've worked with many excellent directors who have never been actors, but 80 percent of my favorite directors have been actors. I am saddened by how difficult it is these days for actors to make the transition into being directors.

Actors continue to live on the fringe of society. What are you? Are you a celebrity, are you a slacker? What's the deal? You don't really work. You tell stories for a living. I think we'll continue to fight those stereotypes, as actors. Someone asks, "What do you do for a living?" *"I'm an actor."* "Oh, what shows have I seen you in?" *"I haven't done a lot of film and television."* "Oh, you're not really an actor, then." We have that conversation. Even with educated people. People don't understand how you can go there, and not really go there, how you can feel those emotions but not feel those emotions. The idea of acting is very foreign for some people. They have preconceived constructs of what it is—not quite scared the way they were in 1590 about being possessed by demons, but a moral objection. Metaphorically, we're still buried in paupers' graves, "outside Christian burial."

I've been blessed with some great parts here, playing less than likeable guys that you're supposed to sympathize with. There's a fine line. My job is to very carefully craft those few moments where I crack open and show the humanness, and then close that shell back up and become that guy again. There was a whole string of roles—Coriolanus, Bertram, Brick, even Bassanio—that make you wonder, "Who is this guy?" Even Mark Antony last year, who can be seen as a hero but is first and foremost an opportunist. I would throw in Orlando, too. The male lead in *As You Like It* is a great exercise for male actors to experience what actresses often go through in plays written by men. It's a lot harder to create an arc when the other person—in this case, Rosalind—does all the talking. I enjoy those tricky nuts to crack, I really do. I find them challenging and complicated.

They keep me up at nights, but they're so much more rewarding when I feel like I've lived up to the words offered me by the playwright.

Even Hamlet, on the page, is not all that likeable a guy; he's pretty mean to a lot of people. You have to figure out where his emotional turn is, where's that moment? One of the big turning points for my Hamlet last time around was finding a little more closure with Ophelia, which allows me to get to the point where he can say "There's a special providence in the fall of a sparrow." Everything for Hamlet moves towards that line with Horatio in the play's final scene. Emotionally, he's completed his arc. What's left to do is just the final thing. He's learned what he has to learn, and that's why Shakespeare allows him to die in the next scene.

My first time playing Hamlet, I felt that Shakespeare didn't give the character of Hamlet any sense of closure with Ophelia in the grave scene, which becomes all about Laertes. This time I took that first line—"Hear you, sir! What is the reason that you use me thus?"—to Laertes, then shifted my focus to Ophelia, holding her dead corpse in my arms, and said: "I loved you ever." I was very proud of that discovery. Then I was talking to Dan Donohue when he visited, and he said, "Well, I kind of did that in our production at OSF"—very subtly, by dropping the letters into the grave and looking down at Ophelia on "I loved you ever." How many actors have stumbled upon a choice, thinking it solely their discovery, only to realize it too has been done before? Dan and I shared a good laugh on that one. But finding that moment allowed me to go where I needed to go for "fall of a sparrow." Maybe the audience didn't need that moment, maybe they could get there without it. But it doesn't have the same impact. If I can't believe myself in that moment, I can't bring you along. I think that's an important part of what actors do and an important part of storytelling.

We have the power to highlight, to connect the dots in a

particular way. When Hamlet finishes his biggest soliloquy, "Now I am alone. / O what a rogue and peasant slave am I," he runs offstage for a two-minute break during the quick little court scene, and comes right back in for "To be or not to be." So Hamlet's arc goes directly from "Now I am alone" to "To be or not to be." There's no break in time for him; those two big soliloquies bookend each other. What connects them? Why does he go off with such certainty at the end of "Now I am alone" and come on with such trepidation for "To be or not to be"? Marco and I discovered in the course of the build this time that the big theme linking both soliloquies is cowardice. How did I miss that the first time around? I don't know. He only says it once in "Now I am alone," when he stops and asks very candidly, "Am I a coward? Who calls me villain?"

I made a false exit upstage just before that line, as if the soliloquy was done: I can't avenge my father, what's wrong with me? Then I saw the throne, stopped, turned back downstage, and asked the audience very directly, "Am I a coward?" Marco wanted that to be the hardest thing I could say to the audience, because cowardice in a prince is unacceptable. Being that vulnerable in front of everybody is huge. So we tried to play "To be or not to be" as a sequence of discoveries to get to the final discovery, "Thus conscience doth make cowards of us all." How did I skip such an obvious parallel between those two pieces the first time around?

In that Utah *Hamlet*, whenever I was onstage alone, the throne *was* Claudius, to me. That inanimate object got the brunt of my frustration. In the middle of the big "Now I am alone" soliloquy, when I got to "remorseless, treacherous, lecherous, kindless villain!", I would pound on the throne—it had a four-inch pad on it—at "O vengeance!" Four shows after opening, I pounded on that throne, and I knew immediately that I had broken my hand. My overacting in the moment was responsible. The very next words that I had to say to the audience, as Hamlet, were "Why, what an ass am I!" I had always felt that was a big laugh line for Hamlet, if you could do it right, a great moment. That changed after I broke my hand. That line became my moment to re-check myself, to go inward, to reflect how Hamlet feels in that moment—embarrassment, humility, frustration, anger—all the things that I felt when I broke my hand. From that moment forward, I didn't get laughs anymore. I didn't want laughs anymore.

Acting is a combat sport. I feel like we're athletes of the imagination. We go to extremes to tell these stories, and we pay a price for it, like Jamie Newcomb playing Richard III. It looked amazing when he came down there like a spider in that opening moment. But he paid the price for it. Both of his shoulders will never be the same because of those crutches. Physically, *Coriolanus* was hard on me. Michael Elich (Aufidius) and I were remembering the other day just how excruciating our big first-act fight scene was. For me, it was like, "Now I gotta do the rest of the play?" Early on, as we were going into previews, Michael peeled off his T-shirt in the dressing room. He had twelve or fifteen bruises on his torso, from me, where I would pop him on the chest, because we were building the piece and had to do it over and over again. I felt quite guilty over it—and I had a few bruises myself.

On double days of *Coriolanus* I learned an invaluable lesson: I don't have to do this play twice today. I have to do this play once, two times. That's equivocating, but it's very liberating to think you only have to climb the mountain that's in front of you. You don't have to worry about the peak that's behind it. You don't get many opportunities like *Coriolanus*. I hold that experience, both as a person and an artist, close to my heart. When a forty-five year-old blue-collar, rugged outdoorsman comes up to me with tears in his eyes and says, "I never thought I could experience something like that in the theater," that means a lot, and we did that with *Coriolanus*. I'll hold on to that forever.

Ultimately I find when you're out there on the stage, you only have a few things that you can hold on to for dear life and this is one of them: it is selfish to rob the person who paid good money to sit in that seat of the first-time experience. I don't like to play jokes when I'm on stage, I don't like to pass the apple or engage in any of those other bad behaviors actors can fall into, because I don't want the twelve-year-old in the third row to see that I winked at another actor. Likewise, when I'm out there in the fifth act exhausted and not feeling I can go there again, or when I'm feeling self-conscious in a moment, I remember being taught the old adage that "that's about you, but it shouldn't be. Make it about the other person."

There are so many "rules" with Shakespeare: don't stress the personal pronoun, don't hit the negative, hit the qualifier. But that's not the way we speak in real life. Sometimes even in the strictest iambic pentameter line, you favor the pronoun a little bit because that's the way it flows naturally. Another rule some people believe in is that we're meant to take a breath at the end of each line—that it helps with memorization and understanding, and that most lines are intact units. But some lines need to flow together. They don't work with that pause at the end. Strict adherence to any set of rules is limiting.

I will say this: it took me a long time to recognize the importance of not gliding down on the end of every line. I'll still do that occasionally because it's very American, it's the way we speak. With the long thoughts that often appear in Shakespeare, however, particularly in monologues and soliloquies, all the verse starts to feel the same if you drop the pitch on every line. If there's not an upward lift that allows you to go on to the next line, then it falls off. It took me a long time to embrace that. Know the rules so you can break them. There's something very powerful about a dropping, end-stopped line—but it has to be used sparingly and for the right reason.

With Shakespeare, I try not to sacrifice flow for meter. Although I believe in scanning a line and knowing exactly where those feet fall and how all those sounds and poetry play off each other, that's all for naught if the audience doesn't understand what you're saying. If the meter dictates a line reading that doesn't have flow to it, why do it? It's got to sound natural, it's got to sound like people actually coining these thoughts and speaking these words fresh for the first time. It's like being a jazz musician, where you learn the scales so that you can then play with the notes in between. The music is not about the notes, necessarily, but about the silence in between the notes. I think the same can be said for poetry, certainly for Shakespeare. Although I scan all my lines, I don't adhere to it as gospel as much as I used to. For me it's all about phrasing.

With Shakespeare, taking all of the commas and semicolons and dashes out of the script is one of the best things you can do for yourself, because those are editors' marks. Often those were inserted hundreds of years after the play was written. With modern scripts, you know exactly where the author put a comma, but with Shakespeare you have no idea. So get rid of those, because then you can look at the page with fresh eyes and begin to figure out your own phrasing—where your own parentheticals go, where your own brackets go, where your own dashes and semicolons go. I try just to be true to myself when I'm looking at these words and the way they string together to form sentences and thoughts. Flow and phrasing trump meter and strict adherence to rhetorical devices. I'm not discounting them; I just err on the side of flow and phrase.

I break the rules more now, but I think it's important to know the rules that you're breaking. For centuries, actors have experimented with these different techniques. I try to embrace those who trod the path before me. That's one of my frustrations, at times, with younger actors. They don't take the advice of colleagues around them who have been acting for ten, twenty, thirty, forty years. You think you're inventing the wheel but you're not—particularly for the stage, since training programs have all shifted towards camera work. I got the chance to do *Streetcar* with Bill Geisslinger, who's played Stanley twice, as our assistant director. I'd be an idiot not to heed his advice. If Dick Elmore or Robynn Rodriguez gives you a suggestion, or if Jimmy Edmondson or Dan Donohue or Jonathan Haugen or Robin Nordli or Demetra Pittman says, "Hey, how about this?" you're a fool if you don't at least go down that road and explore it. We are torchbearers. Getting to play Coriolanus here after Derrick Weeden and Dennis Arndt did makes me feel like part of the Coriolanus club. I feel part of the Mark Antony club. I've taken that torch, and I've passed that torch on.

Michael Elich as Petruchio in *The Taming of the Shrew*. Photo: T. Charles Erickson, OSF.

Michael Elich

In 20 seasons at OSF, Michael Elich has played 59 roles in 47 productions, including Harold Hill in *The Music Man*; The Pirate King in *Pirates of Penzance*; Thersites in *Troilus and Cressida*; Marcus in *Party People*; Buckingham in *Henry VIII* and *Richard III*; Aufidius in *Coriolanus*; Petruchio in *The Taming of the Shrew*; King John in *King John*; Harry Van in *Idiot's Delight*; Antonio in *The Merchant of Venice*; Orsino and Feste in *Twelfth Night*; The Actor in *Enter the Guardsman*; Hotspur and Bardolph in *1* and *2 Henry IV*; Torvald in *Nora*; Charles in *The School for Scandal*; Hap in *Death of a Salesman*; Mr. Dussel in *The Diary of Anne Frank*; and the unforgettable Prince John in *The Heart of Robin Hood*.

WELL, IF WE GO BACK REAL early, I did not come from an artistic upbringing, although my Mom had a tremendous singing voice. I was in a blue-collar, oldest-of-five, barely-making-ends-meet family. It was mostly a matter of getting the next meal on the table. My mom was a teenager when I was born. My father was a troubled soul and died at a young age, alcoholism and drugs, problems there. So I was not one of those kids who said early on, "Oh, theater work is definitely for me."

Looking back, acting was like stepping out of the world you are in and finding something that was kind of freeing. When I was in junior high, a counselor said to my mother, "Your son is so withdrawn that we really need to pull him out of himself, so why don't we put him in a drama class?" And they did. I did *You Can't Take It With You* and a few other plays. I can remember thinking it was almost like flying, in a way. You escaped into this imaginary world. I just gravitated to it. But in no way, shape, or form imagining that I would do anything like this professionally.

As a little kid, I had a record of Richard Burton's *Hamlet* and I didn't have a clue what he was saying, but I played it again and again. Its musicality and heightened sense of storytelling was just glorious. But I wasn't a particularly good student in high school, and like most kids, I tried sports. I was on the track team, and I'd also auditioned for *Oklahoma*! I got cast, and then missed track practice. The coach saw me in rehearsal and kicked me off of the team. After a few shows in high school, I back-packed through Europe, worked on a farm in Norway, did some community theater plays. While in a production of *Volpone*, I remember an actress I thought a lot of asking me, "Why are you doing this?" I told her, "It's a kind of hobby for me." She sat me down and said, "This is *not* a hobby. You've got some talent, you need to develop that, and you need to move *forward*. This is not just a way of picking up girls." That resonated with me.

I briefly wound up at the University of California River-side, and there I met my lifelong, best friend Marco Barricelli. I worked with some instrumental people in productions, but, ironically, there was really little in the way of an actor training program. I had the great good fortune to work with Richard Risso, who was a director and an actor at OSF in the 1950s and 60s. Richard's advice to me was to consider applying to a conser-vatory theater program like Juilliard or ACT, so I auditioned for Juilliard and was accepted into the four-year program. It was the best thing that could have happened to me. It changed my life.

At Juilliard, I was an older student, but the upside was that I had more life experiences to draw from. It was really about stripping you down in that program. They see the essence of the talent you have and then they break down your habits—the way you move, the way you speak, the way you approach a text. It's not about acting in those first two years, although you are doing shows where nobody is invited in. You are immersed from nine in the morning to eleven at night in classes or rehearsal—doing speech and movement and text and verse and poetry. The very first year, I did the "Discovery Project" with the extraordinary Marian Seldes and played Edmund in *King Lear*. Without actually directing, Marian did a "let's see what you've got" guidance into the world of the play. She'd say, "I want you to relax with it, breathe and move with it." In this way, the faculty evaluates what they have in a raw form.

The template for the first two years of training was the building of technique working with experts like Tim Monich in speech, Liz Smith and Robert Williams in voice and text, Moni Yakim for movement, the superb neutral and character mask work with Pierre Lefevre. The Alexander technique was taught by the wonderful Judy Leibowitz. These were the people who were giving me the tools that allowed me to keep working all these years. I would not be doing what I am doing today had it not been for the amazing faculty at Juilliard. For example, it's very important in the Bowmer Theatre, and particularly on the outdoor Elizabethan stage—that *you get the story out:* you are heard, understood, you know what you are saying. It's not *just* about feeling and emoting: it's about melding all that technique so that there is a naturalistic playing style *as you work with* a heightened classical text.

The role models I was drawn to were Laurence Olivier, Derek Jacobi (as Cyrano and Benedick), Peter O'Toole, Ian McKellen in his one-man show *Acting Shakespeare*, Roger Rees in *Nicholas Nickleby*, Christopher Plummer in *Othello* with James Earl Jones. We'd see their performances and then the actors often came to Juilliard to talk with us, which was one of the huge perks of New York training and a school like Juilliard which "gets" the value of bringing in quality professionals to work with students.

After graduating, I was doing a lot of commercials and I didn't like much of it. But the money was good, and it allowed me to pay off student loans and live in New York. I found myself, oddly enough, getting further away from theater. I was tracking my friend Marco's extensive career at the Oregon Shakespeare Festival. He is the one person I like most to talk with about the work in a very straightforward and honest way—we've both done a range of projects, and the trust runs deep. Ultimately, I decided to audition for the Festival. In retrospect, the worst thing I could have done as a very young actor would be to audition for OSF and get hired, because I would have lasted only a year or two. To train at Juilliard, and go work in the real world, act in different theaters on different shows with a variety of actors and directors, *and then go to OSF,* I was in a completely different place—more mature, a larger skill set, more stage experience. I was hired by Henry Woronicz. I'm very grateful to Henry for hiring me, because I met my soul mate Robin Goodrin Nordli. Libby Appel succeeded Henry, and she was enormously generous to me, as has been our present Artistic Director, Bill Rauch.

I love researching, going back to New York City and going into the Performing Arts Library to see video-recordings of stage productions. I'm not a good mimic, so if I steal an idea, I make it my own. I love Picasso's line, "To copy others is necessary, but to copy oneself is pathetic." Robin and I collect old theater memorabilia and we love going into used bookshops and finding early editions of Shakespeare. The truth is that research fires me up imaginatively, but once I start rehearsals, I stay away from it. I just let it percolate in.

When Robin and I were cast in Bergman's *Nora,* the adaptation of Ibsen's *A Doll's House*, we went to Norway to do research. Standing outside in the cold of winter in the middle of the night, you understand what Strindberg and Ibsen are all about. With *The Diary of Anne Frank*, I went to the Frank house in Amsterdam, and then researched in the Dutch Resistance War Museum, and later in an antique shop found a pair of glasses from the period that I used in the production. It was important to humanize these events as much as possible for myself. I also enjoy researching a good "Shakespeare in performance" book where I can read about different actors and the choices they've made and what their process is. In studying text, I always look at the Oxford edition, the Arden, the Riverside, and the Norton Facsimile of the First Folio. I want to examine all the notes, not just the ones that come with the production script. You can often tell which edition the dramaturg used most. I thumb through everything, in hopes that the discoveries will allow me to go into the lines and make a *specific choice*. Ultimately, it's the text where all the answers are. The language mustn't become secondary to the production's visual image or to the blocking and movement. Actors should be *leading* the production with the language.

I don't go into my office and try to learn lines. I'll read a script so many times, hundreds, I daresay, that when I hit the ground in rehearsal, it's not a matter of being memorized, it's a matter of *knowing*. Then I don't have to fish back and find a line. I read an interview of Anthony Hopkins which was very informative. He reads the script, aloud, quietly, countless times, until he is so comfortable with it that he can follow any direction he is given. I want to be so comfortable with the text so that I can *play* in rehearsal.

By researching as many productions as I do, getting on top of the material and doing all my homework with the *Shakespeare Lexicon* [Alexander Schmidt's *Shakespeare Lexicon and Quotation Dictionary*], going through all the word meanings,

I can make the language as accessible and as conversational as possible. For me, it's homework first. You think you know what a certain word means, and then you look it up in the *Lexicon*, and you find out that it may have meant something completely different four hundred years ago, so you discover you may have to completely change the line reading. I can't study a script indoors—I have to go outdoors and be moving. My teacher, Robert Williams used to say, "Don't go home and memorize that Moliere monologue. Verbalize it, physicalize it, let it come out of your body. The whole process is connected with your instrument."

In dealing with Shakespeare's language, you need to follow the natural rhythm of the text. Too often actors break / up / the / text / and put mammoth pauses in the line. What happens is that you lose track of what you are saying. What's really happened is that the actor is not being specific in what he is saying. Directors sometimes feel that pauses make it more immediate and heartfelt. More often, these pauses break into the sweep and flow of the inherently long sentences Shakespeare has built and you lose the meaning. You discover the meaning *on the line*: there's an alacrity of thought and the idea and the spoken word happening *at the same time*, in the moment, so fresh and spontaneous that it surprises you and you *don't* know where it's going—as you drive through to the end of the thought.

Actors need to approach the text like a detective. Shakespeare gives you the keys—but *you* have to open the door. This is what training unlocks. At Juilliard, we would take a passage, let's say Berowne from *Love's Labors' Lost*, and we would spend three weeks on one passage! The choral pieces in *Henry V* are so good to work with, because the language is storytelling at its absolute best: "Now entertain conjecture of a time / When creeping murmur and the pouring dark / Fills the wide vessel of the universe." Sheer visual poetry. It's magic.

Those elements of storytelling, punctuation, and also antithesis, where contrasts and oppositions are set up by Shakespeare to make a point—are paramount. In a large passage, I do this exercise where I say to myself, what are the five words here that are key—what are the *operative words*? Don't emphasize every word. Especially when using antithesis, you learn to leave the voice up, sounding unresolved, while you give the first idea, and then let it emphasize again on the second idea. What took me forever at Juilliard was getting control of the American actor's impulse to let the voice drop at the end of every line: the dreaded "downward inflection." It's a tough habit to break.

Actors are so good at faking things. Sometimes in rehearsal, someone will run through a long speech, and I think—you don't know what you just said because you haven't done your homework. I know because I've cheated in the same way. Looking at all of the research gives you guidance. There are those Shakespeare-for-Idiots editions where the text is on the left side and someone has written out what s/he thinks is the meaning of those lines on the right side. From a teaching standpoint, having worked with people who have never read Shakespeare before, that's not such a bad idea.

A flexible voice takes awhile to develop—genetics factor in hugely, because that's where it starts, what you are born with. Next, how do you use your vocal equipment. Early on, I was influenced by a lot of cultural things, that backward placement of the voice that those smooth DJ's use. It took a long time to get to a neutral palate, where it was easier to manage certain dialect choices or the musical cadences I needed in playing Shakespeare, to where my voice was something that freed me rather than got in my way. I had West Coast regionalisms, heavy sibilants, hard R sounds, that I was completely unaware of.

When I got out of Juilliard and was doing voice-overs, I found that working on commercial copy professionally was very challenging—the choices you make with your voice when inflecting a single word or phrase. Training the voice is comparable to an athlete developing a certain muscle. If you don't use it, you lose it. I couldn't have done *Troilus and Cressida* or *Party People* without some vocal damage had I not known how to warm my vocal cords up, which I do at home. I go into the study and put on headphones and get involved in what I have to do that night. I fear that it's only a matter of time before the outdoor stage will be fully miked. I am continually harping on the idea that it's not just about volume. It's about clarity.

My vocal warm-up starts by humming. Before I even speak, I'll get out of bed, walk the dog and hum. No talking. I gradually work that throughout the day. I will compress that preparation before a matinee. It's a matter of keeping the instrument warm. I run through a litany of speech drills and vocal gymnastics—twenty minutes of tongue twisters I've done for twenty-five years.

I was tickled when I learned we were doing *The Music Man.* One actor told me, in all seriousness, "You do know that Harold Hill is the Hamlet of musicals." If it's a big theater role like that one, I'll do much more singing in the daytime. I'll often re-visit the text that morning. Both the Pirate King and Harold Hill use language in a heightened way. Ninety percent of what the Pirate King does is singing in an operatic style. I wanted to have an open, free voice, along with all the physical movement in that show, helped tremendously by Gary Busby, our Music Director. The reason you sing in a musical is that you get to a point where speaking can no longer express your feelings, so the song is an extension of your speaking voice. Ultimately, technique needs to be completely invisible.

When I was younger, I used to shy away from *me*, thinking, no, I don't like that. For so many years, it was a matter of *not* being myself, shutting that part down and creating something or someone else. I was terribly insecure. I still have a hard time opening out to the fourth wall in rehearsals. I can see that I am pulling away from the very people I need to open up to. It takes me awhile to get comfortable, until I'm fully grounded in what I am doing and can just "release." However, my intuitive side has grown tremendously. You reach a point when you are a little older where you don't have to worry as much about the other stuff—like going into that first rehearsal and thinking, "What are they going to think of me, I have to impress so-and-so." Leave all that crap at the door. I don't need to dazzle anyone right off the bat.

I like working with an actor I've worked with before, where we have a kind of shorthand communication, and we know each other well. We go further faster. Who? Without a doubt, Robin Goodrin Nordli. Also Demetra Pittman, Vilma Silva, Robert Frank, Mark Murphey, David Kelly, Kevin Kenerly, Robynn Rodriguez, Armando Durán, to name a few. We're all quite different. You can tell after a first reading so much about people. I love it when new people come in and they have a skill set—it's like, okay, here we go. Let's play.

In 2004, we took David Edgar's *Continental Divide* to England, playing it both in the Barbican and at the Birmingham Repertory Theatre. That was *huge*—to be on that stage where Jacobi and Ralph Richardson played. To go there with a core group of OSF actors, with a Tony Award-winning British playwright writing about American politics—it was extraordinary. The excellent Tony Taccone directed.

Thersites in *Troilus and Cressida* was a difficult role because the language is so dense. I had wanted to play it because of the sheer fear factor of "can I pull it off?" Thersites is a choral figure of sorts; it was a huge challenge to make this character accessible. Director Rob Melrose was moving the play into the contemporary Middle Eastern world. I had all these ideas about having Thersites legless, initially. He could only move on his hands on a little cart with wheels.

A good director will open you up to new ideas, and then you say to yourself, "Wow. What was *I* thinking. Let's go with *that*." I wrote Rob long e-mails ahead of time about who I thought Thersites was, what he was, his background, how he got back and forth, and about 90 percent of it was vetoed because of the world of the play he'd decided on. In rehearsal, I made the leap by trying different things on my own. You get out there and make a ton of choices and you winnow them down—blow it all out, be bad, make mistakes, fall on your face, risk. That's tricky and scary. That's what rehearsal is for. I don't like to chat a lot in rehearsal—I prefer to just do it.

My biggest fear, in Rob's modern military setting, was how does a character like Thersites *get away with* doing and saying the kinds of things he does without someone actually putting a bullet in the back of his head or carting him off somewhere. That's when the darker, black-market side of the character started to come to life, the drug-addled supplier of goods. He was needed and pro- tected by the drug-addicted Achilles. Problem solved. Thersites is a fatalist but also views the world in the most honest way, seeing its hypocrisy: "Wanna come along with me? It's not gonna be pretty! Our side sucks, but so does theirs. So let's just go along for the ride." His point of view is bloody and dark. He has no illusions about love or war, everything is "A cuckold and a whore."

It was emotionally draining and physically exhausting but also kind of freeing because it was a long run, where you could just play and discover in the moment. My viewpoint is—even though you are performing the play 120 times, you're really just playing the role once, that day, that second. If you're listening and responding, that's the way to keep it fresh and to rediscover it, allowing the performance to go where it wants to go within the framework of what your director and the design team have come up with. When you're working with really good people, it's like sports. They're going to elevate your game and you will do the same for them.

Structurally, I had many asides to the audience, a sort of running commentary of the events. Act V is the big observation scene with the spectators: Thersites, Troilus, and Hector, all watching and talking about the lustful interaction between Cressida and Diomed. Thersites is the ring-leader, saying, "Look at the absurdity of what's going on here." He's an outsider, and he speaks the truth. I'm surprised Achilles doesn't backhand him and blow him out of the camp. There were a few shows when Peter Macon came close. There were nights when I thought, "Well, I'm gonna back off a bit." Deep into the run I was finding some great things in Thersites. Less is more. Less pounding the audience and hitting them over the head with things.

The performance group, UNIVERSES, had seen my work as Feste, as the Pirate King, and as Stephen Price in *The African Company Presents Richard III*. They were looking to cast the double role of Marcus, the 60s Rainbow Coalition radical and the nameless FBI interrogator, in their production of *Party People*. The play is a look back at the Early Black Panther and Young Lords movement mixed with a lot of music and a sort of "where are they now" coming together twenty-five years later. To be honest, I was hesitant, in large part because of my whiteness. How would I fit in this story? I'd ask Stephen Sapp, one of the UNIVERSES founders: "Are you sure you want . . . me?" In no time, the group embraced me in their loving arms. And I was the better for it.

New actor challenges have always excited me. As the character Marcus, I led the cast in a song called "Free Fred Hampton." Hampton had started the Rainbow Coalition in Chicago and was murdered at the young age of twenty-one in a hail of Chicago police gunfire in his bed. His wife (carrying Fred Hampton Jr. at that time) would be attending our matinee. The excitement was palpable—here was Fred Hampton's grown son sitting in the front row. I have to say that the chill factor was off the scale, the hair on the back of my neck was standing up. (In no small part because I didn't want to screw up the song.) We all spoke with Fred Jr. after the show, and he was profoundly moved by the performance, this gentle giant of a man. For me personally, this was live theater at its heartfelt best.

Petruchio in *Taming of the Shrew* turned out to be extremely rewarding. Kate Buckley directed it, and Vilma Silva was my wonderful Kate. Buckley is a great believer in "let's find out what this relationship is and try not to tack on some kind of politically correct element. Let's not start by laying out all those gender issues." We had a marvelous journey. It was an exacting, exhausting, exasperating rehearsal time. It took Vilma and me awhile to fully connect, which was the exact parallel of the relationship you saw onstage, because in rehearsal (and Vilma would agree with this) we did not always see eye to eye. However, a parallel growth got to working, and ultimately, it just rooted us in a great way. The bond between us was very strong.

I wondered what should Petruchio do in the wedding scene when he finally shows up. I'd seen countless choices. "Hmmm—make me the most gorgeous wig in the world and when I arrive, after all that anticipation, I tear off that wig and I'm bald." The audience gasped. It worked beautifully. Vilma and I were on the same page from the get-go that this was a real love story. They are not cruel and abusive, but their actions might be outside of today's politically correct norm of how a relationship happens, of how you communicate physically and emotionally with each other.

Robin Goodrin Nordli was playing my servant Grumio and suggested that we try to incorporate our corgi, Marlowe, into the role of Troilus, the dog that lived at Petruchio's manor. Corgis are short-legged, funny-looking creatures. I worked with him on Mondays, teaching him the commands, giving him a treat, and then he'd run off into Robin's arms and be put into his crate backstage, while the scene continued.

The drill in performance was that I'd call him, he'd come flying in from stage left, I'd throw a piece of chicken onstage, he'd stop and stare at it as Vilma and I continued the action. I'd give him another visual command and he'd take the chicken and run off to Robin. The audience loved it. It worked believably alongside the chaos in Petruchio's household, where no one was particularly competent.

We'd practice every night during fight call. However, one night Vilma cooked up some delicious dog cookies which she gave to Marlowe after the fight call. So, that night, during the performance, I yelled, "Troilus!" and he came running on, got his chicken, ran over to Robin, and then . . . beelined right back onstage and slowly sashayed over to Vilma. Her eyes were the size of cantaloupes. Marlowe was not following protocol. From that night on, Vilma's cookies had changed the pattern of the scene—some nights Marlowe would want to stay onstage, *just* in case. It was hilarious. People still ask me, "When is Marlowe coming back to do another show?"

If I can find the physical essence of where I am going, a character voice generates from that. Petruchio is always on the balls of his feet, leaning forward—he's a character who takes a bite out of the ass of life—he's full. What he wears, he looks good in. If he walked out there in his boxers, hey, it's a good day. It's wonderful he can show up in the wedding scene and be so discombobulated. He's not just trying to show Kate the irreverence of it all, he's saying *this is who I am*, and I don't give a crap what anyone else thinks about me. It's all there on the page—come with me Kate, and let's fly to the stars. She's really that way, too, but she has a hell of a time admitting it. In Vilma's hands, we were able to ride the world we had created. You saw a great deal of love and respect, but you also saw Kate saying, "This is who *I* am." They are equals. Petruchio changes by the end, and there is a deep and proud sense of admiration and love for this woman. They're kindred souls, both alphas. If you were to see the next chapter in this play, I think it would surprise people how well they get along domestically.

The flip side of that play was *King John*. When I was first cast, I kept telling director John Sipes, "The Bastard—that's the real role here." Well, I was wrong because he was very clear about what he wanted John's world to be. It was all about the relationship between King John and his mother Eleanor (played by Jeannie Paulson). There is not much text between them, but what there is in a strong actress' hand creates a binding relationship, although not a particularly loving one. Of all the characters I've played here, this was one of those remarkable times when the penny just dropped for me.

I immersed myself in reading about the family. John was a spoiled kid, completely ill-equipped to lead. The She-Wolf Mother dictated what John should do. She used him as a pawn for power. We set that up in the beginning, where all alone I'd watch a film that covered the entire back wall of the theater showing the horror of war, row after row of soldiers were killed, and I just stood there in full royal regalia watching them die. Sitting on that throne by myself had a profound effect on me. John makes some horrendously bad choices—he's not a character that is warm and personable, not a leader people gravitate to.

Sipes said, "This is where I want to go with this role, that veneer of leadership—you've been thrust into that role but you've never been allowed to lead, only to *play* as a leader." There is the heightened moment where he's told that his mother is dead; John's whole foundation begins to crumble. He's never been alone in his entire life, always been *told* what to do. Shakespeare uses only three spare words: "My mother dead." Sipes said, "If that moment needs to last a half hour, let it happen." I was sitting there, on my throne, by myself, in rehearsal one day, and I just completely lost it. It was so overwhelming that we didn't talk about it a lot.

The costume department was wonderful. They provided the regal trappings of a king—and yet nothing fit. The crown and the cap were just a little too big, the pageantry a bit too much. John was like a dress-up doll.

I was fortunate to play King John, and I am very glad that I didn't turn it down, yet I had wondered what the hell do you do with that role? This production was a perfect example of a smart director using a text-based conceit, in a specific time and space, working with strong actors. Sipes was brilliant about laying out the psychological aspects of the journey. Especially in a difficult play which is almost never performed.

I've had the good fortune to work with Robin Goodrin Nordli in eleven shows, and one of the best was Robert Sherwood's *Idiot's Delight* directed by Peter Amster. We had great one-on-one timing, it was comic, in that 1930s genre I love playing. There's a touch of Bogart in the Harry Van character, a second-rate song-and-dance man. War is on the horizon, and Harry and Irene are in complete denial. Just as they find each other and come together, the bombs start falling and they realize that their lives are growing shorter by the moment. I found it very moving. Especially on the heels of 9-11.

I loved playing Prince John in *The Heart of Robin Hood*. It's a different side of King John, and I wanted to somehow tie together, in a Princess-Bride sort of way, the two different sides of his persona. Robin Hood is the hero and everyone loves him, but you gotta have a good villain in there too. I needed to create a three-dimensional villain, who had his own idea of how to court and woo women. Early in rehearsal I noticed how sweet Kate Hurster smelled (Maid Marian) and I thought, "That's it!" From that kernel, I was smelling everyone, even props. This quirk helped show that Prince John was just a little bit *outside* normal. Joel Sass, our director, loved it. He'd yell out, "Keep sniffing, keep sniffing!"

In the costume drawings, Prince John had a short wig, and the designer insisted he was a real nut about his hair. I said to her, "Look at everyone else in this cast, then look at me. If you really want to make him a rock star, let's go Breck-Girl-Jesus-long and see where that takes us. After much collaboration, the long hair was a go. A perfect fit with the red-and-black Dracula costume, creating a bouncing villain with a need for entitlement.

Our dialogue coach, the excellent David Carey, said, "Think of him as a velvet glove on a steel hand—attack the dialogue with that sense of authority—and when he toys with someone, put on the velvet glove." In this panto-styled script, it was important to make Prince John real. You layer things in, the hanging, the cruelty to the children, the need to control, the lust, the power. Our fight director, the marvelous Chris Duval, worked wonders bringing out the inner swordsman in Prince John during the climactic fight with Robin Hood at the end of the play. It was fun and it worked surprisingly well. This was one of those big, fun action shows. A number of the actors carried small "cheat-sheets" backstage. There was lots of comedy going on as we were all running around trying to keep our entrances and exits straight. Kate Hurster was marvelous, leading our band of players through this merry romp.

You could not have two roles further apart on the spectrum than Petruchio and King John. The same with Buckingham in *Richard III* and Feste in *Twelfth Night*, or Antonio in *The Merchant of Venice* and Aufidius in *Coriolanus*. These are wonderful examples of the fullness of my OSF seasons. That's the beauty of a rep company. You get to play a huge range of parts, parts so rich that you continue to mine them all season long. Sometimes magic happens when the Muse is with you: you're spontaneous and in the moment and you just fly.

Of course, there is always that fear of failure. Those demons sitting on each shoulder whispering paranoid thoughts: "You're really going to screw up today—who are you kidding?" I used to deny that the demons ever existed. Now I embrace them. And conversely they fall away more often than not.

This is a ten-month *marathon* here at OSF. You need to pace yourself. You do each particular show once—you do it *one* time, and you give 110 percent. You should be completely *spent.* I'm always astounded at how fast everyone gets out of the dressing room. Within ten minutes, everybody is gone. I'm still sitting there taking in what happened after the show. I love the silence of the theater after everyone has left.

Nell Geisslinger as Kate in *The Taming of the Shrew*. Photo: Jenny Graham, OSF.

Nell Geisslinger

In 10 seasons at OSF, Nell Geisslinger has played, among other roles, Kate in *The Taming of the Shrew*; Stella Kowalski in *A Streetcar Named Desire*; Nina in *Seagull*; Louison in *The Imaginary Invalid*; Doll Tearsheet in *2 Henry IV*; Lady Mortimer in *1 Henry IV*; Tigress in *Tracy's Tiger*; Perdita in *The Winter's Tale*; Elma Duckworth in *Bus Stop*; Chorus in *Oedipus Complex*; Cordelia in *King Lear*; Liesel Schell in *The Visit*; and Aquarius in *Daughters of the Revolution [Continental Divide]*.

TO BE HONEST, I'VE ALWAYS been headed toward an acting career. Some of my earliest memories of Ashland are Festival memories—being down in the green room, the distinctive sound of the monitor, the quality of light in the dressing rooms, the smells, feeling so happy. I was a loud and out-of-control kid, but all my father's (actor Bill Geisslinger's) friends were able to embrace that. So I always felt at home. When I was ready to go to college, I had been acting throughout my childhood in community theater and school productions, and I had spent my high school years focusing on drama, at a performing arts high school in Los Angeles.

I made the move there when I was fourteen and transitioning into high school. After spending so much of my childhood in Ashland, I was a little stir-crazy and excited to go to the big city. In Los Angeles, at Crossroads School for the Arts and Sciences, I took four morning hours of academics and spent the rest of my day, into the night, in the little black box theater on campus. Just classes and productions of the classics—*Into the Woods*, *Assassins*, *Uncle Vanya*, *Wild Oats* (the James McClure version), and *The Two Gentlemen of Verona*.

I had been living, breathing and eating theater when I graduated. I wasn't sure about college but couldn't think of anything better to do, so I went to Bennington. I decided not to do theater for my first term or year—the only time I've ever said no, I'm going to put that aside. I focused on Spanish literature and dance, which I had studied in high school. Bennington was very unstructured, a perfect school when it comes to the arts. I remember watching the MFA students, who were all so self-directed and knew what they wanted. But for somebody like me, so far away from my family on the West Coast, still floundering a bit, it was really hard—partly because my first day of classes was September 11, 2001.

The good thing about Bennington was the fieldwork term. From January to February, you were required to get an internship or job in your field of study. I called Penny Metropulos at the Festival because I wanted to come back to the West Coast. I thought, well, I'll bring coffee to rehearsals or sit in the box office and field phone calls. When I asked Penny if I could have an internship, she said, "Let me get back to you." A few days later she called me back to say, "I have good news and bad news." I said, "What's the good news?" And she said, "We'd like you to play a small part in *Idiot's Delight*." I never even imagined that could happen, but they needed a local non-Equity person to fill a role. Then I said, "What's the bad news?" and Penny said, "It's a six-month gig." I made up my mind instantaneously. I had just turned eighteen. I did think about whether to go back to college later, but things snowballed. I auditioned for the next season and was hired as a non-Equity OSF company member, working in *Continental Divide* with David Edgar and Tony Taccone and in *A Midsummer Night's Dream* with Ken Albers.

Because I didn't audition for that first, tiny two-line role in *Idiot's Delight,* I felt very uncomfortable about the chance and the nepotism involved. I spent the next three years trying to prove myself in my own right, attending every possible rehearsal and taking on as many understudy assignments as I could. I remember saying to myself, since you're not in college, this is what your school is going to be; make the most of it. I had the opportunity to work on *Oedipus Complex* with Frank Galati and on another Ken Albers show, Durrenmatt's *The Visit* (translated by Doug Langworthy). Ken was a generous mentor, who took me under his wing. I would come in to rehearsal and there would be new pages because he had written in extra lines for me.

When I had the good luck to be put in David Edgar's *Daughters of the Revolution,* I was so young and green that I didn't realize I was seeing a brilliant writer put together a play before my very eyes, taking what we were doing in the room in the workshop stages and rewriting, based on input from actors and the director and the dramaturg. I took it completely for granted. By the time *Tracy's Tiger* rolled around, I understood. That was formative for me, especially because I am interested in the writing and directing side of things now. *Tracy's Tiger* gave me a lot of respect for how brave it is to build a show from the ground up—how much guts it takes to say, "I've written this," then for somebody else to say, "Put it in my hands and I'll direct it," and then for somebody else to figure out how to make it work technically. Where do we place the band? What does the orchestration sound like? All that work—it's such a huge, mys-terious process that I got to be a part of in *Tracy's Tiger.*

There have been a couple of breaks in my OSF career. I had thrown my hat in the ring for the 2005 season, but I was also thinking it was time for a change. My mother (actor An-nette O'Toole) encouraged me to come back to Los Angeles to look for work and spend time with the family there. So I turned down an OSF offer for 2005 and spent late 2004-early 2005 in Los Angeles. I got very antsy, because while there were things I enjoyed in L.A., I'm not cut out to work there. Visiting Ashland in the spring of 2005, I felt emboldened to ask for a meeting with Libby Appel, the artistic director. She met me on the Green Show stage. I don't know how I had the courage, but I said I'd like to come back as an Equity actor, and to be in *Bus Stop*. I just thought I'd throw something on the wall and see what stuck. She nodded her head. In that moment I knew it was a possibility, and it happened. I like to think Libby admired my forwardness.

For an actor today, Equity membership is a huge decision, which sometimes gets made for you. I think it worked out for me because I happened to be the understudy for Julie Oda, whose pregnancy started showing in 2004 when she was playing Cordelia in *King Lear*. Libby may have seen me when I took over the role for Julie for the last two months of the run. I've had qualms about putting Cordelia on my résumé, but it was a real turning point for me, the first time that I had lots of Shakespeare text on stage, and, I think, part of the reason I was cast for 2006. I was still new to professional theater, and I thought that my duty was (and it partly is) to maintain what the actor before me had created. But I had to approach Cordelia entirely differently in some ways. Ken Albers, who was playing Lear, encouraged me to make my own strides in the part. He would take me aside and say, "Yeah, that thing you did—good job." I never worked with the director, Jimmy Edmondson, whose hands were off the show by the time I stepped in, so I had to take over the role with just a couple of understudy rehearsals.

Cordelia was hard for me for that reason, but I also had trouble with the kind of forgiveness that she is able to give her father after he has publicly shamed her—to go through that, to become the bride of a man she may not have any real feelings for, and then still to come back for her father, to go along with the relationship he starts to reconstruct, which is oddly like a marriage. "We'll sit in a cell and sing and everything's going to be great. All I want to do is be with you." *Incestuous* is too strong a word but there's a dis-ease, prevalent through all of *King Lear*, that Cordelia comes back and subjects herself to again. It's bound up with love for her father, control issues, wanting to look at her sisters and say, "I was right about you"—a million different things.

The role of Cordelia is complicated. Because Shakespeare is telling King Lear's story, the play can't focus on the equally strange journey that Cordelia, as a woman, makes. When she returns to England (wearing pants or military fatigues, in many productions), that has been as exquisitely complicated a journey as Viola's or Rosalind's, but we don't get to see it, because she has been offstage. When my friend Susannah Flood played Ophelia here, she also used the word "underwritten" to describe that role, and I agree, because so much of what makes Ophelia complex (like Cordelia) happens offstage. What we do see of Ophelia is there so that we can see the effect on Hamlet, or Claudius, or Gertrude. How are they reacting?

After Cordelia, Libby Appel gave me incredible opportunities to play parts that she sensed would be good for me, growing experiences—specifically *Bus Stop*, my first big role. But even earlier, she helped foster my career by casting me in plays with David Edgar, Tony Taccone, Frank Galati, and Ken Albers. I didn't actually work with Libby until 2006, in *Bus Stop*. That same year, she cast me as Perdita in *The Winter's Tale*, which was a totally different world, totally different character. Libby understood that I function best when I'm doing varied work over the course of the season, and she never shied away from giving me that kind of work.

That was my first year as an Equity company member, my first time running a Shakespeare all year long, and my first time playing a significant Shakespeare ingénue. It was also my first and only time playing a royal—although Perdita doesn't find that out until the very end of the play. Perdita is a little bland, but she has an interesting emotional journey, the surprise and shock of discovering that you're not who you thought you were. That whole arc, suddenly coming into a mother and a family, takes place within the second act. Miriam Laube, who was playing Hermione, was so present and emotionally available in the statue scene that I felt I needed to rise to the occasion as well. For the ingénues in Shakespeare, that is the emotional journey you go on: you're even-keeled, then you spike, and by the end of the play you're in tears. Something huge happens. What I learned from *The Winter's Tale* is that that journey takes a certain stamina.

The rural Bohemia scenes, with singing and dancing, were lots of fun. I remember watching the shepherds and shepherdesses developing their parts in the background. For the first time I felt like I didn't have to do much. The requirements of the Perdita part are that she be graceful, well-spoken beyond her apparent means, regal and lovely. When I look back on my performance, I'm not totally happy with it; all those things seem to me to require just stillness and a sense of focus. For me the wild and kooky character parts have always been more interesting, so I remember watching Geoffrey Blaisdell, one of the shepherds, come into rehearsal and develop a distinctive character that he called "Ruprecht." Seeing him make such specific choices galvanized everybody else. People can get bored and frustrated with the long-running Shakespeare plays when the parts they're playing need to fade into the background. You can choose to be bored or you can choose to be invested. I choose to be invested no matter what part I'm playing. It's important not to steal focus at certain moments when you're in the background, but still to develop a character specific and interesting enough to carry you through a run. That's not easy.

I think sometimes I crossed that line playing the wench at the top of *Henry IV, Part One*, but walking that thin edge was a good lesson. Because I wasn't carrying the show, I could devote myself to the exercise of playing different parts in the ensemble, from the wench to Lady Mortimer, trying to be as believable and different in each world as I possibly could, down to the makeup and the physicality of each character. That's the stuff I really love. Penny Metropulos, the director, has always encouraged me to play—that's just how she is with young artists. For many directors, the large budgets here are an opportunity to go crazy with production values. What sometimes gets lost in the Shakespeare plays is the grimy, dirty quality of Shakespeare's underworlds. The production value sits on top—guys have colorful doublets that don't belong in that world as it really existed in Shakespeare's time. So part of the fun of creating that character, the wench, was to push the envelope with Penny and see how far I could go. You look at old engravings, descriptions of those people on Gropecunt Lane, and it's crazy. Penny let me go there. My wench's name ended up being "Nell" because when Penny did the cutting and formatted the script into our first reading draft, she knew she wanted a "wench"—that's how her original script credited the role—but in that first-reading script, she had indicated that I was in certain scenes by the stage direction, "Hal, Falstaff, and Nell enter." By that happy accident, the character took on my name. Shakespeare would approve, I hope.

The wench re-appeared in the second act of *Henry IV, Part One*, after I had played Lady Mortimer, when Falstaff comes to tell Mistress Quickly that he's going off to the wars. Penny wasn't sure she wanted me in that scene but said "Come to the rehearsals, we'll try you there and see if it gains us anything." One day I bundled my sweaters up and held them like a baby, made my entrance, and sat upstage at the top of the stairs. When the scene was over, I expected Penny to say, "What the hell were you doing up there?" Instead she turned to the stage manager and said, "Would you note in the *Clarion* that we now have a baby in the scene?" Then I started building a backstory about that baby, how it was either Falstaff's or the Prince's. We started our production with all three of us in bed, so there had been some hanky-panky and it could easily have been either one's child. The baby gave another level to my character, who was otherwise just a wet-brained syphilitic wench, and it also gave another layer to Mistress Quickly. In the kind of place she's running, there would have been children in the back, in the kitchen, in a little wooden crate next to the fire.

When I got cast as Lady Mortimer in the same play, I found out that I'd be speaking Welsh. No version of *Henry IV, Part One* actually includes the Welsh called for by the stage directions, so Ursula Meyer, our voice coach, sent me some Welsh text written for other productions. Once we were in rehearsal, she invited a local man of Welsh descent to speak with me and Tony Heald, who was playing my father, Owen Glendower. We recorded him speaking Welsh and English and talked with him about the culture. He ended up coming to see the show—even though he said the history of the fifteenth-century Welsh revolt against English rule is still so fresh in the minds of Welsh people that it might be upsetting to him.

Hopefully, even if they didn't speak Welsh, people could understand the father-daughter relationship between Tony Heald and me. Putting Lady Mortimer and Lady Percy in that scene shows Shakespeare's genius. He knew he was writing the play for everybody, not just the guys who'd want to see the war bits, but all the women out there in the gallery, too. A tight, interesting, well-made play can't all be on the same note, the same tone. You see what those men have to lose—not just the political machinations but the family life. The two marriages are completely different. Mortimer and his wife are newlyweds, and the only connection they have is physical, because they don't speak the same language. The bloom is off the rose for Hotspur and his lady, from what we see on stage.

When I got cast as the wench, I wasn't looking ahead, but halfway through the season I realized that Doll Tearsheet in *Henry IV, Part Two*, would be a great follow-up. I asked for it specifically at my meeting with Bill Rauch, who had become artistic director in 2007. I really wanted to continue the *Henry* cycle and work with John Tufts again. I had the feeling that I wasn't going to get the role, because traditionally at the Festival it's been done by an older woman—or even a man, as in the Libby Appel production with David Kelly as Doll and G. Val Thomas as Mistress Quickly. I thought it would make an interesting dynamic with the older Falstaff for Doll to be this fiery, sexy, street-dirty younger woman. With Michael Winters' Falstaff and my Doll there was a quality—I don't know that we used the phrase "father-daughter"—but this other layer of safety. I was so much younger than Falstaff, and he was most likely impotent. At the end of the night, we probably went off in the back room and just fell asleep together. There's a trust between Doll and Falstaff, and some odd comfort they were getting from each other that they couldn't get from anybody else.

I was glad that we kept the scene late in the play where Doll and Mistress Quickly are arrested. It's one of those delightful scenes that doesn't necessarily move the plot forward, in terms of where Hal or Falstaff is going, but just checks in with real people. It's a necessary bookend for those two women. The more pressing issue is that Doll is arrested for being Pistol's accomplice in a murder. We talked a lot about Doll's relationship with Pistol. Lisa Peterson, the director, was interested in pursuing the idea that Pistol had been Doll's pimp in the past, partly because their relationship in that first encounter in the tavern scene is so inexplicably contentious. There's no way to tell the audience that history explicitly, but we needed to flesh it out for ourselves, to explain how they end up murdering somebody together by the end of the play.

About halfway through the run Pistol (Rodney Gardiner) and I started connecting in the moment at the end when Pistol comes onstage with Falstaff. He'd look up at me and I'd look down at him from my place above, stage left. With that look, we resolved the strife of our earlier tavern scene just for ourselves: "Ah, we're gonna be okay. We're survivors." I had a great time doing that show—especially the tavern scenes—except for the escape from the Beadle (Mark Bedard) arresting me. Lisa kept saying, "Can you get up the ladder quicker? He's chasing you!" Try climbing a completely vertical ladder in five-inch stiletto heels! When I finally got up onto that deck for the last time, the night we closed the show, I was so glad I'd never have to do it again.

John Tufts (Prince Hal) and I go back now, I was calculating, to 2004—almost ten years of working together. I had played Miranda in *The Tempest* opposite John as Ferdinand and Dan Donohue as Caliban in Libby Appel's final season as artistic director. Sometimes I still call John "my patient logman" (we have lots of jokes about that line). It makes a difference to work with people you've known ten years. There's a shorthand and a trust and an easy camaraderie that I have never felt anywhere else, because we all live together in Ashland ten months out of the year, sometimes more. The stuff of life happens, like John and Chris (Albright-Tufts) having a baby.

Before that production of *The Tempest*, I had never really played on the stage with Derrick Weeden (Prospero). I was anxious about even sitting at the table with somebody of his ability and stature within the company. A turning point in my relationship with Derrick came when we were working on the scene in *The Tempest* where, as Prospero, he is about to tell Ferdinand and Miranda that his punishment of Ferdinand has been a test and that he is glad they have fallen in love. On the page, the scene jumps suddenly from "we have to hide our love" to "everything's okay." We were puzzling through how to make that abrupt transition, to finish one scene thinking that they're on unsound footing with Dad, then to enter the next scene and suddenly discover that he approves.

So I had an idea—when I was still not used to saying ideas out loud in the room—which I shared. It was a huge season for Derrick, it had been a long day, and when I said "I have an idea," Derrick kind of snapped and said, "What is it that you expect me to do?" Had I had time to think, I'd have been terrified and upset that I'd offended him in some way, but I didn't. For some reason I saw him in the moment as just another actor in the room, so I said, "I don't *expect* you to do anything—but this is my idea." His eyes opened and he took a step back and said, "Okay." And I shared my idea with him, which ended up being in the show. Prospero would bring us in very forcefully, holding both of us by the arm. Ferdinand and I didn't know what was going on—like, "Oh God, we're in trouble, we got caught making out under Caliban's rock" or whatever. But Prospero was only play-acting anger when he brought us in. Suddenly his whole demeanor changed, and he played the moment as "Now I'm going to tell you that everything is all right. You've got my consent to wed."

I realized from that experience that if I try to be my open and authentic best self, willing to play, I can hope that other people will, too—and, of course, Derrick was right, you can't *expect* anything of anyone. Mostly it comes down to looking each other in the eye and listening. Every time I get off track and feel like I'm having a bad show, if I let my stupid ego go away, I can say, "Well, this is what I've got to work with today, and part of what I've got to work with, even if *I'm* failing, is the other person on stage." If I just look at him and listen to him, hear what he's saying and how he's saying it, that in itself is real and authentic and, I hope, worth watching.

I went down to Los Angeles after that season and auditioned successfully for the role of Desdemona in the Los Angeles Women's Shakespeare Company's production of *Othello*.

I hadn't met any of the company, but Lisa Wolpe, their artistic director, had seen my work in Ashland. Lisa was playing Iago. People were blown away not just to see a woman be so thoroughly male, but by her ability with the text, her nuance. It was the first time I had ever been in an all-female production—actually, the only time. It's exciting to work with an all-women cast on that big robust text. As much as I enjoyed playing Desdemona, I remember feeling a little jealous that I wasn't playing a male role. I've never played one of the pants roles, and I'd really like to take on Viola or Rosalind especially, in the future.

When I was cast as Kate, I'd heard *The Taming of the Shrew* described as a "problem play," but I hadn't ever sat down and read it. I was surprised by how unproblematic I actually felt it was. David Ivers, the director, didn't want to approach the play backwards, trying to fix the "problem" of that last speech. He worked forward from the beginning, so we didn't know finally what direction we were going to take with the ending until very late in the process. Even in our first preview, it wasn't entirely set. I think that's why it seemed to work for us on stage, because we built everything in front of that speech first, so it ended up an organic and logical extension of what we laid as a foundation.

David and I talked a lot about Kate's backstory. The first and most obvious thing was the absence of the mother from the play. She's not once mentioned, totally a blank—which to me says death or desertion. I tend to walk the road of death. Instead of trying to play Kate as the shrewish maid of twenty (David initially wanted to cast somebody in their mid-thirties or early forties), I started to think of the role in terms of an experienced woman, one who's had love and lost it. That became an important touchstone for me— that Kate not only has lost a mother, a female figure that she can look up to, but she's been betrayed or left or her lover died. I'm thirty, and I wanted to approach Kate from that angle—someone with a little more Beatrice in her.

There is a lot of animal imagery in *Shrew*, which helped as I got into the rehearsal room, focusing on the *commedia* aspects of this play. "Caged animal" is a good description, definitely part of Kate. There's Petruchio's "haggard" speech, comparing Kate to an untamed falcon, and the play likens Kate to the non-metaphorical shrew, the actual animal, in her mannerisms and the instinct for self-protection that is a counterpoint to Petruchio's groundedness, his "I'm here, this is me, deal with it" energy. I was also shocked by how much money comes up. I knew the concept of dowries, I knew that Petruchio's wanting to "wive it wealthily," to buy a rich bride, offended some people. But for everybody else in the play, even the clowns, money matters, too. How much money must mean to the women is pushed aside, because the men do most of the talking about it.

That idea seems very accessible and modern to me. In order to be settled in this marriage, in this society, they're going to need money, and she's willing to play the game, in the play's final scene. At least that's the way I'm playing it. Initially David was interested in the idea of Kate sneaking back onstage after she dumps Bianca and the widow offstage, rejoining the party just in time to overhear Petruchio suggest that the men make a wager about which wife is most obedient. We tried it and tried it until one day we looked at each other and said, "Let's not do this." There were good reasons to try having Kate witness the bet—to show her ability to roll with the punches and fit into the plan she sees her husband devising—but we felt it would mean more for her to come in of her own volition, not knowing (as Shakespeare's text indicates). David did want it to be a big bet, for high stakes, so that when Dad says I'm going to give you twenty thousand more, "another dowry to another daughter," it matters—it's a nest egg, to help our life as a couple.

My entire process changed in 2012, before *Shrew*, because Lue Douthit [Director of Literary Development and Dramaturgy] introduced me to charting in the Black Swan Lab. Basil

Kreimendahl, a young female playwright, had written a play called *Orange Julius*, about a father and daughter. It was a good play to chart in the Lab, because Lue felt that Basil didn't entirely know everything that was in her play. She's a very gifted writer—gorgeous images—but Lue wanted to show her exactly how and when things paid off, where images appeared, and whether they should come back later. What does it mean if you show Agent Orange powder falling here, but don't use it later on?

No one does all that better than Lue. When I watched her open Basil's eyes to what was actually in her play, the structure she had built instinctively, it completely converted me to being a "charter." That's where I start now. It's also part of what I'm starting to consider my director's brain. But having gone through the process with Lue and Basil, I realized that I needed to chart the play in order to make informed choices as an actor, to know what to look for. Oh, this word needs to pop. Why? Somebody else may *tell* you that, but it doesn't always make sense, and you're doing it just because somebody asked you to.

You need to know the entire play, not just your role. So over November and December, I started with *Shrew*. I didn't have butcher paper, so I took 8-1/2 x 11 sheets and taped them together and got my colored pencils out. I decided to start by charting elements that I wanted to focus on in *Shrew:* war imagery; wildlife and nature imagery; certain words like "shrew," "curst," "law," "money," anything to do with the word "marriage" or the uniting of two people; and the spectacle in the play: bad behavior, silence, music, pageantry, disguise.

I knew from the essays I had read that for all Kate's vociferous expression of herself, there are great chunks of the play where she is silent, so I graphed where and when that happened and who else was silent. It took me a couple of weeks, but by the end I felt I had a comprehensive knowledge of the play that I didn't have before. I knew going into rehearsal that certain moments and scenes needed to be highlighted, that a specific word needs to be heard, that if I don't really land on a particular idea, I can't build to anything. When I leave Petruchio on stage alone, what do I need to highlight for myself earlier in the scene to enable him to say his lines? It was mostly about knowing what I was saying and why I was saying it.

I did that kind of charting both for *Shrew* and for *A Streetcar Named Desire*. It was interesting to observe the differences between the Shakespeare play and the modern text, specifically in the stage directions—which may or may not be Shakespeare's and differ depending on the Folio or Quarto or whatever text you're looking at. Tennessee Williams, in the Signet version of *A Streetcar Named Desire*, gives very full, specific stage directions, focused on color and sound or the quality of a character's movement.

Because my casting as Kate in *Shrew* came as a complete surprise, there was suddenly this big thing to do. So I focused before and during rehearsal on *Shrew*, and let *Streetcar* slip for a while. I'm a little embarrassed that I had never done anything like charting before. Seeing its value, feeling confident about making informed choices inside the character work, I think it's something I'll continue to do. Simple things came up for me in reading and rereading the text so many times—like disguise, in the sense of people dissembling. Kate isn't. She's never in disguise. So many people are pretending to be somebody else, speaking in somebody else's voice, but at least on the page, she's completely authentic. I noticed Kate's early line, "I'll not be gone till I please myself." Her very last line of the play is "And place your hand below your husband's foot, in token of which duty, if *he please*. . . ." There's no way I'd have realized that without the charting work, looking for things that pop. When I started to move into the character work, I saw that this is a woman who is so hurt and upset, so judged by her society, that all she can hold onto is: "I'm only going to do things if it's okay for me, if I'm happy"—and ironically, she is miserable! By the end of the play, that person who was like a caged animal is opened up to love enough to say, "I'm going to do something for somebody that I love, and that is going to give me pleasure, because it pleases him."

I don't studiously avoid watching other actors' performances of a role, but I don't try to track down every recorded film and television version. Watching another production, I try to get past my judgment about what worked and what didn't, try not to focus on line delivery and specific choices but on the production as a whole. If I'm having trouble understanding a line, why it comes where it does, or what I want to say, I'll look at other people's choices, to round out my library of options. Typically I'll find my way to my own choice; sometimes I'll blatantly steal something if it's really good.

When I try to memorize a part sitting at home, it never works out for me. I mis-memorize, or I get married to a choice and can't see beyond that. After a lot of trial and error, I've realized that the best course—and Derrick Weeden gave me this advice—is just to read the play over and over. Don't focus on memorizing, just read it and become familiar with it. And I did that, through the charting. When I get up on my feet with script in hand in the rehearsal room, as soon as I start attaching actions to words or thoughts, it sticks for me. It's about listening, too. The way I'll memorize a line is listening and watching somebody deliver the line preceding mine. My emotional reaction to that, then looking down on the page and seeing my line, lets my brain make a connection. It's not just the words but all of what I'm receiving in this moment that leads into the next line. I envy the people who can memorize quickly, because I can't until I'm up on my feet. Staying home alone, I can't do it.

Stella in *Streetcar* was a really different process for me from Kate in *Shrew*. From the very beginning I knew it was a role that I wanted to tackle, and I had high hopes of getting cast. I'd been familiar with the story since I was a small child. My father (Bill Geisslinger) had played Stanley; I went to see Marco Barricelli play Stanley; I loved the movie version (well, most of it), and I read *Streetcar* several times over the summer of 2012, so I put that on the back burner. When *Streetcar* rehearsals came up a couple of days after *Shrew* opened, I had a moment of absolute terror. I hadn't finished charting *Streetcar* the way I had with *Shrew*. I felt like "I DON'T KNOW WHAT'S IN THE PLAY AND I DON'T KNOW WHAT MY JOB IS AND I THOUGHT I KNEW!" So I rushed the charting and didn't do it as thoroughly as *Shrew*—but then Stella was not as mysterious to me as Kate was.

That's not to say that Stella is not complex and wonderful in her own right, but Kate's silences and anger were more of a mystery to me. Stella is for the most part the consciously light counterpoint to what Blanche brings into her house. Stella knows her sister well; she knows there's this undercurrent and history of suffering. So I had this realization: don't go to the dark place until you *really* go. Stave it off, stave it off. You're sending your sister to the mental institution but you have to, because it's for the good of your family. You can't stay with that man and sleep with him if you think that Blanche's rape allegation is true. Wait until the moment where the darkness actually hits—which isn't until the last moment of the play.

At some point I realized that Stella's journey is the inverse of Kate's. Where Stella ends the play is comparable to where Kate begins her journey, and where Stella starts is where Kate ends. Christopher Liam Moore, our director, wanted the last moment of the play to be one of complete frozen indecision— comparable to that "caged animal" predicament of Kate. I agreed wholeheartedly. Some productions choose to insert material— in the movie, Stella leaving Stanley, or on stage, something the actress does to indicate that she's going to be out of there on the next train. Some productions go the opposite way—"Okay,

I'm here, I'm going to stick it out for the long haul, that's done," with sobbing and relief and commitment to the decision. Chris really wanted to end with the indecision. Let the audience walk away with strong opinions one way or the other, or see the indecision: "O my God, what's she going to do?" We wanted it to be unsettling, not easy to wrap your head around, because it's not easy for any of us on stage.

As an actor I'm often presented with cultural and historical situations utterly different from now, Shakespeare included. I don't think it would do any justice to our history as a society or to Tennessee Williams talking about America in the 1940s to sweep under the carpet, or downplay, the violence that Stella and Blanche undergo. Because it happened—it's still happening. At least as Williams saw it, that's the way things were, and it's a worthwhile perspective to examine. We pretend that we don't abuse each other in that way—backhanding your wife in a poker game—but perhaps the abuse we involve ourselves in is emotional, on a similar scale. Have we really changed all that much?

Four people come to mind who together comprise my ideal director: Ken Albers, Libby Appel, Chris Moore, and David Ivers. I'm lucky to have worked with them, some more than once. A director has to recognize the importance of trusting the actor, bringing her into early phases of the collaboration. That allows the conversation to go deeper when you do get into the room. Shared language and rapport with the director make everything better, especially when you're playing a large role. The ideal director depends on the role I'm playing. For example, David Ivers allowed me to leap into the territory of co-creation with him, but it's just not useful or possible for a director to invite that when you're playing the third soldier—there are too many voices. You can't have everybody behind the table conferring with Penny Metropulos the way she did with John Tufts, our

Prince Hal, in *Henry IV, Part One*. David Ivers is collaborative, yet at the same time he's able to say, "No, that's not the direction we want to go in." We're all big kids and can hear that. More and more, I feel that good direction has to do with making sure that everybody knows they are heard. We try so many things—which is lovely—but David has the ability to do that and then say no. That's as good as hearing "Yes, do that," because everything informs our path.

And we as actors—I find myself now walking the line of "Does my voice need to be heard at this moment?" I spent a lot of years being quiet and just listening, and then I went through a phase of "Oh, I have an idea! I gotta share it from the mountaintops." Now I'm more moderate. "Pick your battles" implies a war, and it's not that. It's about being sensitive, in the collaborative process, to when you can interject a thought, when it's valuable for it to be heard, and when it's better just to hold that idea and see what plays out organically as we work through this in the room. Maybe something even better will happen.

I was having a terrible time in the *Shrew* scene where I brought Bianca out to tie her up. David early on wanted Bianca to be on roller skates, at the end of a long rope that gradually got more taut as I trudged onstage, so that she would eventually whip out past me like a slingshot. I tried and tried, but we couldn't make the rope behave the same way every time with our human bodies. That's the only time I came close to a meltdown in rehearsal. I finally went to David and said, "I can't do this, I can't make it work, and emotionally it feels wrong for me to let Bianca get that far away, to lose that closeness and control when I interrogate her." And David said, "I didn't realize there was an emotional component that wasn't lining up for you. Let's figure it out." He could let go of the roller skates, something that had been locked into his mind from the early phases of the design process.

David Ivers is an actor. When an actor/director asks something of you emotionally, there's an implied understanding of what it's going to cost you to get there. If today was not your best day, that's okay. This is a generalization, but actor/directors tend to be less goal-oriented and more process-oriented. They understand the value of continuing through a scene even when it's not working. They see the value of failing a couple of times. Actor/directors understand that a performance has to be sustainable, repeatable over the long haul, in our case sometimes for ten months. People who have done the kind of season we do here know what is possible within those boundaries.

Tracy Young is another actor/director whom I admire. She doesn't beat around the bush—and I actually prefer that. She used her strong *commedia* background with The Actors' Gang, in Los Angeles, to shape Moliere's *The Imaginary Invalid* and *The Servant of Two Masters*. She was able to see potential, to think "that person could do it," when she cast people who lacked *commedia* training or were new to the company. Not all of us have the same facility as David Kelly, so she offered clowning workshops to give us the tools she knew we were going to need. We'd have *commedia* half-days, when we would just do games and exercises.

I've had wonderful mentors here: Ken Albers, Catherine Davis, Derrick Weeden, Demetra Pittman, Robin Nordli, Robynn Rodriguez, Libby Appel, and my dad, Bill Geisslinger (working on *Streetcar* with him as the assistant director was wonderful). I have never studied formally under one school or teacher; I can't claim to be a Stanislavskian or anything. I just take what's useful to me from what I learn. I'd say I'm a repertory actor. The directors and actors that I've mentioned—that's the kind of actor I am, or want to be. My résumé is limited, because I've spent so much time here, but because this is a repertory company, I've worked with a lot of different people. The older I get, and the more shows I work on, the more I realize that even after a hundred-plus performances of *Shrew*, if I can be awake and present in the moment in every show we do, I'm still learning. But that's also exhausting, and I am ready for a break.

For the last couple of years I've been fairly certain that directing and writing is where I want to head if possible, as much as I love acting and will want to continue to do that. I've been getting antsy watching in rehearsal. I keep thinking, "Oh, the focus is not good!" I'm probably only occasionally right, but I still feel the urge to express myself. We'll see if it pans out, when I work this year as associate director for David Ivers's production of *Cocoanuts* in Mark Bedard's new adaptation.

I'm getting to the place in my career where I have the connections, the relationships with people, where I can go to an artistic director or a director and pitch an idea or project. I feel empowered enough to say, to the right person, "Hey, here is something I really want to do. I think we could do it. Are you interested?" But it's all in the timing. And for me it's more about *who* I want to work with now. You can make any part interesting and fun to play, but you're going to have to do it a number of times over a number of weeks with a certain group of people. The people are actually more important to me than the parts. There's something to be said for doing work for work's sake—but in our case, it's easy to actually enjoy it if you open yourself up. And that's more fun. Why not?

Jonathan Haugen as Henry Higgins in *My Fair Lady*. Photo: Jenny Graham, OSF.

Jonathan Haugen

In 16 seasons at OSF, Jonathan Haugen has played, among other roles, Henry Higgins in *My Fair Lady*; Gov. George Wallace and Walter Reuther in *All The Way*; Brutus in *Julius Caesar*; Antonio in *The Merchant of Venice*; Sir Robert Cecil in *Equivocation*; Capulet in *Romeo and Juliet*; Doctor Faustus in *The Tragical History of Doctor Faustus*; Talbot in *1 Henry VI*; Bertram in *All's Well That Ends Well*; and Christy in *The Playboy of the Western World*.

I GREW UP NEXT TO A TRAILER PARK in Arizona. I left high school—this was in Phoenix—and got a job, moved into my own apartment, and within a very short time I was twiddling my thumbs. I had friends who did community theater and cabaret acts, so for grins I auditioned, and got into a play. I thought it was great. All during this time, and before I dropped out of high school, I was studying to be a musician. That was the big push in my family. Neither of my parents were musicians but I think—in retrospect—they believed that you need to give your kids a discipline that is not necessarily applicable to how to make money, not "This is going to be my job." For lack of a better way of putting it, an impractical discipline, that later in life gives you an immense form of joy. By the time I dropped out of high school, I had started singing and studying opera. Even while I was working and doing community theater, I was also taking singing lessons, and I thought that's what I would go off and do. And I did for a while.

I did gigs in New York, in Orange County—nothing huge, but good money and a way still to grow professionally. Like a lot of young singers I was given parts too heavy for me, but I was thrilled to have the opportunity, so I barreled my way through. After five or six performances, though, I couldn't sing for another month. By comparison with what we do here in Ashland, there's a lot more money in the opera business, but it's a lot more brutal. I had vocal problems, and it became clear that I wasn't going to get what I wanted out of singing. When I had to rest my voice for three months and lost a job, I got a professional acting gig by accident.

It was a production of *Hot l Baltimore*. A friend said, "Do this! Just do this!" so I went in and auditioned. I was a kid and I didn't know what the hell I was doing, but why not? The very worst that could happen was they'd find me out, they'd drive me away, and I'd sneer and have a great story. Who cares? Then I got a callback and thought, "Gee, this is interesting," and I got offered the job. As much as I enjoyed theater then, I didn't have a lot of respect for it. I didn't get it then. Good theater has an ephemeral quality that's very hard to determine, to rank. When you see an opera, if the person is singing flat, you can take out a mechanical device and confirm they're flat. The same is true of a ballet dancer. If that's not a 90 degree extension, all you've gotta do is check it.

Acting's not that way. I know actors who have horrendous skills, you can't understand a word they're saying—get them up on stage, they're riveting! They're absolutely illuminating, not only to the human condition but to a piece of text, and they may not even know what's coming out of their mouths. Who cares? It doesn't matter. That mysterious quality of acting drove me crazy as a kid. How do you get better at something like that? How do you measure it? Something you see a lot in our culture is people trying to gain status, by saying, "I can hit a 90 degree doing the *Black Swan*," or "Look, I hit the high F at the end of the *cabaletta*." We don't really have that in acting. You see some people wanting that: "Well, I'm Equity. I've worked at. . . ." But whatever those status rungs are, who cares? Now, that ephemeral quality is one of the things I love most about theater. You can take somebody who works at a 7-11, and if it's the right role, and you talk to them in the right way, their need to get out there and say their part may illuminate it far better than somebody who's been in the business, training for thirty years. I love that. It's a very ego-busting art.

So I fell into theater. I kept doing both theater and opera, but in time my hearing failed enough, and I had enough vocal problems, that I thought, "I've got to put this aside." And once I did, I said, "OK, acting, then. That's what I'm gonna do." I should preface this by saying I was raised with Shakespeare in my home; it has always been a passion of mine. I wasn't much interested in any theater outside of Shakespeare. The parallel between music and the poetic math, the rhythmic math that's in Shakespeare seemed very clear to me. I could grab onto that: "Look at all those *m*'s, look at how this beat falls here, look at how this line runs over—look at that." The sound, the musicality of Shakespeare made sense to me. So I went whole hog into becoming a Shakespearean actor.

I went to Cal Arts for training, where I met Libby Appel. Cal Arts was not a big Shakespeare school, but Libby was a big Shakespeare person. I loved the school, loved her, and I just grew there. Cal Arts at the time had a wonderful blend. All this fantastic craftsmanship—here's the appropriate way to speak, here's how to scan—was sitting right there for you. But that was counterbalanced by many different approaches to acting, many versions of the Method, whereas in music, all you're given is the math, the technique. Anything else has to be yours, private-ly, and that element—what way down the line will make you Wynton Marsalis or not Wynton Marsalis—is not discussed in music school. So Cal Arts was a wonderful environment to get a feel for acting, a really good blend of technical information and voodoo. Most schools do one or the other.

It's not as if Cal Arts *worried* about the balance. They were up front. We were told from the day we walked in, "You choose. You learn what you want to learn. Nobody's going to kick you. We're not here to be your parents. The library is open, our doors are open, all this stuff is going on that you have access to, but you have to have the gumption to do it. If you're late for class, nobody's going to care. That's up to you." I loved that—what you want, you get. Perfect environment for me, because at that point I was voracious for anything.

When I was in school, Libby Appel was simply the most interesting person I'd ever met— not apologetic, full of fabulous information, like a house on fire. I still view her as a teacher, and I think in her mind I'm probably still her student. There were many other great teachers there as well—Rodger Hender-son, Susan Hegarty. But I was also mentored by other students who taught me so much—people I still am friends with and rely on artistically. That was my first real foray into an artistic community, surrounded by people who were filled with self-motivation: "I'm gonna start a production company, we're gonna put on these plays. . . ." It was amazing.

If you're an actor, all you've got is your résumé. Walk in, don't get the part, go to the next audition, go to the next and the next. And it is an art form you must practice with other people; you can't practice alone. You paint, you sculpt, you garden alone—no problem. But you act with somebody else. For me, what was amazing about Cal Arts is that I ended up with a team of people who did everything. We started a production company in Los Angeles and made money—not a lot, but enough for everybody to have a drink and pay for gas at the end of the night. It wasn't "we need a designer, we need a leading man." Instead it was, do you know how to sew? No? Then I'll show you. Everybody doing everything—not necessarily by consensus, but it was a production team. I would love to see a school now that taught specifically on that line—how to build your own theater company, how to learn to do everything, so that it ceases to be specialized, it ceases to be "I don't know, ask the designer," or "Gee, I don't know about this light, can you make it more blue here?" I don't want to take anybody's job away—but I miss that collective feeling that happens in the room. It's why I still go away and do smaller projects, because I want to get back there. At a certain level of financial success and business structure, that's harder to sustain, but of all the places I've worked, OSF is my favorite.

There have always been lots of little start-up companies. The trick of it is, do they hold? Do they live? I had a company for three years, stayed in the black, but sustaining it was impossible. Sustainability cannot be based on money. Sustainability is based on manpower. Overworked people are usually what cause these businesses to collapse—or mismanagement of money, of course. But I tend to be one of those Pollyannas who say you don't need money. You want to put on a play, get some crepe paper and put on a goddamn play. What I don't want to hear is another excuse why you can't. I had a gal come up to me a number of years ago, a playwright who had seen something I had written and was very kind to me about it, and she said, "Oh, I'm just dying to get back to playwriting, it's been months and months and months." I said, "Oh, what's preventing you?" And she said, "My computer's down." I said, "You know what? I have a bank receipt in my pocket that I don't need anymore, and surely you can find a pen." I'd love to have my feet tickled while I write. I don't get that, but I still write. Little companies with no resources, out there putting on plays—that's the stuff I want to see.

I played Laertes in a production of *Hamlet* in Mendocino-Ft. Bragg, just a few years ago. A buddy of mine who has a company called Rock the Ground produced and directed it. Full text, every single word. Four hours long, two intermissions. Most of the people had never been in a play, let alone a Shakespeare play. We sat down with these people and we explained, this is what this line means, this is how this scene works. They marched out, said their lines, marched away. But it was a huge success, completely sold out, in an area where most people had never seen live theater in their lives. There was a response at the end, in that applause, that I've never heard anywhere where a ticket cost more than $20. Beforehand my partner Eddie, who's seen many *Hamlet*s, and acted in a few, said, "OK, I'm braced, I'm ready." When he came out, he said, "It's the best *Hamlet* I've ever seen." How can you say that? "Well," he said, "they were alive."

That language was so big and so huge in them. They had to juggle twelve balls at once. Yeah, some of the words were said wrong, yeah, you could tell they weren't professional actors. I don't care. That's the kind of stuff that makes me love theater, and not regret being away from an art form that's based as heavily on math as music is. You want an art form that's not elitist, it's acting. Which is what I love about it. If I could make as much money and have as much stability working with a guy from the 7-11, making cardboard sets and polyester costumes, I would go off and do that in a second. It just doesn't work that way. We need the money, we need the stability of the Festival, without question. I used to travel all over the place. I still want these other experiences, to meet new people, but I don't want to go away and work at another big theater. OSF to me is just perfect.

My first year at OSF was 1990; I was in two outdoor shows, *Henry V* and Libby's *The Winter's Tale*. The following year I was in Jim Edmondson's *Our Town* and an Ayckbourn play, and then the third year I did *All's Well That Ends Well* and *Playboy of the Western World*. Bertram, in *All's Well*, is a great role, but if you don't arc it, it doesn't work. If you start out the same, you're too despicable by the end. You have to show that Bertram is somebody who has been driven away by the woman he thought of as his sister, who went to war, got injured, and came back as a very different person. If he's just the guy who didn't like Helena because of her class, the play sucks. We wanted it really clear that I thought of her as my sister. From the get-go I tried to have a physicality with her that would be inappropriate with somebody other than your sister. So when she's going "Marry me, marry me," it's like "Gross!"

I've done *All's Well* a lot. People dwell on the ambiguity at the end—the "if, if, if, if." I don't believe in it, because I think they're misusing Elizabethan words. "The king's a beggar, now the play is done: / All is well ended, if this suit be won, / That you express content; which we will pay, / With strife to please you, day exceeding day. . . ." People always construe "if this suit be won" as referring to Helena and Bertram, but it's not. "If this suit be won" refers to the players—"if you liked our play." I don't think *All's Well* is an easy romance, but I do think it's a romance. Most directors now are directing the play for Helena, who would most likely have been perceived as a villain. It's one of the reasons she's given so many soliloquies, which are usually given to people of questionable ethics in the plays, so we can understand their point and say it's okay. Now in our view she's a proto-feminist hero. The same thing has happened with *The Winter's Tale*. They're viewed as devices for female liberation as opposed to liberation generally. Twenty years ago nobody was doing *The Winter's Tale*. When the BBC televised the whole canon, the ad called it "Shakespeare's rarely seen *The Winter's Tale*." You can't swing a dead cat now without hitting *The Winter's Tale*.

I'd do Leontes or Prospero in a second, with the right person. One of the worst things in the world is getting a chance to play the role you've always wanted to play, but with the wrong director, because then the role won't *be* the one you wanted to play. There are also roles you think you don't want to play, and then in the middle of the run you think, "Oh my God, this is my favorite role ever"—like Albany in *King Lear* or Cerimon in *Pericles*. Leontes to me is tricky, like Iago. I'm the last person anybody should have to see play Iago. I might as well have written across my forehead, "*He* did it." Because no matter what I do, on stage I'm going to look more sinister than most people. The person who should play Iago is someone like Ray Porter, someone you see doing Bottom or Costard or Falstaff. Leontes is the same way, a role you'd expect me to do. But as I get older, I'm pushing away from what we know. It's tough going to see *Shrew* again. How many have you seen, how many have you been in? From an actor's standpoint, the canon is limited. It's different for playgoers. Even though we have people who've been coming here for thirty years, OSF always has an influx of new playgoers. I really want to try to foster new stuff, not just the occasional Marlowe play, not just "Oh my God, someone is doing a production of *Endymion*." There are tons of anonymous Elizabethan plays that no one will do because they're anonymous, but they're great plays. Even *Edward III* is stageworthy, but I don't think you'll see it soon anywhere where anyone is making much money.

As a Shakespeare geek, I love the histories. I played Talbot in OSF's last adaptation of *Henry VI, Part One*, which was heavily cut. It was a great role that I thought fit me perfectly, though most people wouldn't think so. I had very different interpretations of it than Libby Appel, the director. Most of the play's other characters talk about how noble and wonderful and heroic Talbot is, but everything that comes out of his mouth is grisly and awful. I wanted to play that. The dramaturgical response was "Well, you're looking at it with contemporary eyes. In Shakespeare's time they wouldn't have seen these features as

JONATHAN HAUGEN | 113

bad." And I said, "No, what the play is doing is offering us two different perspectives." Libby said, "Look, honey, if you're character is this mean at the beginning of the play, when you do the death scene with your son, nobody's going to care." And I said, "I can do anything I want to, I could kill kittens on stage, and once I get to the scene with 'Oh my son is dying,' they'll love me." That's the point of the role, it's a common dramatic device in Shakespeare. Set the character up as this horrible person, and then you go, "Oh, I feel so much for him now." That's what's so awesome about the role: Talbot is a monster—and then you get to see him turn into a human being, and die. It's amazing.

I was thinking the other day about *The Merchant of Venice*. It's such a hard play to do now, the play's just so dastardly—but I liked our last production, when I played Antonio. I really liked the moment (it's not in the text—who cares?) where the gondola crosses behind the masquers partying and shouting, and after they've left, Shylock and I accidentally encounter each other, awkwardly. In the Elizabethan that summer, it seemed to rain on every show, while we all had to sit there through the long courtroom scene. Throughout the trial, I was laughing, joyous about paying Shylock's bond "with all my heart." Gregory Linington (Gratiano) said, "I don't understand what I'm supposed to play if Jonathan's doing that." And Bill Rauch, the director, said, "He's going crazy, that's what you play." Antonio finally gets to do something cool, noble, big—something other than the nothing which is mostly what his life has been.

That last scene in *The Merchant of Venice* is a bear. I've never done a production where everybody doesn't end up arguing about that last scene, because nobody wants to look like the bad guy. The *Merchant* where I played Bassanio fell apart because the Portia didn't want to look bad. The set was a big palace with a pair of staircases, and the director wanted us to come in together downstage, but then go up the opposite staircases and exit separately. She would have none of it: "No, they live happily ever after. Everybody gets theirs." In our OSF production, Bill Rauch and I were really simple with my Antonio; we just did it. Eventually Bill asked me what I thought my Antonio would do in that final scene at Belmont, and I said, "I don't go in. I let them go in. They forget about me, and I leave. That's the role. Everybody's coupled except for me. They're all married, they're all happy, they're all home. They sweep in and go 'Oh, wait, wait a minute'—but I'm gone."

Every role, every show, is different. How you prepare for a role depends on the text and the director and where you're coming from—what shows you've just come off, what other shows you're doing in rep. How I prep for Bill Rauch is completely different from how I would prep for Amanda Dehnert—two of my favorite directors, with vastly different rehearsal techniques, vastly different approaches. If Bill had been directing *My Fair Lady*, I would walk in the door knowing absolutely everything I was doing, technically—every note, every line, backwards and forwards. Amanda is exactly the opposite. I want to walk in the door knowing nothing, nothing. The only thing I did for her production of *My Fair Lady* was watch two clips from the movie. When Amanda texted me to ask, "Will you play Henry Higgins?" I texted back, "Yep." That was it. I didn't know *My Fair Lady*, but I know her. I felt I owed her, and the minute she called in a favor it was, "Done."

Julius Caesar was my first outing with Amanda. I had never met her before, although I had heard people talk about her rehearsals, and everything I heard I hated. Then I went and saw her *All's Well*. My mind completely changed, and I said, I want to work with that woman. When they announced *Julius Caesar*, I said, "I want to play Brutus with that woman." And most people said, "You're wrong for Brutus, you don't want to play Brutus." I said, "Nope. I want to play Brutus with that woman"—not Cassius, not Caesar. They're great parts, but Brutus is an impossible role. I wanted to do that role for that woman.

In rehearsal, every single time an actor's acting, Amanda watches. Show me another director who does that. Most don't. They eat, they multi-task, they look up. Every single time, no matter what, she watches. She knows every single word of the script backward and forward. If I said, "You know that part when I don't know why I'm sad but—you know, that part, where…," she'd say, "Start from 'In sooth, I know not why I am so sad.'" Boom. Every single word, she knows. She could get up and act, if somebody was sick. We had a joke about Danforth Comins going out so Amanda could play Mark Antony. Because she could have.

She and I work together very well. For many people she can be scarily direct. Once when we were rehearsing *Julius Caesar,* Gregory Linington stopped the scene and said, "I really want a chair in here." And Amanda said, "Why did you stop the scene? Just go get a chair!" Gregory: "Oh, can I do that?" And she laughed and said, "Am I gonna get up and stop you? Get what you need. Don't stop and give me a list, just get what you need." Very empowering. And very different. Actors are trained to be obedient. It's very clear, in our union, who has the power and who doesn't. So we're used to saying yes, and then trying to get what we want. Well, the older you get, the less you want to do that, even if it costs you your job. And then there are the people you don't understand, like Ping Chong, a great gentleman I enjoyed working for on *Throne of Blood,* where you say, "Tell me what you want, man. What do you want—the hand here? A little higher? OK, got it. There? Great, perfect." I'm not going to give him anything other than obedience because of the nature of the project. I just want to make sure I am there to respond to what he wants. But there are other instances—don't put me in a Shakespeare play unless you want my opinion. If you think you've figured out *Love's Labor's Lost,* or whatever, and you cast me in it because you think I look right, you've made a mistake.

I know *Julius Caesar.* I've been in the bloody thing a few times, seen it a million times. We didn't have a script till first day of rehearsal, and the poor cast was panicked. Not me—I had seen what happened with Amanda's *All's Well That Ends Well*. Fifteen minutes into watching that show, I was frowning. By the end I was transported. I felt the same way when I saw Bill Rauch's *Pirates of Penzance*. The first fifteen minutes I just wanted to take a fire extinguisher and spray everybody. By the end I was higher than a kite. Maybe it's because I started skeptical and ended amazed, but I saw what Amanda and her cast had done with *All's Well*—they ripped it apart, they re-wrote it, they expounded on it. Hitherto I was a man who did not believe in cutting a word. I didn't want your Civil War concept, I just wanted the text. She changed my mind.

Amanda is one of the few people I believe really knows how to cut Shakespeare. Now when I go to see Shakespeare plays that have been cut and are still three hours long, I want to say, "If you cut it, why do you need three hours?" I would suggest that you didn't cut it enough. You're walking a fence, trying to appease people. Don't. If you're going to cut the play, cut the damn play. Know what you're doing, and cut the play. Amanda did that with *Caesar*. I even remember wanting a line back, and planning to tell her that I wanted this line back, and I never did. You know why? I didn't need the line back. Everything I needed was already there. If you're experienced, you know when you want the lines. Just because there are more lines doesn't mean that you know what to do with them. You may have the top line count in a Moliere play, but you're still not the lead; you just have a boring, non-funny role with lots of lines.

I'm a musician. How do you cut five bars? How do you cut the second movement? But music isn't information; plays are. It's interesting how traditions become The Way It Is. It's one of the big problems we have dealing with Shakespeare because everybody knows how it goes and what it's supposed to be. It's like Varya and Lopakhin in Chekhov's *The Cherry Orchard*. The text never explains why he doesn't propose to her, but ask anybody, and they'll tell you exactly why, because they have built an answer in their own heads. Go back to the text, it's not there—and it's not there on purpose. That obliqueness is why Chekhov is the great modern playwright. He refuses to show cause and effect, doesn't base his psychology on that. People just do stuff. Which I love, because I tend as a spectator watching a play to want to get my own story, not what they're telling me. I don't like it when I *know* everything an actor is playing, because it's usually too simple. That story is there for me to get, not for you to tell me what it is. People feel that Shakespeare needs to be explained, but I don't. Most of the people who had no education still got it. Just do the play. March the characters out there for four hours, and when they die, let them lie on the stage.

For me, character work happens at different moments, different times. In certain circumstances there are modifications you want to make—rhythm, temper, physical traits—but never in rehearsal. I'm not going to wait, and make my colleagues wait, while I try to figure out my limp. I take that as my responsibility, as secondary work on my own time. If I'm worried in the rehearsal room about my carriage, my rhythm, my gestures, then the job's too hard. In some roles, there isn't much of that work, but there are other roles where I need to do more. I knew right out of the gate that I wanted to gain weight when I played Brutus. I knew. All of the things that Cassius says about him are from long ago. Brutus is dilapidated now, not the young idealist. Why hasn't he acted? Has he just been waiting? He's thought revolutionary stuff, but he's never said it. He's been enjoying his wife, he's been eating candy bars, he's been friends with Caesar. He knows it's not great but…. Let's make no mistake, Cassius is the catalyst for change, and he's the one who says, "You used to be so cool, man. You were like the sharpest, the best. But you're just gross now." That's where I wanted to start from: "Yeah, I was a lot better than I am—but my knees didn't hurt then. Well, no—Cassius is right. I've become fat." What I didn't want was to be "the noblest Roman of them all." What does he need Cassius for then? Why have a partnership? Why does he need the spurring?

So going in, I knew that I wanted weight on me, and that I wanted to be more of an everyman in that world of hotheads. Between Greg Linington (Cassius) and Danforth Comins (Mark Antony), I did look kind of normal—but over time, things happen. There were a few hallmarks in the script that I felt I needed from the very get-go. To me, the Caius Ligarius scene is crucial. After the conspirators come to persuade Brutus to kill Caesar, there's all this discussion, they decide to assassinate Caesar, they wait while Brutus has the moment with the wife. She goes in the house, Caius Ligarius arrives, and Brutus says, "I'll be in, I just need to deal with this guy." Caius Ligarius and Brutus have a very long scene, which is usually perfunctory, or even cut, but I thought the entire play turned on this one scene. It is why he is able to do what he does to his wife, why he is able to destroy his country. To have this person who is physically compromised, dying, come to Brutus and say, "You are the soul of Rome, you are noble," is everything. Earlier in the scene the conspirators are arguing; they act like infants, like animals. But Caius Ligarius calls Brutus "Soul of Rome!" Forget the wife. There is no wife, and there is no soul of Rome—I knew that from the get-go. We never had to talk about it because Ako was playing Caius Ligarius, brilliantly. After we read the scene once, Amanda turned to me in rehearsal and said, "Do you need anything?" and I said "Not a damn thing. That's exactly it." But from there on, as you're rehearsing, you find more physical stuff, how the body needs to move, what you need to do to portray that person, in that state. All of that stuff for me gets done in secondary rehearsal at home.

When we were rehearsing *Doctor Faustus*, I was having trouble with my prayer to Satan. I knew the lines, I knew how to do the incantation, waving my wand, but it just wasn't right, and it was driving me crazy. So I went home after rehearsal, late at night, and worked on it for three or four hours. I lit all this incense in my shop, got a broomstick, set up my little scene, trying this and trying that to feel how it should work, and how it should grow. All of a sudden the lights flicked on, and I whipped around. Eddie was standing at the door. It was 3 o'clock in the morning. He said, "Are you okay?" And I said, "I'm just praying to the devil, for *Doctor Faustus*." It's a running joke in our house. I need a little privacy to try to get the character stuff in the body, to get the body in the right rhythm and carriage, responding in the right way to my character's thought process, making it second nature so I'm not thinking about it on stage.

During the show's run, that deepens more and more, but you have to be careful not to gild the lily, to go too far. There's a point where you have to back up and say, "Let it alone, stop." I know. When I played Malvolio at Cal Shakes for Jonathan Moscone a number of years ago, I would run home from rehearsal and go into my shop to work on my little behaviors for a few minutes more. After the second or the third night, I knew I was ruining it, so I let it alone, even though I wanted to keep playing. Instead I ate or watched TV or some stupid thing like that. But when I performed, my Malvolio was living there on stage, instead of left in my shop. I've seen people who were breathtakingly brilliant in the second week of rehearsal, and when the show opens they suck, because there are too many bells and whistles, too many quirks, too many little mannerisms. It's just whipped cream, sprinkles, cherry, more whipped cream.

Learning lines, I use my house. I walk and I move and I do physical things. If I'm doing the lines with my body, I can get it. If I have to go in as an understudy and don't have much time, there are other techniques I can use to download that information fast. I'm not going to keep it very long, and it's not going to be as accurate. But normally, if I'm building something big, I have to physically move while I'm doing it. It doesn't necessarily mean I'm acting the role, just that the brain function and motor skills and body have to be engaged all at once, so that language becomes secondary. Once I've got it, I can choose to do with that language anything I want, as opposed to "The line goes like this, because I've memorized it like this." The process has to leave you flexible when you walk into the rehearsal room, or in performance, or wherever you want to be responsive with the language. But I'm a slow study; I'm terrible. If I'm actually going to perform a role for a long run and really learn it, it takes me forever. I enjoy it, though, because that's when I learn things about the role.

My joke at work is "Oh, I'm not memorized; I just know what to say." One night, during the last OSF production of *Henry VIII*, we were doing a really hard ensemble scene toward the end, which nobody understands. It was freezing cold, and we were dying out there. I was playing Gardiner, the Bishop of Winchester, who is plotting against Cranmer, the Archbishop of Canterbury, played by David Kelly, an actor I've known for years and a good friend. In the middle of a long speech, David started screwing up. This is a guy you don't need to help across the street, who knows what he's doing, and like most of us, he usually can rewrite, just making stuff up on the fly. So David got back on track. But then he got lost again and couldn't get out. He came to an absolute stop in the midst of our big argument in the council scene—I'm the bad guy and he's the good guy— and turned to me and said, "I know not what to say, my lord." I turned around and said, "I do." And I finished his character's speech.

I like distractions; they help when I'm learning lines. Get that language so that it lives somewhere, even if the phone is ringing. Shakespeare is the easiest stuff in the world to memorize, because it's metered and I know the genre. Most stuff that has a lot of formal conventions is easier. Writing that requires a more natural delivery, that doesn't have any obvious poetic math to it—that's the stuff that's hard, because it's all based on the memorization of your thought process, and the language becomes a much greater part of the body product. I'm not saying there's not subtext in Shakespeare. I'm not one of those silly people who say, "It's all the language." Of course it's all the language, but the brain does a lot more things than just talk. Shakespeare still gives you much more guidance than Mamet or Pinter. But over time, those writers' plays reveal their structures, and you get them. I always find that the weirder it is, the easier it is. *Doctor Faustus* was like that, because it was so intensely different from Shakespearean structure.

I never got to see the *Doctor Faustus* I was in. That's the problem with being an actor. I saw Jessica Thebus's *As You Like It* in the Elizabethan and just loved the production, the use of the women above. Then I had to go into the show as understudy for Howie Seago for the end of the run, maybe five performances. Once I calmed down, I started noting my character's track, and the tracks of the people around me, but as actors we never really see the entire play; we never really hear it, have no idea what we're in. If I just walk my track, I do not get the sense of the show as a whole, even from an understudy tape.

People told me Robert Schenkkan's *All the Way* was breathtaking, but I didn't really get to see that. It was cool to be able to play several different people in the show—George Wallace, Paul Douglas, Walter Reuther—with different wigs, but if people knew what the backstage track was, they'd have a better idea of how hard the job is. I'm busy running to do a quick-change every time, down to my skivvies and changing everything else—glasses, wig, mustache—and trying to find my props. "Where's my fake cigarette?" Vroom, and back, vroom, and back. It's a lot of fun, but exhausting. It's also important for the actor, walking his particular track, to trust the whole. With somebody like Bill Rauch directing *All the Way*, I know that he knows what he's doing, so I'm not going to poo-poo a choice, assuming that I'm seeing the big picture when actually I'm only seeing a corner and missing the rest of it. That's one of the reasons why, as you become older, directors you can trust become so much more important.

The best working circumstance of my life was *Equivocation* with Bill Rauch (the director) and Bill Cain (the playwright) and the rest of the cast. Not the friendliest by any stretch of the imagination, but absolutely the most rigorous, to great effect. We, as actors, had no idea. I was convinced nobody was going to understand a word of the play, and I was angry that I had been cast in it. And, of course, after we all edited it and illustrated it and made it clear, it was spectacular. Bill Cain and Bill Rauch made a fantastic team together, because they were not complicit, not working from any collective standpoint. I viewed them as rivals, enemies. And it drew the best work out of both of them, just so potent. Bill Cain is a curmudgeon, but a magnificent thinker. It became important for us to be able to work on the play in the most efficient and truest way, and sometimes that didn't mean being polite. Sometimes it meant saying "Give me a break!" to the author, to all of us. I remember John Tufts and I getting into it, teasing each other back and forth, until he was really getting pissed—but eventually he started laughing, and everything was fine. It was this incredible working situation where we didn't need to ask somebody if they needed a coaster. We didn't need to worry about honoring each person. If you had something to say, get me to shut up and push me down and say it. Nobody needed a talking stick.

Chris Albright-Tufts (Judith Shakespeare), the only woman in the cast, finally stepped up and said, "Let me tell you what this play is *really* about . . ." That was a wonderful, powerful moment. Not for one minute did anybody worry, "Did they like me?" "Am I being mean?" "I shouldn't have said that, I went too far," "I need to remember he's my boss." To hell with that: you're building something, you're building something incredible. When you get to this level—and OSF maintains its integrity more than most places—it's easy to forget that, and to think about finding the next gig, getting to meet so-and-so, how you'll be perceived, whatever. And you forget it's just about building this cool show and driving it down the road. I suppose I'm a little sentimental that way. I vividly remember taking Bill Rauch out of an *Equivocation* rehearsal during a break and saying, "Thank you, you were right, I was wrong, I'm glad I'm in it."

I loved playing Sir Robert Cecil. Doing a part like that on the Elizabethan stage with sixty people, that's one thing. To do it with five other people—that's what was fun. To me the most dramatically fantastic turn comes when Cecil prophesies the future and sees his progeny. In that moment, at the end of the play, after he's been duped, Cecil is made so powerful by what he's learned from this artist, Shakespeare—something you don't get until you deliver that speech on the stage. Shakespeare's company has performed *Macbeth*, they didn't do what Cecil wanted, he's lost, they've won, the King gives the company money, and Cecil's humiliated. He could easily have the players ruined—and he doesn't. He's nice to the actors—"Hey, I thought your play was great"—and he's nice to Shakespeare's daughter. What is he doing? People thought Cecil should be pissed. No—they're missing it. There is no cat and mouse in the play. At any point Cecil can say "kill him" and Shakespeare's dead. Instead Cecil's using him, he's learning.

I really liked the character of Cecil quite a lot. No, I don't think he should cut people's heads off, but there are other things about that spirit that I loved. I actually did a lot of research for *Equivocation*, and I'm not a researcher. I don't believe in research at all. If you're acting the role, it's what's on the page. Stop there, or it's going to be too much—unless the role is so thin that you need more material to put in there. That wasn't the case with Cecil. But somebody gave me all of his extant writing, and it was mind-boggling. When his daughter, who was also deformed, first went to court, Cecil wrote the most beautiful letter of instructions on how she's to be treated, how she's to be dressed, how everything must be arranged so that her deformity is hidden. He basically says I know, from growing up with this deformity, what it's like, so I will protect you. I stopped, jumped off the research track, because the history became more interesting than the play. That's where we don't want to go as actors.

One of the things I admire about Bill Rauch is his risk. Sometimes I think it pays off wildly and sometimes it doesn't. People ask, why can't we just do only the really good shows? No, it doesn't work that way. You can get consistency if you stay in the middle, but I admire that risk that gave us *Equivocation*. I would like to see less emphasis on new work here, having seen enough pieces that I don't think we should have done. But I would have said the same thing about *Equivocation*, too, so I'm glad I'm not the boss.

I personally would love to see more obscure works come up in our repertory—more obscure American works, more obscure poetic works, translations of great European writers like Rostand and Victor Hugo, who was a playwright foremost, not a novelist. Works like these reach across to you over a hundred-year period of time, saying we have information we want to give you.

And yes, I believe that Shakespeare should be lauded, but there are a lot of kings, knaves, queens, all these other positions to be filled. I loved *Doctor Faustus*. There isn't a role in Shakespeare that large, not even close. There's other Marlowe I would love to see—*Tamburlaine; Dido, Queen of Carthage; even The Massacre at Paris*. Not to mention the Jacobeans. Jerry Turner did them, but he didn't do them with respect. He started read-throughs by saying, these are badly written plays. People know Shakespeare so well, and know the sound of it so well, that when they hear something different, they say it's not as good. But how can you possibly say Puccini, or Wagner, is not as good a composer as Verdi is? They're just different. You can say you prefer one, but if you take a set of ideas from one and bring it to the other, they're not going to apply. *The White Devil* is a magnificent rollercoaster of a play, but Jerry was doing it as "bad" Shakespeare rather than good Jacobean tragedy. You have to look at it in a very different light.

When I was a kid and decided to be an actor, all I wanted to do was bring that stuff back, to show people why *The White Devil* is a great play, show people that the world is larger than they thought. What would be very interesting, not that it could ever happen: do the whole Shakespeare canon in chronological order, with the same actors, then start doing the Jacobean plays and see what happens. My guess is, they'd really get the Jacobean plays, because they've gone through all of Shakespeare. They've done it; they don't want to repeat. They would be able to see what came next. They'd have better appreciation for it. One problem. You've gotta sell too many seats and the shows run too long. What you need—and I would love to see OSF do it—is limited runs. I'd kill to see *The Maid's Tragedy*. It's the lost stuff, all of the lost stuff. Somebody said to me, "Well, don't you think maybe that it deserves to be lost?" I don't know. I'm not comfortable thinking so until I've turned it over in my own hands.

Anthony Heald as Shag in *Equivocation*. Photo: Jenny Graham, OSF.

Anthony Heald

In 10 seasons at OSF, Anthony Heald has played, among other roles, Duke Vincentio in *Measure for Measure*; Shag in *Equivocation*; Iago in *Othello*; Shylock in *The Merchant of Venice*; Tartuffe in *Tartuffe*; Stage Manager in *Our Town*; Wolsey in *Henry VIII*; Rosmer in *Rosmersholm*; Alfred P. Doolittle in *My Fair Lady*; Simyonov-Pischik in *The Cherry Orchard*; Patrick in *The Further Adventures of Hedda Gabler*; and Otto in *The Magic Fire*.

I GREW UP IN A HOME WITH a heady mix of culture, in a family that loved the theater and valued language. My father, who was English, studied Elizabethan literature at Cambridge University. When he came to this country, he became a college textbook editor, mostly in radical psychology. He was a brilliant man—national vice-president of MENSA, and at one time the educational director of the New York Communist Party.

My mother had grown up in New York City and Europe. She was best friends with the daughter of Norman Bel Geddes, the famous Broadway set designer, and she got to go to tech rehearsals and dress rehearsals of projects he was working on.

When my parents moved with the three kids out to Long Island in the late 1940s, they felt that they were out in the wasteland. It was all potato farms and new developments of tiny bungalows. So they started a play-reading group, which soon developed into a community theater

Though I acted in plays in high school, I never thought seriously that theater would be a possibility as a life for me. Then the second week of my freshman year at Michigan State University, I got cast in a production of *Zoo Story*. It turned out to be a massive hit among the theater students, and our cast, though new to the department, instantly became part of the in-crowd. I was being invited to parties and asked to be in various acting and directing scenes, and got a lead in a major production my second semester. I began to realize that this was something I had an affinity for, and that it gave me a great deal of satisfaction.

So, I decided to keep doing it until somebody I respected told me to stop. And nobody ever did.

I had two important mentors at Michigan State. The first was Mariam Duckwall, who taught acting. She did a lot of Readers Theater, *John Brown's Body*, for example, which had *wonderful* language, and also an adaptation of Camus' novel, *The Stranger*. She really understood me as an actor, challenged me, and I found her classes thrilling. She was very much about "the voice" and encouraged me in my interest in Shakespeare, giving me great instruction and advice. Then there was Sidney Berger, an amazing and inspiring teacher, who later became Director of the Houston Shakespeare Festival and head of the University of Houston's theater program. I hadn't seen him for forty years, and then he showed up at the Festival year before last at a performance of *Julius Caesar*.

In the middle 1960s, there was a program at Michigan State called The Performing Arts Company, where graduate students were paid to act in plays and teach some of the courses. I was asked to photograph their auditions, which determined what each of them would play that season. I was doing that at the back of the auditorium, and this guy got up and did Malvolio. I didn't take a picture! I just sat open-mouthed, watching him do this brilliant performance. He was named Eberle Thomas, and I then learned that he was Co-Artistic Director of the Asolo Theater Festival in Sarasota. He directed a play in the department that year with an actor named David Colson—whom he then invited to play *Hamlet* at the Asolo.

I thought—if Eb directs a play next year, I am going to try and get into it, and if I do a good job, maybe he'll invite me to the Asolo, too. The next year he directed his own translation of Goldoni's *The Lovers,* I got the lead, and indeed he asked me to join the Asolo acting company. I left Michigan State two terms shy of graduation, gave up my student draft deferment (this was during the Vietnam war in 1967), and became an Equity intern that summer. I was quickly called to my pre-induction physical in Miami, which I failed due to asthma, and I stayed at Asolo for a season and a half, at a time when the regional theater movement was coming into full flower. One of the directors in the company, Paul Widener, was named Artistic Director at Hartford Stage, so I got into that company, and from that point on, I was working professionally.

In the 1970s, I got out of the professional theater track, went back to college and finished my degree, and worked for two years as an anti-war activist, directing a street theater company. Directing became my passion.

However, the more I directed, the more I realized that I was hurting my acting. As a director, your obligation is to come up with a concept, then take what the actors give you and work with them, modifying, changing, shaping what they're doing. But as an actor, the minute I start doing *that* with my scene partner, I have completely violated the trust that has to be there. As an actor, I have to take what my scene partner gives me and accept that as reality, as truth. Whatever he does, that's what the character does. As soon as I start thinking about that partner,

"You should do that faster—you are missing the joke—you are hitting the wrong operative word," then I am out of my bubble. I am being critical of my fellow performer and I've violated the basic, fundamental bond that has to exist. I am seeing as if I were a director (which also has me "out of character"), and I've had enough actors look at me that way to know how horribly destructive that is to any kind of ability to be creative. Even if an actor is whispering my cue to me and my response is "Stop shouting at me," I wait for the director to notice that, or I try to go through the stage manager and not inject myself into my scene partner's choices.

One of my most important acting challenges was in *Equivocation,* a play by Bill Cain about Shakespeare and his company, which premiered at the Oregon Shakespeare Festival. It was memorable for the sense of ensemble that emerged through the rehearsal process. The highest goal for me is to be an ensemble player. I was originally cast as Richard Burbage (the lead actor in Shakespeare's company), but Bill Cain pushed Rauch to cast me as "Shag" (the character of Shakespeare). Rauch was resistant, and I agreed—I said I wasn't interested in that role, I didn't see myself as Shag, I was too old. Cain asked me to read the play again, and I did, trying to put myself into the mindset of Shag, and the minute I finished it I called Rauch and said, "I'll do anything to play Shag!" He had me audition, and I worked with Chris Albright-Tufts, who was cast as Shag's daughter, on one of our scenes, and after the audition Rauch decided Cain was right.

Later on, my wife asked what the play was about and I was *stumped.* I tried to tell her the plot and kept getting lost and could not figure out what the real story was. So I suggested that the cast get together at the Black Sheep, a local "English Pub" restaurant, and talk about the play and how the hell we were going to do it. That was the first gathering of the ensemble and the beginning of a real sense of ownership for the six of us (Jonathan Haugen, John Tufts, Chris Albright-Tufts, Gregory Linington, Richard Elmore, and myself) on that project. We still had problems figuring it all out, but we had the luxury of three eight-hour workshops in December with both Cain and Rauch, and we spent a lot of time analyzing it.

On the third day of the workshop, Rauch had us get on our feet and work our way through the entire show, carrying scripts and improvising blocking, to see if that helped us find a physical approach. There were places where I completely dropped out and sat down and did not physicalize, and I apologized to Cain afterwards for what I saw as a failure on my part. He said that for him it was the most instructive thing possible, that if there was a problem or a disconnect in the play, those "failures" helped make that clear. He was a terrific playwright to work with because he had a strong directorial sense, and he was so fearless about how he approached people. He was not at all about to sugarcoat things or be diplomatic, and yes, he is still a practicing Jesuit priest. There were also times when he was infuriating and intolerable.

After the workshops, we had three months before we started rehearsals, and in that time, I learned the whole text and also did an enormous amount of research about Shakespeare's life, concentrating on what his relationship was with his company, what the work method was, what the touring schedule was like, what his relationship was with his wife, Anne Hathaway, and his children, how long it took to get from London to Stratford—trying to build a backstory specifically around the death of Hamnet, his young son and twin to his daughter Judith.

There would have been times when Shakespeare's company was out touring when the London theaters were closed because of the plague, so I imagined his wife trying to contact him to tell him his young son was fading. I was building a sense of who the boy was and how he was different from his twin Judith, in order to help explain the relationship between Shag and Judith. Often one twin is dominant, and I felt strongly that Judith was the sturdy one, the bright one. I thought Hamnet might be in some way disabled or deformed, somehow compromised, and that stimulated nurturing feelings in Shag. Perhaps the boy was physically affectionate, curled up in Shag's lap and asking to hear a story. Whereas Judith was the hearty one, and felt a bit guilty about taking the vitality that should be shared between siblings.

I also thought in terms of Shakespeare's repertory—the plays being done one time and then not again for weeks or months, how probable it was that there were frequent discussions the morning before a play went up again for a matinee: "You know, Will, I've always hated this speech," or "Can we make this a little smoother here?" or Will saying, "I've rethought this transition," or "I have a new speech for you." Since scripts were not all printed up and ready to go off to Samuel French, they must have been treated in a more fluid and organic way. That meant trying to figure out where Shag was during the course of the play, because he was also in rehearsal for this strange, new beast unlike any other he'd written, *King Lear*. There's also the good-daughter-bad-daughter-bad-sons-fathers-and-children theme in that play, no mothers around, that might have been on the playwright's mind at that point. Or perhaps frustration with the company, or the sense of not being satisfied with the artistic routine he'd established, trying to break out and find his way to new ground? All of that informed very much how I approached the scenes.

There was an interesting dynamic in the rehearsal hall because the playwright and the director each had their own ideas. Then too, there was Shana Cooper, the assistant director, Barry Kraft and Lue Douthit offering dramaturgical ideas, and of course, six actors with very strong opinions. There were occasional conflicts and eruptions, and in the third week we spent several hours doing a "Let's-calm-down-everyone." Nonetheless, it developed into an amazing creative partnership.

In terms of rehearsing, we'd get on our feet and do a scene, just improvising the physical life to see what would happen. Rauch is not the kind of director who says, "I think you should start here and during the scene, you need to be doing this particular thing." Instead, he watches for what the actors come up with, and works with that. And he maintains a wonderful willingness to keep open to new ideas.

You know, we get only two previews of shows, and it was the Saturday afternoon before our opening. In the first scene of the play we had done it from the outset with me coming in and taking a seat and sitting during the whole scene. That afternoon I said, "It feels wrong for me to sit—it's too comfortable, and it's hard for me to share the scene with different parts of the theater audience because I am locked into facing one direction. I'd like to try it with no chair, with me standing." Instantly it was much better.

We made major adjustments to three scenes that afternoon, and it paid off wonderfully. I said, "Something feels wrong about the second scene with my daughter Judith." Rauch asked what was wrong. I said, "I feel like we're coming together—we're reaching a strong point of connection. I've been told by Father Garnett, 'Look to your daughter. That is the penance I demand of you. Look to your daughter and you will see your son.' I feel now that I am seeing her, connecting with her, a resolution is happening. Yet, in another fifteen pages, I say to Garnett, 'Your penance can't be done. I've tried.'" I said to Rauch, "That second scene needs to be about trying and failing, rather than trying and succeeding." Both Chris and Bill responded to that. We re-rehearsed the scene and changed the dynamics of it.

Chris Albright-Tufts is one of the half-dozen smartest people I've ever worked with. In rehearsals there would be the male egos battling here and there, and she would simply say, "What about such and such?" and we'd say, "Well, *yea-ahh.*" In the later production at Arena Stage in Washington, D.C, there was a moment when Bill Rauch came in and wanted to cut a certain bit, and the men said, "Oh, great, that makes it all go faster," and then Chris pointed out, "but if you do *that*, then these references ten pages later make no sense." She just thinks so analytically.

I adore Jonathan Haugen. You *never* know what he's gonna do. Sometimes it's infuriating, but most of the time it's *absolutely thrilling*. He totally obliges you to stay on your toes, and you can never give a pat response. I tend to be extremely methodical and consistent; Jonathan tends to wing it. I can say to him, "You know, I'd love to try it this way this time, or when I do this and you're doing that, it makes it hard for me, so is there something else that could happen there?" I can get into nuts and bolts with Jonathan, and he's *very unthreatened*. I'm the anchor and he's the sail, or I'm the post and he's the tether ball!

Rauch is the kind of director who is endlessly willing to explore ideas alternative to his. He would cede the floor to Bill Cain for an hour and watch as Cain gave notes to the actors. Cain would say, "Is this okay, Bill? Am I going too far, talking too much?" Rauch would occasionally say that the two of them disagreed on smaller points, but most of the time he'd tell Cain to go ahead. Rauch is so secure in his artistic ego that I've never found him to be threatened by ideas that are not his.

Bill Cain gave me an interesting critique during this show. He told me I was a very generous actor onstage: "You're aware of your fellow actors and you throw focus to them and make the connection. I urge you to grab the ball and take the shot. To be more selfish, to take the focus, to be a little less generous, to be a little less of a team player and a bit more of a star." As I tried to put this into effect, I began to see the reason for his comment. There are times when you want a character to grab the performance, especially if the character is one who can—then the actor needs to embody that intention.

One of the truly great things about *Equivocation* was going immediately to Seattle after the run here, and then on to that

Arena Stage production in Washington, D.C. two years later. Inevitably in the rehearsal phase, you gloss over and pay short shrift to certain gnarly problems. You find a way to get through them into safe territory, Scotch-taping over some deep gashes you never found a way to heal. You lose sight of them when you are acting in a group, then you come back to them two years later and at one of those points, your body says, "Oh! This is the spot that I always hated—I've never understood this part." Then you can flag it and finally take the time to deal with it. So when we got ready for the Arena Stage, it was a phenomenal process and we had the opportunity to do it on the set, which was set up in the OSF paint shop, and we really delved into it. The life of that production in D.C. was the best of any of its incarnations.

One of the reviewers for the *Washington Post* came to see it and he hated the play. His complaint was that it was too full, there were too many ideas. I thought of the Emperor in *Amadeus* telling Mozart that there were too many notes. People would come to see it seven, eight, twelve times—one woman came all the way from the West Coast to see it her eighteenth and nineteenth time, since she'd also seen it in Seattle. It's because the script is so rich, it's such a Thanksgiving dinner of a play that you can continue to find nuances and to clarify what is going on. Each time you see it, it rewards you.

We finally decided that what *Equivocation* was about at its core was "a co-operative venture." The most satisfying aspect of the performance of it was what the audience saw in the six actors who played so many different roles. It was about being a family, about the interrelationships and interdependence and the love and the forgiveness, everything that goes along with being an ensemble. Shag says, "Theater is a small world, but it is built on affection and trust." Later on, I talked to one of the actors in the New York production at Manhattan Theater Club (with the Irish director, Gary Hines), and he said when they were in rehearsals, when that line came up, Gary said, "I don't believe that. Theater is not a small world built on affection and trust. That's bullshit." Also, they cut forty minutes out of the play and asked Bill Cain to leave the rehearsals.

I don't think they understood what the play was really about.

As I get older, I realize that what I need as an artist is to be excited and stimulated and challenged by what I am having to face in constructing a character. I'm looking for experiences that call upon my command of verse, the ability to untie the knot of a character who is deeply enigmatic, to really answer those questions about a persona in an organic way that feeds me as a performer and unlocks the play for an audience. Being part of *Equivocation* certainly did that.

One of the great assets of working in Ashland is the Margery Bailey Renaissance collection in SOU's Hannon Library. Typically, I read dozens of texts to get very clear about the range of critical and professional opinion in approaching a character. For Shylock or Iago or the Duke in *Measure for Measure,* there is a wide range of possible interpretations. I look at the aspects of the character that critics have commented on. If a review talks about a successful interpretation, what made it that? If unsuccessful, what factors determined its lack of success? If you are lucky, there are performance histories that describe the performances line by line—what each actor did when. Then you see the enormous range of possibilities at every moment in the arc of the character. It opens up myriad choices and I think, "He gave the line *that way?* What an interesting idea." You know, we're all magpies as actors—we go around finding bright, shiny things and we take them back to our nest.

Also, what was Shakespeare reading when he wrote this play? So much of *Midsummer Night's Dream* is about metamorphosis and change—happening to all of the characters. We know that Ovid's *Metamorphosis* was something he read, and *Pyramus and Thisbe* was in that book, as was the Theseus and Hippolyta story. So, what's in his mind as he's writing this play that influences the choices he makes? He could have written *anything*— any story, any dialogue, any way to bend his plot. My questions are why this plot—why these words—why this particular word? He is constantly making choices, not just word and verse choices, but from all the different forms of language at his disposal. In *Dream,* he goes from rhymed couplets to trimeter to tetrameter to prose and so on, using a dozen different ways of manipulating text as he proceeds. Why does a speech go along as unrhymed and then all of a sudden turn into couplets? All of that is there for a reason, and maybe that's why I'm obsessive about research. I'm always terrified that someone will say, "I loved your performance, but did you ever consider such and such?"—that there will be some fundamental, obvious, crucial consideration that has entirely escaped my attention.

One of the recurrent things I found in researching *Dream* was the number of times that women were forced to terminate their relationships with other women and accept a subservient relationship to men. We see it with the friendship between Hermia and Helena, which is upended and causes both women to be absolutely silent, without words through the whole fifth act. We see it in Titania when she refuses to give up the changeling child out of loyalty to its deceased mother. Finally she does give up the child, thus breaking her word. For Shakespeare to be writing women's perspectives of that density and maturity and complexity, knowing that they were going to be played by fifteen-year-old boys: it's a strange concept to wrap your head around.

So what we're supplied with in a script or play text is conversations between imaginary people—that's all we have (unless you are doing Pinter's pauses or Shaw's elaborate stage directions). The behavior that gives rise to these conversations is only available to us by inference. The actor has to try and figure

out, "Why do I say this, what's going on physically, emotionally, spatially, during the time I am saying these words? Why
do I choose to say *this*, what does the other actor/persona say,
and how can what I say (or the way I say it) influence what the
other person says?" If in *Julius Caesar*, Mark Antony comes into
the scene after the murder of Caesar in an angry and provocative way, it's impossible for Brutus and Cassius to agree to let
him speak in public. Antony has to approach the scene in a way
that enables the other characters to trust him. You can't whisper
a line to which your partner responds, "Don't shout." You are
bound not only by what you need but by what your scene partner needs as well.

If I weren't an actor, I would have been a cartographer. I love
maps. Years ago, when I was a director, I got into the habit of
doing what I call "plot maps." It's a way of outlining the play in
a visual sense. I get an enormous sheet of paper, and I draw a
small column down the left hand side. I divide that column into
a page-numbering system that corresponds to my script, and
then halfway across the sheet, I'll draw a second column. I now
have a sheet of paper that shows me about the first fifty pages
of the play, so I can see a lot of the play as if I were two stories
up and looking down on all of the pages laid out on the floor.

Then sometimes, using color-coding, I'll show where the
key characters enter, basically dividing the space up into French
scenes. Then I'll find the key events, the "hinge moments" in
the play, where those fall. Where do these scenes change from
one large section to another? What is the event, or the thematic
shift, or even the specific line that makes that happen?

When I go back to look at it, I might see, "That first beat
goes on for four pages!" Or, I might make that discovery and
then four more shifts happen, which means that something key
is going on. *All this enables me to step back and see structure.* I
have to know structure—to find out how B leads to C. I do that

for the whole play. I used this method as a director because I could draw a red line whenever a character entered or exited. It was great for making rehearsal schedules. I began to understand how important it was for an actor to get a handle on what the play is structurally.

Then when I began to work on Shakespeare roles, there were significantly large speeches, and this same technique worked for those. I always take a longer twenty-line speech and see where it hinges, where it changes. If it's a series of speeches where specific points are being made, what are those points? How do they arise in that speech? I need to do that kind of structural work before I learn them, because then I *know*—that's the speech where I have a three-line introduction, then I list five things, and then I have a two-line conclusion. Once I've figured out the structure of the speech, I start looking at language, word choices, why this word and not that word.

If I am trying to memorize a speech and I keep making a mistake on one word, then I need to understand why that word is there. When I played Iago, Nancy Benjamin, the voice and text coach, introduced me to the idea of rhetorical devices—such as *thesis* and *antithesis,* the juxtaposition of opposites—and also just plain persuasive speeches. Finding out how Shakespeare has structured them. Then it is easier to go through and find the *key word*, which I need if I am going to make sense of a long sentence. I know that I have to set up the sentence beforehand to prepare to emphasize a specific point, and then vocally lift the key word.

I download the Shakespeare text script from the Internet and then go through and make whatever changes are in the rehearsal script we've been given, or I have the office email me an Office Word file of the script, so that I can go through with different colored pens, underlining certain words, drawing arrows which point to the next idea and the one after that, and so on to the conclusion. Then I can *really* understand the structure of the speech. If, as in the case of both Oberon and Theseus, there are a dozen major speeches, I make a list of those—longest first and then down and down as they diminish in size, to ten-line speeches. I make sure I have a separate file of each of those speeches so I can go through and dissect meaning and structure. Then I check them off as I get them memorized.

Once I've got the major speeches memorized, then I memorize the scenes in which they take place. The speeches are like tent poles to the dialogue. I start with structure, then word choice—then out of word choice, meaning—then out of meaning, objective and interpretation. If I made mistakes as an actor initially, it was often allowing interpretation to be the first step. If you just *begin by* interpreting it, you have no basis. I've actually seen directors do this just to "come up with" an interpretation. These often make no sense, or are fascinating but don't mean anything. The progression needs to be structure first, then meaning. I don't think I "get" meaning until I get the structure.

I have very conscious ideas about text preparation, obviously. Regarding punctuation, I'll consult as many different versions of the text as possible. We have text meetings with Bill Rauch, the other actors playing major roles, and the dramaturg—taken up with "Now, is this a colon, semicolon, comma, or period?" Compare it with Pinter—is it a beat or a pause or a silence? I like to breathe as infrequently as possible. I find it irritating when a performer takes a breath every four or five words. I prefer to speak whole sense units. In reviewing the text of *Measure for Measure*, it was so noticeable which words were actually the *operative* words, and which words were *parenthetical* to the actual crux of the idea.

I use the computer very consciously. I take a speech or a scene, copy and paste it as a new fresh document, then I go through and bold-face operative words, put parentheses around parentheticals, italicize certain words, then go through with a red pen and draw lines connecting words. I found in *Measure for Measure* that the word *haste* had immense importance to Vincentio. In the end, he uses that word to Angelo, "Haste still pays haste, and leisure answers leisure, / Like doth quit like, and measure still for measure." To really mine the text, not just in Shakespeare, but for every play, teasing out every possible clue that makes the text a *story-telling tool.* The goal is to make everything as clear as possible so that the audience can follow the story.

The crucial thing with any text is to have it make sense and to have the text sound like it's actually spoken by a living person. So whether I am working with a living playwright—Terrence McNally or Bill Cain—and I have questions about what something means, they can adjust or explain the line. But Shakespeare's not here to do that. That's why I read as much as I can. Finding out what other people have thought is helpful to me.

I think the vast majority of actors here at the Festival do text work. Vilma Silva is an intense note-taker. I shared a dressing room with Josiah Phillips, and each night he'd go over the text with a pencil to remind himself that this sentence only made sense if, five lines before, you had lifted a certain phrase. Actors are constantly writing in their scripts—all those who are serious about work and their textual study—I see those scripts lying around. There may be some younger actors who don't. In the recent *Dream* I acted in New York, a young actress who had no verse experience with Shakespeare was playing Helena and working on that long speech of Helena's, "How happy some o'er other some can be!" A very difficult and complicated speech. She was mining the speech for the emotional content first: she should have begun by finding the sense of the words first, i.e., what do the words mean.

It's important not to approach Shakespeare as if you are presenting a museum diorama, not to view it as something for which there's a right way and a wrong way, but rather to view the plays as much as possible as fresh material and to imagine that Shakespeare is in the room while you are dealing with it, as an active participant in shaping this work that's never been seen before. There is something debilitating about the idea of "doing a classic." You need to give yourself permission to treat the material as live text, to say, "Does it serve me to have this long speech at this point? Can we trim it down?"

One of the differences between TV/film actors and theater actors is the attitude toward the sanctity of the written word. Some film actors' attitude toward the text is that the screenwriter has come with words for the character that the actor can kind of use as a road map, but yet feel free to take a detour. With them, there is constant paraphrasing, ad-libbing, playing fast and loose with the text. Whereas the theater artist tends to understand that the playwright has chosen those specific words in that specific structure for a specific reason.

It's fine for a painter to be an abstract expressionist, but he first has to learn draftsmanship, and he has to understand the mechanics of perspective. In the same way, after you've really examined text and really understood why the choices were made to use this word and no other word in order to properly structure the dialogue, then you know what to do. And you can decide, "If we take out these four lines or we reverse this phrase in Shakespeare, it'll help a modern audience to understand." You can alter the text with living playwrights if you have a good enough reason and they agree; so with Shakespeare, imagine him in the room and put to him an informed request.

All that goes with what I feel about not looking at a Shakespeare production as a museum piece. Even though another arrangement of lines might have worked for Elizabethans, modern productions are not bound to perform it exactly as it was written, uncut, not bound to the clothes or the playing space Shakespeare would have done it in. We are trying to make live theater, and we have to be conscious of what we and our audience bring to the experience—then we create our version of the text that tells the story we want to tell. You look at nineteenth century actors like Henry Irving and Edmund Kean, who were cutting and pasting, even eliminating an entire act. Those theater artists were smart, perceptive, theatrical geniuses who used an old text and found a way to present it for their own time. We all need to treat it as if the performance is for *now*, as if the ink is not yet dry.

Bill Rauch is the essential director I enjoy working with, because he is so open to the actors' ideas. In *Measure for Measure*, he involved me and Stephanie Beatriz (who played Isabella—to coincide with this production concept, the spelling of characters' names and other details were modified, e.g., Isabela for Isabella), along with dramaturgs Barry Kraft and Lydia Garcia, in about twenty-five hours of text work. We carefully went over the script to find out what could be cut, what language needed to be changed to make it clearer, what restructuring was possible or desirable. I come into rehearsals with a lot of very specific ideas. I felt that some of the Duke's major soliloquies were misplaced. I wanted to try them out in different ways. I had strong opinions about where the intermission should come, just in terms of clear storytelling. In past work on *Othello* (with Tony Taccone directing), I discovered the value of what kind of information you send the audience out into the lobby with at intermission. So I wanted the intermission to come at the moment when the Duke realizes he's romantically drawn to Isabela, at the end of the first scene of Act IV. Barry was adamant, however, that in Act IV, the first and second scenes are contiguous, basically the same scene. All I wanted was for the audience to go out into the lobby thinking about the fact that I was falling in love with Isabela. I wound up being successful with that.

In this play especially, it was so useful to think about what was on Shakespeare's mind as he wrote it. You can look at the possible early sources of this play, and then contrast those with what Shakespeare did with it. What changes did he make and how did he make them, having known all of the stories that gave rise to the final text of *Measure for Measure*? In none of these is Isabela a novitiate, a novice nun; in none is the Duke disguised as a monk. Those are all inventions by Shakespeare. Why?

The connection with his having grown up exposed to the Christian Humanism of Erasmus—the approach to reforming society structurally—is very much what the play is about. Do you reform society in a draconian way by imposing harsh penalties coming from the ruler, or do you reform it by giving a society a chance to truly see itself—to learn from example and observation, from strong moral leadership and having a key figure to emulate. Also important was Erasmus' fundamental belief in the power of theater and drama to enable people to see opposing viewpoints. In some cases, there are differing characters who are crafted to display a more three-dimensional picture of a moral viewpoint: the fifth act of *Measure for Measure* is a play that the Duke has partially created and partially improvised—which actually breaks down into a five-act structure.

Our 2012 production of *Measure for Measure* was in an urban setting during the 1970s amidst a Latino community. One of the questions I had was—how suited is Isabela for life in the convent? She condemns Claudius mercilessly for his very human impulse of trying to save his own life, yet she places an incredibly high value on her own chastity. She's not really suited to life as a nun, so why is she becoming one? Why is she entering the sisterhood? She says the first time she enters, "And have you nuns no farther privileges," meaning she wishes a more strict restraint. She wants structure, she wants to be confined, she wants very strict morality, and the order of St. Clare is already one of the most restrictive convents. Even Claudio says, "For in her youth / There is a prone and speechless dialect, / Such as move men." We can see in the way both Angelo and the Duke respond to her that she is an electrifyingly charismatic young woman. My take on her is that she's been "hit on" constantly, and she wants to be in situations where her sexuality is out of the picture, to be within a society completely composed of celibate women. She doesn't want to have to deal with the fact that she is so alluring, which is why chastity in her world is such a priority.

We staged one scene with her sharing a cigarette with the Duke, then disguised as a monk. I fought that idea. I felt it said to the audience, "What do you do if you are feeling awkward with the opposite sex, if you are having trouble breaking the tension? You share a cigarette." I argued that this was the wrong message to send, and I suggested taking out a Hershey bar. You see this monk and this nun together and it's got to be so incongruous. I finally said, "I will do this, but my wife is coming to the final dress, and she is fiercely anti-smoking, as am I, and if she has a negative reaction, I'm sorry but I'm not going to do it." So I asked my wife after the rehearsal what she thought, and she said, "Oh, I loved it."

When Isabela took my hand, just before she left, and then I was alone—there was my hand she'd just touched, and I brought it to my cheek, a little flustered. Then I pulled my wig off, literally flipping my wig. I felt it was crucial that when the Duke proposes to her in Act V, that it does not blindside the audience. They need to have some awareness of the effect she's had on Duke Vincentio. The only place to show that is after their first scene when she leaves and he is left alone. At that point, I can do something that impresses upon the audience's consciousness how he feels after his contact with this incredibly magnetic young woman.

Act V is the longest scene in all of Shakespeare, and it has to be. What a thrill it was to perform, because there is some evidence that Shakespeare played the Duke—so here would be the creator of the reformer Duke within the play that he himself created, the playwright of the whole play directing the last very complete act of the play.

How do the Duke's decisions in that last act explain what he is trying to do in Vienna? Why doesn't he tell Isabela that her brother isn't really dead? Clearly, the only way he can make Isabela truly understand the concept of mercy is to have her plead for it for Angelo, the man *she truly believes* killed her brother. If she pleads for a man who merely *threatened* to do so, this is no great sacrifice for her. At the point where Mariana begs for mercy for her ex-fiance Angelo, Isabela directly faces that complicated choice. If she makes that plea, she is now the perfect partner for the Duke. She now has a full understanding of Christian principles. She will have demonstrated compassion, and it is only after she has passed the test that the Duke can propose. He takes everyone right to the breaking point. It's cruel and it's manipulative, but it is for a good reason.

This wide range of possible interpretations is true of several characters, including Iago, Hamlet, and Shylock. A question you have to ask is—where is this character coming from morally? With Shylock, is he an evil person or a good person? I came to the conclusion very early in my study of the role that what Shylock does in society is beneficial. He supplies the lifeblood, the money, the vital fluid that keeps society operating. When Bassanio wants to woo Portia, he needs money. He is able to do that because he gets the money from Shylock. Shylock is a life force, a positive thing. Rather than building him on the image of Fagin, this evil guy trying to get what he can by misleading and misusing people, he's really more like Tevya from *Fiddler on the Roof.*

I look to find the telling detail that helps the story along. In the Elizabethan theater especially, if you are more than ten rows out, subtle gestures or facial expressions won't be seen. In the scene with Jessica and Shylock, I wanted to make it clear that he doesn't find it easy to express affection towards his daughter because she resembles his dead wife, so it's too dangerous for him. Furthermore, if there is a closeness, it's very hard for her to make the choices the text requires her to make later on—to leave her father's house and to take his treasure. So how do we embody that in the scene, telling that story to the back rows of the Lizzie, in a way that is totally visible.

I asked Bill if we could stage their scene together as if in front of a mirror. Shylock is narcissistic and very self-involved, and if he's getting ready for a dinner party, perhaps he's getting dressed. That's the physical action in the scene. Shylock says, "Jessica, my girl, look to my house." Some Shylocks have made that a loving line, filled with tenderness. Instead, I snapped my fingers and pointed to my shoes and said, "Jessica." She came over and knelt at my feet and removed my slippers and tied my dress shoes, while I was looking in the mirror at my necktie. She was clearly there to serve my needs as a servant. Those strokes help the character tell the story.

George Bernard Shaw's plays contain so many complex ideas crammed into one line. He needs, even more than Shakespeare, to be spoken from start to finish in a sweep. If you break up Shaw's sentences, you may lose the sense. You have to speak the whole line through: "My needs are as great as any widow who ever got money out of six charities in one week for the death of the same husband." You cannot break the line up. Consequently, *My Fair Lady,* adapted from Shaw's *Pygmalion,* turned out to be a marvelous but still challenging experience. I had played Higgins in high school and again thirty years later at the Roundabout in New York, so I was thoroughly familiar with the source material. There was much less character analysis work on Doolittle and much more concentration on the nuts and bolts—the choreography, the movement, the singing, the accent. Having done two productions of *Pygmalion* was groundwork that set me up to understand Doolittle and his world.

I had an interesting conversation with the choreographer, Jaclyn Miller, who asked me, "What does Doolittle want in the number *Get Me to the Church on Time*"? I told her, "I think Doolittle wants to get married, that he's ready to get married, even though he's nervous about it. He moans, 'I am a slave to that woman because I am not her lawful husband.' He wants to have a huge block party for his friends, with eating and drinking and dancing and having fun—a big variety show, where everyone gets to perform their numbers. But he insists, don't let me screw up! Make sure I'm there for the wedding."

"Get Me to the Church on Time" was a song developed for one group to perform, then a solo happens, and so on—going along with the theme of the show, that *you learn things from each other*. So the dancers were teaching each other new steps, and it became enormous fun.

In performing Doolittle, I decided to use a trick I saw Sutton Foster do last year in *Anything Goes* on Broadway. I picked out particular faces in the audience while I was singing, using a "sharing-a-secret-joke" look. Doolittle's philosophy of life is "Enjoy it. To the *fullest*." He often convinces his pals not to go home just because it's last call for drinks in the pub, but to stay out longer and drink and party more. Since his day job was to go around emptying dirty coal dustbins day after day, when the work is done, it's time to enjoy himself. At the end of "Get Me to the Church," there's a weird refrain in a minor key, which I was first doing in a sad and weepy kind of way. Eventually I said it triumphantly, with members of the ensemble hoisting me up, my fist in the air: "Yes! I'm gonna do it!"

When I work with accents, and Doolittle's is a tricky one with lots of detail, I write them out in my own phonetic way. Details count. Always do the homework. It's like learning Shakespearean verse: you plot it out, and you go from sound to sound. I got a lot of the accent of the character by listening to Sarah in the first season of *Upstairs Downstairs*. For instance, she substituted the "v" sound for the "th" sound: "without" is "wivout." I worked with text coach David Carey, who was very helpful in keeping me consistent. There's better support at this Festival than any other place I've ever worked. We had a dream team on this show and a great cast to boot.

My priority is *always* to come into rehearsal as far ahead as I can possibly be. Rehearsal is not the time for me to learn my lines, because I'm concentrating on a million other things. Some actors worry they will get locked into a specific approach if they learn the lines before rehearsals begin. I find that learning the lines *while* I am carrying a script and *also* learning the blocking locks me in much more rigidly. If I already know the lines, I can improvise the behavior that gives rise to them with greater freedom. Also, *I can only memorize the lines if I fully understand them.* To try to play a scene when I don't know what I am really saying—my focus is too scattered to accomplish much.

I have to say that one of the reasons that my approach is to have the book out of my hands (have the lines totally memorized) is very much influenced by film work. In 1987, I was in the movie *Outrageous Fortune,* directed by Arthur Hiller, with Shelley Long and Bette Midler. Hiller shoots fifteen to twenty takes of every scene, and encourages the actors to watch the dailies. Shelley Long, a TV actress, would do fifteen takes with fifteen identical approaches to the material. Bette Midler would be big, small, angry, happy—all over the map—she tried everything. What that meant in the editing room was that the director could find anything he wanted in Bette's footage and construct the best possible performance out of the variety of choices she supplied. Much richer. Multiplies everyone's options.

So my early approach to stage rehearsals is to be off book—I am free to try stuff, to come up with many different choices, not worry about right or wrong. Try it angry, even though it's not written angry. Every once in awhile, you are in the middle of trying something, and you feel the spirit just swell you up, and you know *oh! I'm onto something.* Doing Fluellen in *Henry*

V one day—I was shorter than others in the cast, so I saw him as a little bantam rooster who needed to make a large sound when he walked across the stage. So I stamped my feet, and that became the physical wellspring for the character.

The standard approach in acting classes is "Define your objective; be clear about the obstacle; specify the action; and *then* experiment with adjustments." If I know what I am after and really know what's stopping me from getting it, then I can come up with the reason for my actions, including the dialogue. What is the action I take to overcome this obstacle and achieve this objective? The adjustment then is the *how*, in what way. Once you identify an objective, an obstacle and an action, you can approach the how in a million different ways.

That's the source of experimenting with choices—trying the actions with this adjustment or that. If it's not sparking anything in you, then take a longer look at the obstacle. Maybe it isn't powerful enough and you need to find a stronger one. Then you discuss it with your scene partner and the director, and clarify the obstacle: the stronger it is, the stronger the action has to be, and the brighter the colors and the more electricity there is. This business of making different choices is so important for students coming into the profession.

It's like ping-pong when you're working with your scene partner. Any kind of fresh spin that you put on it, that sends the ball spinning toward him or her in a slightly different way, will necessitate a different response and keep things alive.

"Keeping it fresh" figures into OSF work. The longest runs here would be "the long-running Shakespeares," which can be up to a hundred and twenty-five performances. The runs are fifty to sixty performances on most other plays. And it's a blessing that you're not churning out the same show seven or eight times a week. You have the advantage of doing something *else* at the same time—similar to going to a gym and working your biceps and then changing to your triceps. If you are working your comedy and your drama muscles in the same day, it's a full body workout, and you find that the comedy things spark an idea for something you are doing in the tragedy.

The down side is that I don't really feel that I am free from rehearsal choices and fully living in the world of the play until the fortieth or fiftieth performance. By then, the season is winding down or closing. When we did *Tartuffe*, we had only sixty performances, and the last fifteen were thrilling, with new discoveries happening all the time.

When I first performed in the Thomas Theater in *Julius Caesar*, I loved how the intimate playing space allowed me to work with nuance in a much more successful way. A facial expression really pays off. You don't have to be concerned about projection overall, and you can be almost cinematic in your acting choices. It's very similar to the Black Swan, where I did a lot of work in the old days.

I was warned by a fellow actor just after I'd joined the company, "If you are going to stay here, don't do anything in the Elizabethan Theater for a year or two, because it's a very tough space and a hard one to work in." One of the difficult problems is that you rehearse in a different, much smaller room, where if you're playing downstage, the wall of the room is ten feet from you. You can be seduced into making intimate choices in that rehearsal hall, and when you get into the larger venue, you find that those choices don't work. You have to make a tricky adjustment quickly.

My first big role in the Lizzie was the Stage Manager in *Our Town*. So I went out onto the Lizzie stage very early in the rehearsal period. I realized that I needed to get my chin up to be really comfortable with projecting in that large space. I explained all that to my director, and warned him that I would be over-projecting in the hall. Then in performance, the great advantage of playing the Stage Manager is that it is 98 percent direct-address to the audience, so I really learned how to bounce off of certain sweet spots. It became a real laboratory for the performance experience. Voice coach Scott Kaiser was very helpful with this, and I was able to find things that really *pinged,* really sent out a clear signal without being muddied by nuance.

It's also about being blessed or cursed with an advantageous or disadvantageous vocal quality. There are some actors who have voices that play beautifully in that space, and some actors in the company, wonderful as they are, who don't have voices that carry well. It is a great blessing to have three performance spaces, as long as actors are intelligently cast. We have to really resist the growing pressure to amplify, unless it is absolutely necessary. The audience doesn't always understand that it is not their hearing that is compromised, but that sometimes the actor cannot get it out there clearly.

Everyone who has worked in the Lizzie knows it's not about being loud, it's about being *clear:* it's not about volume, it's about *intention.*

I tend to arrive at the theater long before half-hour call. I like to get into costume as early as possible so that I'm walking around in clothes that feel like they belong to me. I like to be on the stage doing physical warm-ups and stretching as early as possible, especially in shows that have a lot of movement up and downstage, dashing here and there.

I try to get in a vocal warm-up, which is problematic at the Festival, because there isn't much space for that. If I am working in the Elizabethan, I tend to get there early and spend a good deal of time pacing through the rows of seats and going through every speech, not for acting values but just getting all the sounds in. I tend to have a messy dressing space. I tend not to wear makeup unless it's absolutely crucial.

One of the first things that attracted me to the Festival as an audience was that while you may not have people of world-class stature in some of the major roles, you have a depth in the company that allows the supporting roles to be played by people who are doing leading roles in other plays. There is a quality to each cast that is very unusual to find in New York, where you get strong people in the primary roles, but the people handling the supporting roles are not necessarily as qualified. Here, you can cast for people who know how to handle Shakespeare's language. Which is not only rare but is still the gold standard.

I took some friends to *Henry V*, and they asked me, "How many audience members do you think have read this script?" I said I thought 10-20 percent or more of this audience has seen previous productions of this play—most likely here, at OSF.

When we were at Arena Stage in Washington, D.C., we were playing to 65 percent audiences. I told the technicians that this was depressing, and they answered that this was great, a very high number. They said you'd never get more than that unless it was a musical! I was offered Prospero at the Hartford Stage a few years ago, and I called a director I knew and asked him how things were going at Hartford, and he said they were doing as well as anyone, 60-65 percent. I told him I remembered full houses there before, and he said, "That was years ago—things are different now."

The Oregon Shakespeare Festival is a "destination theater." So we actors get spoiled. Nine out of ten times, people are in Ashland to see the plays. It's the center of their day, it's why they come. And as you walk around the streets, people are talking about the matinee they saw that day, or are reading a script, or talking about what they are going to see. And the doors close at curtain time and everyone is in his seat. In other places, people wander in ten or fifteen minutes late, so the plays start late. That happens on Broadway, because the theater is an experience people tack on at the end of the day—audiences do not have the same intense focus as ours do. The Ashland audiences are the best audiences I have ever performed for.

Richard Howard as King Henry in *1 Henry IV.* Photo: Jenny Graham, OSF.

Richard Howard

In 26 seasons at OSF, Richard Howard has played, among other roles, Theseus in *A Midsummer Night's Dream*; Archbishop of Canterbury in *Henry V*; King Henry IV in *1* and *2 Henry IV*; Friar Laurence in *Romeo and Juliet*; Jaques in *As You Like It*; Ford in *The Merry Wives of Windsor*; Shannon in *The Night of the Iguana*; Pericles in *Pericles*; Angelo in *Measure for Measure*; Richard in *Richard II*; Hamlet in *Hamlet*; Romeo in *Romeo and Juliet*; and Wesley in *Curse of the Starving Class*.

I STARTED ACTING WHEN I was a junior in high school. My dad had died just before my sophomore year of high school, and then I got right into the theater thing. I needed that outlet, and I guess I had a natural ability. It was like, "Hey, come and do it, you can have this part and you can design the set." I could hammer and nail, too, so the theater was a natural place for me to divert my energies. Ever since then it's been one project after another.

When I was in high school, the nearby College of Marin Theatre Department was at its height, with James Dunn and Harvey Susser on the faculty. They had three theaters, a full scene shop, everything. After high school, it was a no-brainer to go there. I was in the scene shop all day, took all the theater classes, was in all of the shows—couldn't have been better. It was like being an apprentice in a semi-professional theater, because a lot of talented people from the community, not just young students, participated in the shows. ACT [American Conservatory Theatre] was at its height then, too, with Bill Ball as artistic director. I went often. I remember how lively and exciting the theater was in the Bay Area at that time. These things come in waves.

When I got to the College of Marin, in 1975, they were doing a rep of *The Merry Wives of Windsor* and *Much Ado About Nothing* in their barn theater. Dakin Matthews was the guest artist, playing Falstaff and Don Pedro. So I put together an audition, using Mark Antony's famous speech: "O pardon me, thou bleeding piece of earth, / That I am meek and gentle with these butchers!" I didn't know what I was doing. I don't think I'd even read *Julius Caesar*, I just did the speech. Anyway, I got cast as Master Slender—I was the type, that's who I was—and as Claudio, in *Much Ado*. I actually got to act with Dakin, but just hearing him was a learning experience. I would listen to him do Falstaff in *Merry Wives*. It was so musical. I didn't really understand what he was doing, but to me his way of speaking the language was perfect. I can still remember him doing the scene with Ford disguised as Master Brook: "I will use her as the key of the cuckoldly rogue's coffer." He put an imaginary key right into his belly, like it was a safe full of coins, turned it to the left, and recreated the sound of coins falling out. The guy playing Ford was just helpless.

The other seminal moment for me was a line I had as Claudio in the marriage ceremony, when he shuns Hero: "Give not this rotten orange to your friend; / She's but the sign and semblance of her honor." In my California dialect it was, "Give not this rotten 'ornj' to your friend." "Ornj"—sounded right to me. And the director, Jim Dunn, said to me (Dakin's real name is Richard, so in rehearsal he would be Dick and I became Dicky, to differentiate us), "Dicky, talk to Dick about how to say that.

It's orange, orange, not 'ornj'." So Dakin helped me with that, and I realized, "Oh, I have mannerisms and habits that maybe aren't appropriate," that there were things to learn about speaking the language. Anyway, I did two seasons there: I played Bernard in *Death of a Salesman*, with Dakin Matthews playing Willie Loman; Ensign Pulver in *Mister Roberts*; and Rosencrantz in a wonderful production of *Hamlet* that was set in an old opera prop room full of cobwebs, with Kurtwood Smith playing Hamlet.

The College of Marin during that time was kind of a feeder school for Juilliard. So it was natural for me to think, "Oh, maybe I could be that person." I got accepted by Juilliard and Carnegie and chose Juilliard. By the time I got to Juilliard, I was hungry; I really wanted to learn. And that doesn't go without saying. There were students there who came with more experience and may have resented going back to square one. When you go to a school like Juilliard that is so intense and all-encompassing, maybe you have to think that you don't know anything, try to do it their way, and then make it your own. One of my acting teachers said it takes twenty years to be an actor. I didn't know what that meant. Twenty years later, I think it has to do with not doing it for the teacher, not trying to sound like the teacher. You have made it your own. And that takes a while. I still feel like that's what I'm doing now, trying to strip that away and get to my own sound. But when I started, my own sound had a lot of physical tension. I had all of these encumbrances as an actor, I was really tight. On the outdoor stage you need to be able to open it up and relax. There's a difference between intoning and imitating some sound, and really having it come from you. That is a lifelong task.

I was at Juilliard four years. First thing, they throw you into a Shakespeare, to see what you can do without much guidance. We did *Richard III* in a studio with a wonderful director who helped us make sense, but she wasn't trying to make it a professional production. All the teachers could see who you were, where you were, what to work on, when confronted with something as difficult as that. And then it was movement classes, speech classes every morning, and every night you'd be rehearsing a play: *You Can't Take It with You, As You Like It,* Ibsen, Chekhov. After two years some people were cut. The third and the fourth year you're really a company, and you work on productions that you perform in public.

After graduating, I toured for four months around the country with The Acting Company, which the director John Houseman had started with Juilliard's first graduating class of actors in 1972—great experience, being in different venues every night. You'd go out and say, "Oh boy, we've really gotta fill this house," or "Oh, this is intimate," and make your adjustments. And you're sitting in dressing rooms in places like the Victory Theatre in Columbus, Ohio, thinking, "My God, the Barrymores must have sat here!" It was a wonderful experience to be on tour like professional actors in days of yore.

I was a tall, skinny Puck in *A Midsummer Night's Dream.* I was Vladimir in *Waiting for Godot,* directed by Alan Schneider, who had directed the play's very first American production. Then we did *Il Campiello,* an obscure Goldoni play directed by Liviu Ciulei, who later became the artistic director at the Guthrie Theatre in Minneapolis. That's how I got to the Guthrie for three or four years after the Acting Company. Sometimes it's all about connections. I always tell young actors, "Do good work wherever you are, behave well, be professional." That's how you get your next job, really. Directors remember people they've worked with before, and they're more likely to cast somebody that they know. As a young actor, it's a great opportunity to be in a professional situation. The things that you see really working are magical. The things that aren't working you can look at and think, "Why? That should happen faster, make a move there"—and then you're teaching yourself by observation.

After my year with the Acting Company, I went to Europe

with my bicycle and made it back with literally just coins in my pocket. I had to ride my bike back from Kennedy Airport. I was building bookcases for people when I got a call from the Guthrie, offering me George in *Our Town*. Oh God, just to get that phone call—it's the best phone call I've ever gotten! I'm really not very good at that part of the profession—agents and auditions, the business. Perhaps that's why I'm here instead of New York or LA. You have to be as good at the business as the acting to have that kind of career.

I ended up sticking around the Guthrie for three years. Great experience—I loved working in that space, and Liviu hired wonderful directors. I did *The Marriage of Figaro* with Andrei Serban, *Candida* with William Gaskill, a Goldoni adaptation with Garland Wright. I played Peter Quince in Liviu's very special production of *A Midsummer Night's Dream*. One of my smallest roles was Jaques de Boys in *As You Like It* with Patti LuPone and Val Kilmer. I literally entered at 10:55 and delivered good news. I must have been understudying another role, but that's part of the learning process, watching a production come together. It was interesting working with Romanian directors like Liviu and Andrei, who had a European sensibility. Liviu would say, "I want you to just say the line and then let your hand drop," or "Could you just massage your eyebrow?" It was external and specific. He would be shaping you, and then he'd say you had to make it your own. That was frustrating, for a director to give you all the physicality that you're doing, but it was a great experience of working with people who have really different approaches.

My last show at the Guthrie, in 1985, was Emily Mann's play, *Execution of Justice*, about the murder of San Francisco mayor George Moscone and Supervisor Harvey Milk and the subsequent trial of Dan White. I was asked to go to New York with the Broadway production. I did that show and a couple of others that came up, which kept me working in the city for about six months, but something didn't feel right. I hadn't invited anybody to see me, I hadn't hustled. I didn't like living in New York. I was working as an actor, not waiting tables, but I didn't want to have my life and career there. I went back to Minneapolis, got my VW bus out of storage, installed cruise control and a new stereo, and went on a road trip

My plan was to go to Seattle, a pretty active theater town, and think about where to live. I came down to Ashland to visit Marco Barricelli, a good friend from Juilliard, and Penny Metropulos, whom I had met at the Arizona Theatre Company in between Guthrie shows. When I got here, they said, "Oh, they're looking for the young boy in *Curse of the Starving Class*," so I auditioned for Pat Patton and Andy Traister, the director. And then I left to go hang out at my godparents' cabin in Mendocino, all by myself in the redwoods. But they did have a phone, so I got a call, in this remote place, from Jerry Turner, OSF's Artistic Director: "Hey, Richard. We want you to come up here." I was supposed to start with *Curse of the Starving Class* in March, but I came up in December to figure out where to live. I had met Rex Rabold, who was playing Richard II at the top of the season. Because I was his height and looked vaguely like him, and I didn't have anything to lose, I said to Jerry, "You know, I met Rex and I'd be willing to understudy him." And Jerry said "Okay." So I ended up starting earlier, playing various roles, and understudying Rex, which made me all the more prepared when I was cast as Richard II the next time OSF produced it, in 1995.

One of my roles in *Richard II* that first year was the Welsh Captain: "The bay trees in our country are all withered, / And meteors fright the fixed stars of heaven." I got my old friend Tim Monich, my speech teacher in New York, to help me with the Welsh dialect. At some point in rehearsal I thought, "Okay, I'm ready to try it." I got to rehearsal and went "The bay trees in our country..." in my thick Welsh accent. Afterward Jerry said,

"Now, you know, I think people are gonna wonder what the *hell* you're talkin' like that for"—because Jerry had cut out any reference to the Captain's being Welsh. After all that work.

That was my first role here and I wanted to show everybody how great I was. God! I think I've dropped some of that. Now I hope I'm much more willing to just try things and not get too attached to them. For example, in *Henry V* in 2012, Joe Haj, the director, wanted my Archbishop of Canterbury to be played as a politician in that first scene, to differentiate him from the more pious Bishop of Ely when the two characters discuss a bill in Parliament that would appropriate the Church's wealth. One day—and this is unlike me really—I lit up a cigarette at the beginning of the scene. Even if it wasn't going to stick, it was a good exercise for me. My dad was a smoker, and it just helped me go there. Joe said, "I don't want to start the play with something so contemporary." The next rehearsal I pulled out a flask at one point and took a swig.

I wanted to be more inventive in that scene, because I tend to be careful as an actor. I'm still learning to take more chances. But it was fun that Joe liked that. It gets a little response from the audience, when I pull the flask out. They think, "Who is this guy?" That scene is hard to follow, and something unexpected can grab the audience, draw them in.

For classical texts, finding different patterns, shifts in tone or rhythm that are grounded in the text, is so important, because the ear needs that. It's easy to fall into playing one tone, one rhythm, or one attitude. So I'm looking for strong shifts, different attacks, different points of view. What I'm talking about is *unpredictability*, finding ways to re-engage the audience.

Shakespeare's such a good writer that within a speech, even within three lines, there can be some shift comparable to the shift, on a larger scale, from a tragic scene to a comic scene. Those shifts are the things that drive how I approach the text when I first know I'm playing a role. I'm looking for meaning, looking for images, looking for sounds, even just the actual sounds of the words. If something is hard to say, it's not a matter of just practicing it so much that you can say it fast. It's a clue when some words or combinations of words are asking for more time to be taken with them.

The language, not just the meter, is showing me the rhythm. When I first approach a text, the most interesting thing, of course, is, why is this person saying it in this particular way? What does it say about where he is emotionally, about his point of view? Why would he choose that image? How does what he says pick up on what the other person has said? What is his action? How is he trying to affect the other person? I think the best advice you could ever give an actor working on heightened texts is "Why those words?" You should *need* those words. You're not just choosing to be flowery with your language. It's the *only* way to express how you're feeling, or how you're trying to change the other character. Those words. That way, everything becomes very particular.

I can't study sitting down. I tend to walk, whether it's around my garden or with the dog. I'll have the crumpled-up script, with a little plastic over it, and I'll start chipping away at the speech—like the Salic Law speech in *Henry V*, where I had to get through that French royal genealogy and understand the relationships. That speech is like reading the phone book. So you have to make your own connections, your own images. I just carry the words around. I walk. I get a line in my head and contemplate it, think about how it feels in my mouth. Is there a natural place to take a breath? If you take a breath here, does the line have a different meaning?

Breath is inspiration. When you get an idea, you take a breath. There's a relationship between the breath you take and what you say. As Romeo, I used to struggle with the lines in the balcony scene after "O, speak again, bright angel." For me, it never really worked until I had the impulse to begin, "for thou art / As glorious to this night, being o'er my head" and then on one breath say: "As is a winged messenger of heaven / Unto the white-upturned wondering eyes / Of mortals that fall back to gaze on him / When he bestrides the lazy-pacing clouds / And sails upon the bosom of the air." That's one image. That was one breath. You could do it in two breaths, fine, but keep the idea going. Romeo sees it all and just paints it. That's how full he is.

Some people think that you must pause at the end of an iambic line. That's ridiculous. Okay, it's iambic pentameter, so you're aware of that. What's most interesting, though, is when the pattern changes. You should always be thinking about what happens at the end of a line, but that doesn't mean there's some rule about it. I'm thinking, "Where is it a short thought, and where is it a long thought?" and I realize, "Oh, I take a big breath here because that's a big image." After I've been playing the role for a long time, the breaths all happen naturally, because I'm just thinking the ideas. But when I first work on lines, it's useful to think about where to breathe as a way to get to that level of ease.

When I did Romeo, I was perhaps foolishly inclined to believe that it's not good to be too prepared for rehearsal, because then you come in and it's all set in stone. About three weeks into rehearsal, I wished I had worked on the lines more. I wanted to be able to see what Grace Zandarski, my Juliet, was giving me, but I found myself wholly unprepared. I've learned that I'm terrible at rehearsing with a script in hand, so I like to be very, very familiar with the text before I start. If you can be almost off book, not needing the script, you're ready to take it to a different level in your rehearsal.

And if you do your work of learning lines correctly, you're not locked into choices. Sometimes you instantly get a reading that's right, and that's okay. Sometimes there are bits of language that are calling out for a certain rhythm. But as I work on my own, before rehearsals begin, I'm thinking of questions, possibilities. Here's an intersection where you can go this way or that way. When I'm in rehearsal either the answer will be evident or I will put that question out on the table. For example, Archbishop Canterbury in *Henry V*: is he sincere? Is he in awe of this young boy, King Henry? Or is he a political animal, haunted by the fact that he can't figure Henry out? So I'm not going to plan out my performance and have it all set before I walk into rehearsal. But I will be really familiar with the architecture of the language, with choices and possibilities. Then you're actually more free. The readiness is all. But the trick is to find how you can be most ready and most open *at the same time*.

As I'm reading the script, I start to see myself moving in space and relationship to other actors. Would I be far away from my partner, or closer to her on this line? It's just the way my brain works. I think spatially, I think of solutions right away. And that's not necessarily useful because, of course, I'm not with the other actors yet. Since thinking of the scene externally comes fast to me, I have to try—especially with Shakespeare—to focus on the other dimensions, to really get to know the architecture of the language. What is my character thinking that he needs to say this? The emotion will come. What's more useful is: what is he thinking, what's his point of view, what does he want, what's in his way? If you go right to the emotion, your acting is generalized.

When you're in dialogue, you're always looking for what was just said. How is my language not just responding to but picking up on that language? Often in Shakespeare the next speaker takes a word that the other character used, and turns it around or repeats it. We do this in life all the time. I heard what you said, you used that word, so I'm going to use it again, so that you know that I'm paying attention, or perhaps to mock you....

Even in a soliloquy, you have to ask yourself, who are you talking to? Because you're talking to somebody. In *Hamlet* we decided that we were actually talking to the audience, but even then, it's not that simple. Who is the audience to you? What's the assumption about what that audience is thinking? How am I trying to influence them? A soliloquy often might start with a question, have a thesis, a first line that states the problem. In a way it's the same as a dialogue. It can also be a dialogue with yourself or another part of yourself—like Launcelot Gobbo's line, "The fiend is at mine elbow."

The way I approached "To be or not to be" was probably not original—nothing's ever really original—but I was struck by the fact that the speech comes after the soliloquy that ends: "The play's the thing / Wherein I'll catch the conscience of the king." You have to decide who your character is. Hamlet is active, he has a plan. After a short absence he comes right back onstage with "To be or not to be." My choice was to come on with the same energy that I left with, as if I was still in motion. I delivered "To be, or not to be: that is the question" to the audience. It was active dialogue: "I need help. What do you think? Did you hear what I was just thinking? Is that right?" To act, or not to act? To act is to be, to be in motion. Yes, this is good, "To take arms against a sea of troubles" by provoking Claudius with *The Murder of Gonzago*. But then you see Hamlet's mind bring him to stasis, to lack of action. I'm risking my life, because if I find out the truth it's very dangerous. And then "to sleep, perchance to dream…." Pretty soon, by the end of the speech, you've witnessed Hamlet's progression into stasis. So I was thinking through that with the audience, asking them.

In *Henry V*, in the outdoor theater, our whole cast addressed the prologue directly to the audience. I was also in the first scene after the prologue. Early in the summer, it's still quite light outside at 8 p.m. and it's a challenge to your concentration to walk out and see all those eager theater-goers in their summer colors. First scenes are already challenging in these plays, in that you have to tune the audience to the language. You don't have lighting to focus their attention. One of my mentors, Ken Ruta, who played the Stage Manager when I did *Our Town*, used to talk about using psychic energy to connect with the audience. I think this is somehow connected to an actor's desire to tell the story, to draw those people in the back row into your mind, if you will. Never would this kind of thinking be more relevant than in presenting the first scene of a Shakespeare play.

Your mind is always looking for someplace more interesting to go. Nature abhors a vacuum, so if you haven't built your imaginary world—if you haven't thought a lot about where you are, who you are, what you want, who the other characters are to you—then you'll find yourself easily distracted by stuff you don't want to be thinking about, like "what's going on with the guy with the Mickey Mouse hat on, in Row C?" The whole point is to build an inner life for your character that's interesting to *you*, to make choices that activate you personally, that draw your particular imagination into the world of the play.

Ironically, sometimes you are most likely to forget a line when you've been performing a show awhile and are starting to loosen up, be more in the moment, and trust your impulses. My first year, I was playing Malcolm in *Macbeth*. He has the last speech in the play, which ends in a rhyming couplet. Well, I totally blanked about four lines before the couplet. And feeling the momentum of the entire play behind me, needing its resolution, like a wave approaching the shore, I believe I actually spoke some rhythmic iambic nonsense for a few lines, and finally found my way to the final couplet. You can't just stop in that situation. I would rather have the audience think, "Gee, I didn't get part of what he said," than bring the show to a grinding halt!

My pal Jonathan Toppo always likes to remind me of a moment in *Cymbeline* that we did in the little Black Swan Theatre back in 1993. I was playing the doctor and had to explain how I had compounded "a certain stuff" for the Queen, which would give the appearance of death. Well, for some reason I could not come up with "certain stuff," so I paused and said, with great conviction, "a secret brew"—which to the rest of the cast, apparently, was particularly amusing. I was so thrown that I couldn't quite negotiate the conclusion of the speech, so I looked at them all with a straight face and said, "And here we are!"—which, of course, was undeniable.

Dan Kremer told me that, when he was playing the Prince of Morocco years ago on the outdoor stage, Christine Healy, playing Portia, was supposed to come out to greet him and have a seat—just the two of them. A costume change went awry, and she didn't show up. He waited and waited. Finally he took a long cross, arcing down center. He looked out to the audience and said, "Ah, Venice!" So I tell young actors, always know what town you're in, because if something goes wrong and you're left alone on the stage, you can always take a cross downstage and say, "Ah, London!" or "Ah, Verona!"

Being an actor, being onstage and playing a character, is an incredible act of concentration. You have to know your own brain and use your own imagination to wrestle your monkey mind into one place. We learn all these techniques, but ultimately, there are no rules, because every actor has a different imagination. You have to make decisions about other characters that you're interacting with, who they are to you, what you want from them, what you think they think about you. All these things feed your imagination.

When I played Pericles (it's the whole journey of a life, it's boy-to-man, every scene another section of his life), I remember thinking that there's already inherent continuity because I'm playing Pericles—me, the same actor—throughout. What if in each scene I imagined Pericles as a different character in a different play? That was freeing. But you could break Hamlet down that way, too—a series of different characters. When Hamlet gets sent away on the boat to England, and sees the death warrant carried by his ostensible friends, Rosencrantz and Guildenstern, a lot becomes clear there. "Oh, I see. It's very simple. These people mean nothing to me anymore." In that moment, his world turns upside down again. He simply rewrites the letter, making it *their* death warrant. When you see him next, explaining the whole thing to Horatio, he's a totally different person. Now he's a man. He's grown about fifteen years in that one week. You can feel that in the audience. Wow, what's happened?

It's great storytelling if you can find that: how Hamlet has changed. Before, he was like a wind-up toy who keeps trying things, hitting obstacles, bouncing off in the wrong direction. But now, after meeting the gravedigger and seeing Yorick's skull, there's a certain calm; things keep getting clearer and clearer. At the point when Osric announces the duel with Laertes, Horatio can't understand why Hamlet agrees to the fight, but for Hamlet, it's a pathway opening up, his only way to go—the same character, but with real change. The main thing is to keep asking what's the circumstance, what's the problem, and what are the obstacles—internal or external —that your character comes up against. Character comes out of that.

In terms of finding a physicality, if you're playing Hamlet, it's best to be yourself. It depends on the production. What is the period, what am I wearing? That's going to affect how I move. If I'm playing Richard II in period, I have a straight spine, I grew up having dance classes and fencing classes. I've been trained to hold my nose in the air and my head high, ready to wear the crown. It would be ridiculous to slump around and drag my feet. In a modern-dress *Hamlet*, wearing jeans, my power gets expressed by a different physicality. Posture is not as important. In the text there may be other cues as to who the character is, interesting idiosyncrasies. When I played one of the tribunes in a modern-dress *Coriolanus*, my image of myself was a guy with a bottle of whiskey in his metal desk, down in the bottom drawer. I could hear the drawer opening—Jack Daniels, yeah. That specificity stimulates me.

For Romeo—a role I didn't expect to be cast in, a complete surprise—Henry Woronicz, the director, said, "I want you to be just like Wesley," an ordinary, struggling kid that I had just played in *Curse of the Starving Class*. In the balcony scene, Henry wanted me to endear myself, to do something foolish that would make the audience root for the kid, the underdog, to get the girl—Grace Zandarski, who was a more typical Juliet. So I had to win her over with my charm, not my good looks.

On the line about being stabbed by Cupid ("Alack, there lies more peril in thine eye than twenty of their swords"), Henry had me pretend an arrow had hit my heart, and I fell down on the floor, and Juliet laughed. Looking back now, it is a little cliché, but it was Henry's cue to me that it was okay to loosen up. I wasn't self-conscious, just crazy in love, kind of goofy and innocent and free. The arc of the play took me to the banishment scene, where Romeo is a totally different character. After what's happened, he's not a boy anymore. Now he's like a revolutionary, realizing that the adults don't know what they're doing. Then, in the tomb, he's a husband. Understanding that can really help you to get rooted in who you are, because in tragedy what's ultimately moving to an audience—even unconsciously—is feeling that arc. It's important that they care about the hero, that they get invested in this teenager who's foolish and light. So how are you going to do that? Engage the audience, interest them with the way your mind works. Then you've got them, and you take them on the journey. It's not hard with these great plays; they're written that way. The more that arc is developed and has a real trajectory—that's where you earn the tragedy, because you change as you go through the play.

I did one hundred twenty performances as Romeo and as Hamlet. Some days you go to the theater for a matinee and think: "I can't do Hamlet now!" But you just start at the beginning, one thing leads to the next, and afterward you might think, "That was great!" A big part of it is the long run. Fifty or sixty shows in, things start to strip away. You take a really natural breath and speak. You know it's there, you're thinking as the character, you're not trying to control it too much, and it starts to resonate and come from a deeper place in you. Really making that complicated language your own—it's a journey. Toward the end of the run, you look back and think how hard it was and how worried you were and where you knew you were strained. After sixty times, you come to the theater and know you can get through it.

Hamlet was one of the best experiences I've had. I was supposed to understudy Henry Woronicz, who had just taken over as artistic director and was going to play Hamlet. The legendary Adrian Hall, of the Dallas Theatre Center and the Trinity Square Repertory Company, was going to direct—a real coup. On New Year's Day, I was reading a book about Adrian, getting excited about working with him, when Henry called to say that Adrian had to bow out. Henry would take over directing, and he wanted me to play Hamlet. For a moment I was disappointed—"No Adrian Hall!"—but of course that went by the wayside quickly. Henry had played Hamlet before. I loved working with him. I felt supported, to be directed by an actor and friend who knew the route.

I like working with directors who have been actors. Even Liviu Ciulei, who was a bit of a puppet master, was a wonderful actor. It has to do with a certain respect and understanding. A director who was an actor may understand better what that isolation is like when you're trying to create a role. You want a director who knows the play well and who's interested in telling a story. Directors get into trouble when they're so worried about making their mark that they focus on the frame around the play, the concept, instead of the play's events. I like to work with a director who's most interested in what's going on with the characters at any given moment. That's the story. The audience is interested in what characters are feeling, but more importantly, what they're thinking. The characters' emotions are revealed in performance; what's mysterious is what are they thinking? He said that . . . but does he mean it? Is she exaggerating? What does she really want? What made him say that? What's going on in his head? We only get the words, but the event is something much deeper, and must be explored and agreed upon by the artists.

If you're well cast, some directors use what you have and temper the production to that. Mary Zimmerman (author/director of *The White Snake*) works that way. Whatever we gave her, Mary would shape a little and orchestrate. She'd make it work. Her process is unique in that she is both playwright and director. Because she had never created a piece away from her home in Chicago, where she works regularly with many of the same actors, it was important to have somebody who knew her company and her work. So for *The White Snake* she brought her designers, a musician, and one of her actors, Lisa Tejero, from Chicago. Everyone else was cast out of the OSF company.

The way Mary works is that she gets the production designed, creates a world, and then she gets her cast. She works on the story, obviously, but she doesn't write the actual dialogue until she's in rehearsal, because she wants to have those actors and that physical space in her mind as she writes.

Our first rehearsal started with singing auditions. Everybody sang a song. You had to pull it out of your hat. We talked a bit about the story, and then she said, "I have these three pages, let's just read it." After we read it, she said, "Let's just do it on our feet. That's the way I want to start." She placed us on the stage, and we did the opening moment, with the cloth falling over us, a few times. That was it for the day. Then she went away and started writing the next three pages.

Now she had our voices in her mind, our qualities. "Your taste," she said, "your voice, the way you move." So every day there were three or four more pages, which she would stage. Often, whatever she did the first time stayed in the show. Then we'd go back and start at the beginning. After a week we had about twenty minutes, and we'd run the twenty minutes a couple of times, and add a little more. It was layer, layer, layer. Pretty soon you'd get enough so that you could run that section. There was plenty of time to learn the lines. Even for the leads, there wasn't that much dialogue. Because she's so clear about this process, it was very reasonable and calm. She didn't know if it was going to turn out well, but she knew that this was a way of working that has been successful for her.

People in marketing and the artistic staff thought, "You're starting a play without a script?" But there were never any problems with storytelling. She'd figure out a simple way to solve it, trusting her instincts, without anxiety. There's a real beauty to that trust in us and in this mysterious thing that happened to her, that she's creating. I said to her once in a rehearsal break, because we were getting close to the end of rehearsals, that we all were wondering how the play was going to end. And she said, "Yes, me too." I found out later that she actually had written the end, but she held it for three days because it was so personal that she felt self-conscious about it. When we read that whole last section for the first time, it was very moving.

Shakespeare does help you with contemporary work like *The White Snake*. Dealing with heightened language, with poetic language, is like a jazz musician working on a Bach piece, something really structured. When they get back to doing jazz, perhaps their technique is better. When I'm working on Shakespeare, I'm thinking about where he uses onomatopoeia, or lines that have a lot of "k"s in them, or long arcs of thoughts, long parenthetical phrases where you've got to get back on the train and finish the thought. But you don't think about that as often when you're working on modern plays. There's a lot to be said for going back and forth, so that when you encounter a contemporary text, you're more likely to think about how a long speech is arced, about the sounds of the words. Keith Jarrett is a wonderful jazz musician, but he also plays classical music: there's an exchange there that's useful.

Mary Zimmerman's writing for *The White Snake* was beautiful. She gave me a couple of wonderful, very complex narrations, like the one that begins, "I've heard it said that we fall most deeply in love when the other person seems to open a door to an entire world we have not known." The challenge turned out to be owning it, being just me, finding the right tone. She wanted a transparency, a book-on-tape quality, almost neutral but with an empathy for what I was describing. Other narrations went: "Come on! Here's the story! This is what happened next." In my narration, there's no character there—except that I begin, "I have heard it said…." She could have just said, "We fall most deeply in love…." But the speech has authority because it's been said before, an old wise man said it, and it stuck. Was it me? Or am I just somebody who heard this and was moved by it? That was really smart of her.

The ideal director gives a little praise here and there, a bit of "We're on the right track." Directors don't need to be syrupy. Sometimes even when you try something outrageous, they're so glad: "That's good, that's good, that was exciting!" And you think, "Well, it's just an idea. Can I try something else? Or can you shape it? Was it really right, or just unusual?" Actors can be hesitant to try things if a director doesn't know how to incorporate their experiments. Every actor should know how to direct himself, in case there's no support there, but I'd rather have a lot of give-and-take with the director. Part of our job is to develop working relationships, connecting as much as we can and keeping lines of communication open. It's tempting to find a solution and call it good. But I like it when a director encourages me to try things, to take a risk. Rehearsal is the place to be wrong.

One of the best collaborations I ever had was with another actor in my third-year acting class. I was doing a scene from *Who's Afraid of Virginia Woolf?* with a woman who was really gifted and powerful. We did the scene over and over and over and over again. We just played off each other, and hardly had to talk about it, because we knew when something was happening. The next time we rehearsed, we would build on that, and it began to take shape, just by repetition. I love that the French call rehearsal *répétition*. That's their word for it. Of course we didn't have a director because we were just preparing a scene for acting class. We didn't finish the scene and say, "Oh, that was great, when you did this and I did that." You can sometimes destroy the work by talking about it. It's a matter of trusting, when you're in that moment, that this unspoken thing is taking shape—which is best, I think.

In 1999 I had an offer out of the blue to return to the Guthrie to play Cassius. I was thrilled to be coming back, as a better actor. I had never worked with the director, but I had met him and we had a good connection. So I went out. The Guthrie no longer had a resident company, so actors had been jobbed in from around the country, some locally. After being part of the OSF company for so many years, I was aware of the difference. People were generally self-protective, we lacked a common vocabulary, and I had a hard time connecting. When I came back to OSF to do *Three Musketeers* and *Pericles*, I really appreciated, on a different level, what it means to be part of a company—that when you sit down to start a rehearsal with people you know, there's a level of trust and ease. You can say things, you can be wrong, you don't have to prove anything. People trust you.

I was thinking about my friend John Pribyl, whom I love so much. I remember one rehearsal, near the start, when he was very quiet and reserved. Then his work just grew and grew and grew, and he created something that only he could create, so hilarious and wonderful and moving. Now because I know him, I know that's going to happen. I hope people feel that way about me: "Oh, Richard. Well, he always starts really loud and trying to impress everybody, but eventually he calms down." We all have our funny starting places.

You hear about Broadway shows, first readings with producers standing around, and people get fired within the first three days, because there's so much at stake: "This isn't working, there's no chemistry." But that's not the case in our company. I've been lucky to do repertory almost my entire career, because it hardly exists today. Maybe that's why I've been here so long, even though sometimes I'd like to be more challenged. To be part of the company, to have this artistic home, is of overriding importance to me.

David Kelly as Argan in *The Imaginary Invalid*. Photo: David Cooper, OSF.

David Kelly

In 24 seasons at OSF, David Kelly has played, among other roles, Argan in *The Imaginary Invalid*; Garry LeJeune in *Noises Off*; Colonel Pickering in *My Fair Lady*; Benedick in *Much Ado About Nothing*; Bottom in *A Midsummer Night's Dream*; Senator John Falstaff in *The Merry Wives of Windsor, Iowa*; Sir John Falstaff in *1 Henry IV*; Senator Everett Dirksen in *All the Way*; Major-General Stanley in *The Pirates of Penzance*; Richard in *Richard II*; Biff in *Death of a Salesman*; Porthos in *The Three Musketeers*; Launce in *The Two Gentlemen of Verona*; Horatio in *Hamlet*; Antipholus of Syracuse in *The Comedy of Errors*; Tuzenbach in *Three Sisters;* and Detective Hennessey in *The Cocoanuts*.

I'VE ALWAYS BEEN SHAMELESSLY hammy. I had three older sisters who adored and spoiled me. My twelve-year-old and I compete for my wife's attention—sometimes I'm more like the older brother than the dad. I had that performing thingie already going at a young age. I was even a juvenile impersonator—I did Ed Sullivan, a great Richard Nixon, and Flip Wilson was a favorite: "The devil made me do it." I loved Frank Gorshin, who played the Riddler on the *Batman* show. I played Foster Brooks who did all those drunks. Much of my comic gift goes back to watching lots and lots of television and seeing funny stuff there.

I did a couple of classroom plays in elementary school, I was in the band and played trumpet in marching band, I sang in the choirs, and everything came together for me in school. I admit that most of it was social, as it is when you are twelve or thirteen. If you find a place where you are accepted when you are going through that freaky stage, you are lucky to have those friends. I found my place in drama and music, where I was also rewarded by my work. It gave me a personal feeling of worth, success, and social acceptance. You want to do the play, and you want to be around your buddies.

I went to undergraduate school at UC San Diego where I studied with Alan Schneider, the famous Beckett and Albee director there, and I also studied with Eric Christmas, who worked at the Stratford Festival in Canada. Then I got my MFA at the University of Wisconsin (the program later moved to the University of Delaware) and carried out an intense conservatory experience. We studied Shakespeare and the Greeks. You did much more than scene study. It was a three-year program where right away we were working in a repertory system, also performing in *Arms and the Man, Cherry Orchard, Twelfth Night*. The program brought in new people every three years. Our class started with thirty-six students and graduated only twenty-four.

From the start, we had classes in text work and poetry. We worked from the theories of Tadashi Suzuki who is now in Japan and has a school of theater there called Toga, which does an international festival. He was a theorist and practitioner of a challenging boot-campy regimen of vocal and physical training, where we worked to a point of emotional fatigue. His idea was that the expressions we manifest come through all the history of the earth, and then we can bring the power of our voices and bodies from the core of the earth. We would do ninety minutes to two hours of that each day. It was very movement-oriented with strenuous exercises where we pushed ourselves to the very edge of vocal and physical exhaustion; then we went beyond

DAVID KELLY | 179

that to a new place of creativity. Sometimes you were not thinking any longer. You are something else in Suzuki philosophy, and you became the servant of those messages that are in the play and from the earth. Now, that's just the ooga-booga part of it, because we were also aware of how tired we were all the time. That was just one of our classes.

The only thing I can compare it to would be training at the Bolshoi or American Ballet Theater where they start students at nine or ten years old with the rigors of working to become a prima ballerina or a lead dancer. Without that kind of study, I would not be working in the Elizabethan theater outdoors. In a way, the training got me ready for big projects like *Noises Off*.

Ironically, the very first voice person I worked with at OSF (who was all about relaxation and openness) told me I had done irreparable damage to my voice—even though she hadn't heard it because I was at that early stage where I had only one or two lines per play. However, to balance the Suzuki work, we were also taught by a Western-trained voice coach and did Alexander work as well.

We were so exhausted, beginning with movement class at 8:30 in the morning, then back at 6:30 for rehearsals on whatever play we were doing. At this time, a lot of the smaller summer Shakespeare festivals—Colorado, Utah, Montana—relied on casting an army of graduate students. So, I worked at a number of them, for $200 a summer. It was excellent experience, and you could be in more than one show.

One of the great people in graduate school was my mentor Jewell Walker, a practical man and a tough coach. He had been "Mime Walker" on the television show *Mister Rogers' Neighborhood*. His background was movement, and he was responsible for bringing the Suzuki method to the U.S. He'd also trained in the French acting traditions, not only in mime, and he knew a great deal about the American tradition of burlesque and vaudeville. Even though that path seems broad and crazy, it brings such refinement to comedy, making it an enormously detailed and complicated art form, even a science.

Another kind of training that is considered old school and is defunct now was the work of Edith Skinner. She was the one who taught the "Mid-Atlantic" accent to all of the stars and starlets of the thirties, forties and fifties. When you hear Katherine Hepburn or Fred Astaire speak with this perfect accent, an upper-crust, rich, New England slant in the speaking voice, it's not British but somewhere between sophisticated and classy. Our trainer, Susan Sweeney, was a first-generation student of the Skinner method. It wasn't the accent that was important, it was the specificity. In the myriad of choices available about a character—how do I want it to look, how do I want it to move, how do I want it to sound—all of that comes from training.

Early in my career, I thought that if I just learned my lines, I could make up a lot of it, and I was successful doing that. Graduate school improved my ability to make choices from how to speak more clearly to making every point in the dialogue count. It is still very like being a musician and a dancer in that you train your body for movement, and study voice and articulation for more flexible speech.

I'd been coming to the Oregon Shakespeare Festival since I was about twelve years old. I got bitten by the bug in my early teens. This was always the job I wanted to have. My friends in high school wanted to be on Broadway or go to Hollywood, but this place, with all its variety, was the work I wanted to do. In the Festival's earlier years, there were two seasons, which meant the opportunity to do more roles. When they opened the Bowmer Theatre in the seventies, they would perform the first season there with five or six shows. Then they would rehearse and open the Elizabethan Theatre as a separate season, so you could actually work both seasons. This was before union rules came into the Festival, at a time prior to Actors' Equity union requirements. Nowadays, most of us are in two shows, and some in three.

I auditioned at the Festival four times in ten years. My final audition was in 1990 for the '91 season, and one of my favorite stories is that getting hired was total luck, which is pretty much the name of the game in our business: you can build skills which will improve your odds, and you can be the best speaker around, but you still might not get hired. There is no guarantee. It really is about luck. I'd auditioned at OSF right out of high school, twice in college, and then waited until after I had worked at other Shakespeare festivals before I actually got here.

I owe a lot of that luck to my good friend from graduate school, Christian LeBano. He worked for two years in the office here in 1990 and 1991, filing papers and typing. He knew how badly I wanted to join the company, and he'd heard in the early spring of 1990 that Pat Patton was looking for an actor because someone had dropped out of a show. He kept putting my picture on top of the pile of applications from young actors, and he kept saying, "You've got to hire David Kelly. He's great. He can really carry a spear for you." That piece of networking really worked well for me.

Patton called me and said—you are not going to have any lines and this is a bit part in *Henry IV, Part One*. I said, "Yes." He said it was a non-union contract, and I said, "Yes." He said it was only $225 per week, and I said, "YES. I'll be there. I don't care what it takes." I had been playing Benedick in a touring production of *Much Ado* out of San Francisco, and my manager said, "Well, you are going to the big leagues now." I was really nervous because I'd never quit a job in my life, and I said, "I *gotta* go." And he said, "Yes, you gotta *go!*" OSF used to audition between fifteen hundred and two thousand people a year. One friend did eleven auditions and never got in. There were no casting directors then, and nowadays the hirings are winnowed down by them. Two weeks after I began work here, my room-mates from the Bay Area forwarded my mail, and it contained a letter of rejection from the Oregon Shakespeare Festival: "Dear Mr. Kelly, We regret to inform you . . ." And I was already work-ing there!

Then, I began to add on extra work. Sandy McCallum was directing *Taming of the Shrew*, and luckily he needed another servant (Curtis) for Petruchio's household who actually had a couple of lines in a scene with Grumio. Sandy directed *House of Blue Leaves* and also played the Stage Manager in a beautiful production of *Our Town*, directed by Jim Edmondson. When I first got hired here, I had to pay off school loans, and I did a job as house staff, bartending in the Bowmer. That let you have time to sneak into the theater between intermissions and watch the plays, so I snuck into that show a dozen times. Jerry Turner also directed one of my seminal experiences as an audience mem-ber—Shaw's *Major Barbara*. This wonderful history at OSF.

There are so many of those "old acquaintance" moments recently—running into Michael Ganio, my favorite stage de-signer, on the bricks one day, and he said, "Isn't it fun that David Ivers is coming to direct at OSF? David was a student at SOU then, and now he is co-artistic director at Utah Shakespeare Festival and directing *Taming of the Shrew* here." I replied, "Isn't that great—my first year he was in the same show with me from Southern Oregon College" (as SOU was called then). And Mi-chael reminded me—"David, that was the first show I designed at OSF!"

Then there is Nell Geisslinger. I remember her as a little girl. She took dance and ballet and has been around actors and known them all her life because of her parents' work in the the-ater. You see that growth and the culmination of her work as she performs Kate in *Taming of the Shrew*. Her time has come, and it has been thrilling to be onstage with her, in both *Imaginary Invalid* as Louison and now Kate in *Shrew*.

Being in a repertory company is the draw to acting at OSF. In the 2013 season, for example, I developed two roles all year long—a low comic, Gremio in *Shrew*, in repertory with Colonel Pickering, an upperclass, retired military man in *My Fair Lady*. One of my favorite seasons was getting to play Gratiano outdoors in *Merchant*, a flaming hairdresser in *Enter the Guardsman*, and then the pathetic sad, lonely Baron Tuzenbach in Chekhov's *Three Sisters*—a good variety of roles, with three different casts. It's like three different jobs that take place in three different locations.

I learn so much from everyone I work with. You realize that this cast of people makes my performance different from every other performance I've done. It isn't simply my saying how can I be different from the way I was in the last show I was in. It's that I feel I am not owed anything. It is so black and white, concrete and true for me that there are three hundred other guys who are my type, on my level, who could take my place in a minute. That is utterly clear to me. I know I have a wide skill set and a lot of experience, but I want the work to be brand new each time I walk into a different play.

My professor, Jewell Walker, put a question to me in rehearsal, at a point where I did not know where to go with Bluntchli in *Arms and the Man*. He'd already said, "You are not 'getting' this role—you are still too stiff. Who is the free spirit represented that often shows up in Shaw's plays, a character who is always open to the world? Who would you cast in this role?" I mentioned a couple of people in my acting class. He said, "No. Any actor in the history of acting, movie stars or whatever. Who would be ideal in this role?" I just threw it out there and said, "Cary Grant." Jules said, "Good. How would Cary Grant do it?" He wasn't asking me to do an impersonation. Rather to put the essence of Cary inside me—do that, create from that. In the rehearsal room, people reacted to that choice with all kinds of comments: "Whatever you are doing, it's working"—"You are kind of transformed"—"I don't recognize you"—"That's something new for you." They did not see Cary Grant up there. I didn't sound like him, I didn't look or dress like him, nor did they have any idea what I was doing or what I was thinking about.

For me, this idea was the "hook" for the role. Finding who would that be? It might not be as specific as a single performer or a character type. It doesn't even have to be an actor. It could be somebody from history, or somebody from my everyday life: "Oh right, that's *that* person." When I get cast in a role, or when I read a play, I cast it in my head with one of my favorite actors. Occasionally, I'll think, "Wow, this isn't a role for me. This is a role for so-and-so!" My character-building process is more about observation and intuition.

There are actors who are well read and research-oriented. They love it and it gives them so much fuel. For example, you can work on Shakespeare's folios and quartos, and I really loved doing that when I played Richard II. Scott Kaiser, Barry Kraft (who was playing John of Gaunt) and I were invited to Libby Appel's house to work on *The Tragedy of Richard II*. We had three four-hour sessions in Libby's dining room, using all of the different texts of the play that have come down to us over the years. As the director, Libby would err on the side of "Let's make the play shorter so we won't bore the audience. Keep it moving and never over three hours." So she'd say that a certain speech goes on much too long, so let's shave it a bit. Barry would say, "How dare you!" and he would always have a good reason for not cutting it. Scott and I were somewhere in the middle of the road—even though the actor part of me thought, "Yeah, I don't understand parts of it, so let's get rid of it." What was important was to do this early on in the production so you can get down to the specificity of the choices you make as an actor.

Barry would offer that there was a semi-colon in the Folio

version of a particular speech. However, I've had fellow actors and teachers say to me, "Take out all of the punctuation. See how that works for you, and then punctuate it vocally for yourself." That may sound like a rebel, but when you think about all the editors and printers who have handled that manuscript, sometimes just trying to get all the language onto one printed page—between Shakespeare and the "final" copy, who is really responsible for that punctuation mark? Also, many literary people, editors, have made alterations over the years, not always improving the text or making it more playable. So I might have horrified everyone by saying, "I don't know what that semi-colon does for me there."

When Jack Willis was cast as LBJ in *All the Way* and during the workshop prior to the production, he said, "I've got all these lines I need to learn, but I have to stop myself from buying books on Lyndon Johnson." That work was feeding his process in an extraordinary way. His was a case of exploring all the known historical data about a person from recent history. Shakespeare operated in a different way. He wrote about Hotspur as if he had been near the age of Prince Hal, doing this great theatrical version by putting the two opponents onstage together. In reality, Hotspur was considerably older than Hal. Shakespeare's idea of history was very much to create for dramatic purposes, to forge an interesting play using known materials.

Many actors feel the pressure to be original. But Shakespeare's plays are over four hundred years old. Do you really think it's possible to be original? The point is that the performance lives in the moment you are doing it. No one is going to know whether Kevin Kline made the same choice you did, a choice that serves your own production very well. You are acting it for the first time because it's you, and you are creating it from your own personality traits—that alone makes it original enough.

One of my very first acting teachers in college told us about his rather interesting interpretation of the Stanislavski method of acting. He said that a play is more or less a delivery system for the character you play. For example, if I am playing Baron Tuzenbach, this play becomes for me the story of only him, because I am playing that role. What is happening in every single moment affects that character. I was all over that idea as a young acting student. Because if I were playing him, even though the person downstage is Vershynin in his love scene with Masha, I make the scene about how exciting it is to play cards upstage.

As I grew older, I began to think, "This is weird." Am I not then upstaging the scene that's happening? The play is not about my character. It is about a group of people and the trajectory of that story. And now my focus needs to be on the function of the character in that scene, perhaps more likely to create the ambience of someone in the background playing cards. Even if you are playing Hamlet, there are some scenes that are not just about Hamlet.

I have worked with actors who behave—and I have been one of these actors—as if the play is about their character only. Not that they are mean or egoistic people, but some do go about working on a play as if every moment belongs to their character. The work should be about feeding the idea that we are all working to tell this single story that is this particular play. An important question is—what is the trajectory of this play—scene by scene, what is needed and what is the function of each character within this context to tell the story.

A really good example is in *A Midsummer Night's Dream*. You have six guys in that play whose entire job is to be funny. I have seen so many productions where the lovers feel that they have to be funny, too—so they do a lot of goofy things, especially late in the run of the show, where they have discovered places that get laughs. What they forget is that they have a pressing job, which is to solve the problem of "Where am I in my life and why do I totally love you, or not love you" plotline. That's their function. The lovers' scenes are even written in rhyming, iambic pentameter, very different from the rustics' prose—these other six guys have the job of reacting to the comic event of Bottom entering with an ass's head and then playing the Pyramus and Thisbe scene outrageously. Even in the Puck and Oberon and Titania scenes, actors find ways to be funny. I am not saying they should not be occasionally comic, but I am saying that we sometimes forget our overall function within individual scenes. The way Shakespeare uses language directs you to how you play the scene.

This idea keeps coming to me through the comedy work I do, especially in working with Tracy Young in both *Servant of Two Masters* and *Imaginary Invalid*, a show that involved the craziest, broadest acting we do. Her challenge was to focus each scene so that the audience knew where to look at every single moment. I check for that every time I watch a play now. It is not just the director's job, it's also important for the actor to also have the directorial mind. We are part of a team. I've enjoyed working with Laird Williamson, and recently, when he set *Romeo and Juliet* in California in the 1800s, he was still most interested in the relationships of the characters and the language of the play. He is very nuts-and-bolts about telling the story of the two young lovers. The times I am most comfortable are when the concept does not override the plot. The director doesn't merely "have a hunch" about the play: he knows where the plot is going and he moves it there. I'm not saying you cannot modernize a play, but if the concept clearly generates from the language of the play—the who, what, when and where—you could set it on Mars and it would work.

The director can correct situations, can ask you why you are doing such-and-such in rehearsal, and I can respond and say that this was where I thought the focus should be, and the director might say, "No, no, I need you to do something else." That kind of negotiating goes on. Nonetheless, I've had great success working with other actors, knowing that they will focus the play with me, just like a camera. There is a focusing moment at the opening of *Imaginary Invalid*. The hypochondriac Argan talks about how sick and "overcharged" by his doctors he is. The speech is a set-up for the entire play, the description of this character's whole function. He shows all his pills and bottles and insists that nothing is making him better and that his doctors are charging him too much money. He wonders how he will solve the problem, so he decides to marry his daughter off to a doctor. There you have the whole play! When I played Pickering in *My Fair Lady*, I was very much the Horatio, the listener, the facilitator, the sounding board for Henry Higgins. My job is not "Hey, look at me." No. I am the way through which Higgins gets to tell the story.

I don't mean that an actor should tell another actor what to do—one should never do that. But actors can inspire and suggest to each other. I have on occasion in rehearsal said, "Wouldn't it be great if we tried this?" The other actor says, "That's a great idea," we do it, and the director says, "What are you two guys doing? Stop doing that"—or says, "That's fabulous! Let's keep it in." That kind of teamwork can emerge. Although the director has the final say—it's up to the actor to create and provide interesting choices for him.

Just for the record. I don't want this to sound like it's some kind of magic hooha—but I never feel like I am anybody but David Kelly. People sometimes say, "I felt like I was actually in Russia, and I am the doctor." I never laugh at those people— they believe that. But I have never once felt that I am anyone other than David Kelly telling the story in a play.

One of my favorite productions was *Noises Off* in 2002. It would kill me to play that show now and was probably one of the reasons I have bad knees today. The process for that comedy was very hard yet had one of my favorite preparations of all time—it was like a hilarious boot camp. The director was Ken Albers, a terrific actor, and stage manager, who knows about all aspects of putting on a play, but his true specialty is comedy. Farce of that kind is so dependent on exact timing, especially in that show, which had two levels, lots of stairs and doors, and the audience often looking at the back side of a stage set. Everything onstage was timed out from where the furniture was placed onstage when they are looking at the front side of the set, and where the doors and stairs are visible from the back view of the flats.

Ken requested a rehearsal set, and so the crew built a very simple framework of the set into one of the rehearsal halls. It had the basic dimensions, stairs that went up to the second level, and doorframes, but no doors. There were three doorways on the second level and three doors below.

When we started to learn the script and to stage it, we were speaking and running up stairs, so our first line would be "OPEN THE DOOR" (our stage direction) and then we would start speaking the dialogue. Then we said "CLOSE THE DOOR," as we exited, but sometimes we would still be speaking the line after you closed the door. It was vital that we had those obligations every time we went in and out. Once we had a set to work on for the final dress rehearsals and tech rehearsals, we continued to say "OPEN THE DOOR, or SLAM THE DOOR," or whatever our blocking was before or after we gave the line. Naturally, every actor occasionally did this at least once (and in my case two or three times), where the line carried over into the performance and it shouldn't have. I would say to myself, "Darn! I don't have to say OPEN anymore—because I am doing it." It was a joy to be working in that ensemble: in my world, there is just no time for ego in a show.

Another powerful influence on my career as a comic actor was Tracy Young. She trained and has extensive background in *commedia dell'arte*, a type of comedy performed in Italy in the 1600s and 1700s, which influenced Moliere and modern comedy in a variety of ways. A kind of one-page plot was hung backstage, and that was the story to be told in that performance. It would be punctuated by *lazzi* or bits of comedy that the actors in any given troupe had devised. There were character types—such as the Pulcinella, the clever servant, and Pantaleone, the grouchy older man usually lusting for a younger woman.

Tracy Young and her writing partner, Oded Gross, devised a way to use the plot and the subplots from Moliere's *Imaginary Invalid*, so this adaptation was grounded in the story but still had many different facets and influences of theater in it. Moliere has much more of a heart center, and the characters in the Moliere plays are very three-dimensional, even though really crazy and funny antics predominate. However, the original *Imaginary Invalid* included olios, a device where you'd do a scene, then someone would come out and sing a song, and then this might be followed by a sketch or a comic bit which, in the original *commedia dell'arte* form, had nothing to do with the play. In Tracy and Oded's *Invalid*, the sketches and songs were directly related to the performances, which made the plot and dialogue very clear. Moliere had often used characters that mirrored the stock characters in *commedia*, but we coordinated them in meaning and in story, which shaped our whole show much more into an American musical theater piece. There was a further adaptation in that the dancing and the songs were not only an integral part of the play but were inspired by 1960s pop music, created by Paul James Prendergast.

Both the sets and the costumes were designed by Chris Acebo, which doesn't happen often in the U.S., because this is largely a European custom. The result is one person's vision. He created a unified look of a wealthy apartment in Paris in the 1960s, and it was such a fun playground—very open and all in white with splashes of color in the furnishings, the weird mod nude sculpture covered in a blue velvet-like texture, the paintings, the Warhol character. Just genius.

Tracy and I worked on the opening monologue for hours

because we wanted to bring back the original message of Moliere's play. We wanted to build a *lazzi* into it as well. In the traditional Moliere performance, Argan's actions were dark and depressing, and he used an abacus to find out how much money his doctors ripped off. Oded and Tracy wrote instead an upbeat opening song-and-dance number where everyone is joyous, and then they all exit—so Argan has to pull the audience down from that high note. I would spit up in a cloth and be very negative about marrying my daughter to a doctor. I loved that contrast right at the opening of the play.

It was my idea to be in a wheelchair at the outset because it anchored me to Argan's situation. At one point as I was sitting there and thinking, I just walked right out of the chair, clueing the audience that he is the *imaginary* invalid, by the way, forgetting to perform that ruse when he's really angry. At the end of the act, Toinette and I have this great scene where she finally berates him, accuses him of faking his illnesses, and tells him he should shape up. He loses it. I pushed off out of the wheelchair and tried to throw it backwards (I figured out how to get the wheels lined up so it would go directly straight back) and then I laid into her verbally, stood up, and walked off. So, the audience knows he isn't ill.

Then we brought into the mix all those bizarre medicines, which become part of the story. The character of Toinette, played by K.T. Vogt, the cheeky servant girl, showed us the many unpleasant procedures she had to do each day. I wanted to have leeches, which were used in those times to suck blood from the patients to clear their systems. I was constantly inventing ideas and surprising my director with the results, one of my favorite things to do. The prop master, Jim Clark, came up with the idea of rubber fishing lures for the leeches, and I used toupee tape to keep them on my body. I still can't believe I did that. The audience didn't respond all that much, and I thought that's really okay because I didn't want to go on doing that. Afterwards, no matter how much I showered and scrubbed my belly with a washcloth, I still had little black marks there.

If you pull your comic bits out too early, you get "rehearsal laughter" and then this goes on continuously throughout rehearsals and you never know if the joke still works or if it is still fresh. The great ACT artistic director, Bill Ball, had a rule in rehearsal hall that people could not laugh, because your friends do it to keep you supported. I can always tell that fake effort. The director will tell you when you've crossed the line.

The hardest role in the play is Toinette's, clearly the smartest and most strategic servant in the play, so good at arranging plots and pulling the wool over people's eyes. She mocks her master, Argan, so much that he comes close to knowing that. K.T. and I developed a good working relationship where she would make fun of me to my face to the point where I would just about catch her at it, then she'd cover by moving on to something else quickly. The ultimate message for Argan was to have to take responsibility for his actions, and then life goes on, which he finally came around to at the end of the play. He should not go on blaming his various "illnesses" and should learn to face his hypochondria. He can see his daughters for who they are rather than who he wants them to be. The final song of the play says this clearly, "All We Have Is Now."

I think Tracy used more rehearsal hours for this play than were used for Hamlet. There was so much dancing and individual singing numbers, yet it was all the good kind of work where you collaborate and say, "Let's figure this thing out."

Servant of Two Masters was also in the *commedia* style, so we were working from that same vocabulary, with the stock characters and a director who was immersed within a theatrical style that goes back a thousand years and establishes character types and/or "lines of acting," where certain actors have specialty roles.

Modern counterparts are the Yiddish theater, burlesque, vaudeville, the Marx Brothers, the Three Stooges—even modern cartoons like Bugs Bunny play off that tradition. Goldoni wrote this play from the *commedia* tradition and gradually brought more script, language and character depth to it, so it remains a kind of performable record of how the older tradition happened. It was probably written from a plot outline, and the *lazzi* and other inside-the-play entertainments are still included.

Tracy Young's directorial work gets quickly to the physicality of the play, so we were up on our feet right away. Once again, you could see and hear the interrelationships with Moliere and Shakespeare and the *commedia* troupes who were playing around the corner from Moliere's theater in Paris. (In 1996, we did a short play by Nagle Jackson called *Moliere Plays Paris,* and the character of Moliere says, "Those darned Italians—they're stealing all our stuff.")

When we began rehearsals, Tracy asked us to figure out where our character would locate his/her predominant body center. Richard Howard played the Dottore (usually either a medical doctor or a doctor of law), and he was always sniffing around for money, so he could lead with his nose. Richard explored how that would manifest itself in his character's body. His Pantaleone (grouchy old man) was always moving from his middle body, making sure his money was safe in his purse, and at the same time having erections which he couldn't do anything about or with, so he's most certainly not about the "mind centers" of the body.

We spent the first three days working on physicality. Richard and I wore the traditional masks of *commedia*, but mine was only a nose and cheek piece. I dressed my eyes and eyebrows with makeup so you could see my eye movements. We didn't do full masks because those would cover most of our faces, eliminating the emotional color of each character. We knew we would be working in the round in the Thomas Theater with audience on all four sides of the performance space. We had four entrances, one in each corner on this set (designed by Richard Hay). We could work in the corners and on the platforms. People came to *Servant* a dozen times. It was so fresh, and Mark Bedard, the lead *zanni*, would find something brilliant and go off on a tangent in each production. He loved to find kids in the audience, because he could play with them easily and bring them into the performance.

Mark was Truffaldino, the Arlecchino (Harlequin) jokester, and he was granted the license to "go off script." Part of the plot device was that Truffaldino was hungry all the time, so the business with sandwiches could only go so far, because he could not eat in front of his master. He would steal food from people's purses and start a running dialogue about what he found there, occasionally juggling the food. It was the job of the rest of us to tell the story as straightforwardly as we could and to keep it moving—then he would spin off in a comic direction and the job became getting everyone back on track and moving with the plotline again. At the end of the first half of the performance, Mark would put out a bag and then ask people in the audience to fill it for him and he'd be back for it later after the intermission. This trick became another source of jokes.

Sometimes his comic "bit" was so enticing, and he'd make the opportunity for laughs so golden, that we just let it play longer if it was working well with the audience. In fact, the stage manager had to give us notes afterwards to remind us about the rule to keep the storyline of the play going. If we had a dispute, we'd call Tracy Young at her home in Las Vegas and make a request to use a joke we'd found in the play. Richard Howard and I developed a miscommunication and one-upmanship contest with the two fathers vying at the end of the second act, moments we'd worked so much. However, the cast had to clear out at a certain point to make way for an evening show in that space, so that bit didn't always get performed.

One of the roots of the word farce is "to stuff," as if you were stuffing or forcing something into the chicken. That's what a *farceur* does, is to stuff moments full of laughs. You do have to choose when you are going to stuff and when you are not. You have to be judicious when you find something really cute or funny and the audience laughs at it—because you don't want to lose the forward movement of the play.

The pressure of this show and being in the middle of it felt like someone had pulled the cord on a lawnmower. The planning became second nature and there was this feeling of being available to what's happening onstage now. I felt I was in the moment, inventing as I went. That's the thrill of it. When the show is over at the end—you feel that so much energy had been expended vocally and physically, that where did the time go!

Sometimes the old adage, "The show must go on," announces itself like a fanfare. Because actors make mistakes—ask my friends who work with me. I just "go up" now and then, and they are doozies. Jonathan Haugen has saved me several times.

There was Benedick's "gulling scene" in Act II, scene ii of *Much Ado About Nothing*, where he had this soliloquy wondering how Claudio could be so foolish and gullible about focusing on love. Claudio was a brave, plainspoken soldier, not interested in fashion and romance, and suddenly now he had changed. That would never happen to *me* (my Benedick vows). The other men come onstage, Benedick quickly hides in the pool of a fountain and overhears the chat of the Prince, Leonato, and Claudio about how Beatrice, in reality, adores Benedick, pines for him but has to hide her love because he would scorn her for that. The men leave, having completely tricked Benedick into believing their story. He comes out of the pool and gives this soliloquy in a surprised fashion—can it be true? Can she love me? She enters at that point, calls him to dinner very matter-of-factly and ironically, in the manner of most of their conversations.

In the biggest faux pas of my career on one night, I emerged from the pool and did the wrong monologue, totally skipping her curt request for him to come to dinner, and then I exited the stage! Not only did I run out of the scene, soaking wet, I got applause on the power of my exit, so I think I'm the King of Acting, the greatest person ever to play this role. My dresser, Rich, said, "Go back onstage! You have to go back out there. Look!" and here stood dear Robynn Rodriguez, usually such a totally composed actor, now gob-smacked and wondering what to do. I ran onstage and jumped back into the water, all in the course of six seconds. "Will it please you come into dinner?" she began, and we gave the rest of the scene.

Then she left, and I was stuck out there, dripping, because I'd already spoken the closing remarks of the scene. So I just jumped to the end, said, "She loves me" or something similar, and exited a second time. A friend said to me later, "That was an interesting choice."

People just do not *know*.

On the other hand, flubs happen to everyone onstage sometimes. And I executed one of the most imaginative saves of the 2013 season about midway through the run of *My Fair Lady*. My silly but very necessary improvisation had to occur to keep the show going. In that production, we used very few props and almost no scenery, only two grand pianos, played onstage. The Chorus performed all the "extra" parts—Cockneys, snooty horse-race fans, Henry Higgins' house staff—with all costumes being changed onstage. In Act I, my character Pickering brings a beautiful antique telephone onstage, supposed to be moved and ready, near the piano—but that night, this prop never found its way onstage. In Act II, Pickering has to call the police to find Eliza. I looked across the stage at the fellow whose job was placing it onstage, and he mouthed "NO PHONE!" to me, and he ran off to find it. I gave three more lines and ran off to look for it, also. I heard my cue then, bolted onstage, and suddenly saw in front of me the huge man's slipper Eliza had earlier hurled at Higgins. I picked it up, in true Maxwell Smart tradition, put it to my ear and said, "Scotland Yard? Col. Hugh Pickering here on my SlipperPhone." It was silent in the audience and onstage. I said again, "That's right, I'm on my SlipperPhone." Although not known for this, I kept calm and I didn't crack, despite uncomfortable titters from the audience.

The show went on, and for the second phone call I had to make later on in the scene, the "real" telephone had been magically retrieved and replaced.

Kevin Kenerly as Hotspur in *1 Henry IV*. Photo: Jenny Graham, OSF.

Kevin Kenerly

In 19 seasons at OSF, Kevin Kenerly has played, among other roles, Sterling in *Two Trains Running*; Casca, Lepidus, Messala in *Julius Caesar*; Hotspur in *I Henry IV*; Macduff in *Macbeth*; Oberon in *A Midsummer Night's Dream*; Lyons in *Fences*; Citizen Barlow in *Gem of the Ocean*; Algernon in *The Importance of Being Earnest*; Levee in *Ma Rainey's Black Bottom*; Booth in *Topdog/Underdog*; Oswald in *King Lear*; Romeo in *Romeo and Juliet*; Orlando in *As You Like It*; Segismundo in *Life Is a Dream*; Troilus in *Troilus and Cressida*; and Canewell in *Seven Guitars*.

GROWING UP, I NEVER HAD a desire to be an actor. It isn't something I'd always done, like being in the school play. My parents, instead of letting me watch TV or play video games, always made us read books and play games and draw. So I had grown up drawing. Human anatomy really intrigued me. When I was twelve, I tore up my knee playing soccer and had an ACL repair. I was completely amazed that the surgeon could fix my knee, so as I was growing older, I thought maybe I'd be a medical illustrator. And when I took sculpture that led me to believe maybe I could be a prosthetic engineer.

In the beginning I went to Cass Technical High School in Detroit, Michigan. My parents moved us to Kansas City, Missouri, because my father worked for Ford. We were there for a couple of years, couldn't stand it, and came back to Detroit. I ended up going to my neighborhood school, Detroit Central, where all my uncles and my father had gone, so they treated me like I'd been there forever. It was just so strange to go from pearly-white, ultra-rich North Kansas City, Missouri, back to an urban environment, walking through metal detectors at Detroit Central.

My senior year I was taking a class called Current Events. You'd get a newspaper off the stack when you walked into the class at eight in the morning, and you'd write about the most interesting thing you read in the newspaper, so you'd know what the hell was going on in the world. I was so bored in this class. One day the drama teacher substituted and said, "You have a nice voice. Would you like to join my drama class?" And I said, "Can you get me out of here? Will you give me a credit?" So she got me into drama class and put me in a play, and we ended up going to the Thespian Festival in Muncie, Indiana. It was interesting, it was fun. She found me a school—Olivet College, in Michigan—that had a biology program, medical illustration, sculpture, and a theater scholarship for me. Bonny Sheehy Nielsen—she literally changed the course of my life. I'm forever grateful.

The theater scholarship paid for a good chunk of my schooling. It took me five years to get a double major, but I was finally done. Even then I wasn't convinced; I was tired of doing theater because I was never cast. One of my friends said, "Oh, they're doing *Hamlet* over at the Hilberry Theatre, you should audition." The Hilberry Theatre in Detroit is a gorgeous space—it reminds me a lot of the Bowmer. So I went over to the Hilberry to audition, but they said, "No, no, the auditions are over at the University." So I went to Wayne State University, thinking I was auditioning for *Hamlet,* but unbeknownst to me I'm auditioning for grad school. Fifteen minutes later they offered me a theater scholarship. I had a choice to make. I could either pay

$50,000 a year to go to med school or I could take their stipend to go into the craft of acting. I took it.

The theater classes drove me nuts because I liked *doing* the craft—I'm very tactile, I'm very hands on—and I found that the best way to learn it was to do it. I was always working. I'd go off and audition for commercial work, but then I'd have to shoot the commercial when I should have been in class. So they were starting to get upset with me missing classes. But I constantly worked, and eventually I decided to quit grad school. My partner at the time said, "I'm going to hate myself for telling you this, but if you like Shakespeare and microbrews, you should go out to the Oregon Shakespeare Festival." So I came out in 1995. I belonged to SAG [Screen Actors Guild], but I wasn't an Actors' Equity member yet, so I had to show up in Ashland for auditions. I saw *Richard II* here and loved it, loved Oregon. It was July, but when I woke up in the morning, it was so cold, maybe 40 degrees. In Detroit, at seven o'clock in the morning in mid-July, it's already eighty degrees. But I woke up, threw on a sweater and boots and went to the New Place to audition for Pat Patton, Associate Artistic Director. They called me five months later and I had a job. Long history—I came here to work for six months, and eighteen years later I'm still here.

Every time I'd get the impulse to leave to do another show somewhere else, Libby Appel, the artistic director, would say, "You don't want to do that. I have something beautiful for you. You don't want to do that." She would discourage me, but she always did have something lovely for me to play. Libby was instrumental in keeping me here. I've spent the bulk of my time here on the West Coast. I occasionally do commercial stuff elsewhere, but that's it, never theater. It's lovely. It's uncommon. Most people need four or five gigs over the course of the year to pay their bills, but I have that seven-to-ten month period to settle into the work and not fret about my next job. I also record books on tape for Blackstone Audio in Ashland, everything from Stephen King's *The Running Man* to *Whoreson*, a book by Donald Goines, another Detroiter. It's cool, because I get a chance to tell a story, to play different characters interacting to move that story forward.

My first show at OSF was Poet Laureate Rita Dove's *The Darker Face of the Earth*, in 1996. In the Shakespeare plays, I started out in ensemble roles. That first year I learned a lot playing a Volscian soldier in Tony Taccone's *Coriolanus*, a very athletic, muscular show, with Derrick Weeden jumping down to the main stage of the Elizabethan Theatre from the balcony. I played a myriad of servants and messengers for the next couple of years, then Thaliard and Bolt in Laird Williamson's *Pericles*. In 2001 Libby Appel finally said, "Okay, here you go," and gave me my first lead, as Troilus in *Troilus and Cressida*, with Ken Albers. That same year I also played Segismundo in Calderon's *Life Is a Dream*. I guess at some point she believed I could do it. But by that time I had definitely cut my teeth, I had paid attention, to watch and learn what was required to play these roles.

I had been in five productions of Shakespeare before coming to Ashland: *Hamlet*, *Much Ado About Nothing*, *A Midsummer Night's Dream*, *Romeo and Juliet*, and *Twelfth Night*. So the Hilberry program was really good training, because like OSF, it's classically-based repertory. We were doing two or three shows at the same time: Shakespeare, Moliere, Chekhov, all the greats. For familiarity with the plays, there was nothing like it. Two years of theater history was instrumental in being able to come here and know what I was talking about. Period styles—to be able to move in these shoes and wear these wigs, know what these costumes do to your body, how to glide across the stage with some semblance of elegance. You wouldn't think Russian ballet would play a part in doing Shakespeare, but for fluidity of movement it does. All of those things really trained me to do Shakespeare.

When I first got here, I listened to Dan Kremer and J. P. Phillips and Dennis Robertson speak in the Elizabethan. I learned how to play that space because of them, because of people with strong voices—Derrick Weeden, David Kelly, Robynn Rodriguez, Michael Elich—who can play the outdoor theater well without looking like they're cheating out all the time. Voices do drop off in the middle of the house, but it's not just about volume. You can bark in that space all day and still be inarticulate. Vilma Silva, who has a lighter voice, has the vocal support and technique to be able to "ping" in that space. That is key to playing the Elizabethan. People come to OSF to see that. Point and shoot: you stop and land, you lift your head, and you throw your voice. I don't know that training programs do that anymore. But somebody must. Training programs now are focused on film and TV, not outdoor theaters. I'm very proud of the fact that someone taught me how to speak in the Elizabethan, that every word I say there can be heard. It seems important to find and train people who can speak in the space, like Nancy Benjamin and Scott Kaiser and Ursula Meyers [OSF voice coaches] trained me.

Most people don't know that physical intimacy on the Elizabethan stage before twelve hundred people is standing two feet apart, not right up on someone. That's a trap. You see actors who want to play intimacy there as if they were in a tiny space, but that's not what intimacy is on that stage. How do you teach someone to speak with enough vocal quality so that the audience looking at the side of your head can hear you? How do you teach someone to stage whisper to twelve hundred people? That's a skill essential to being a good, solid actor. So it makes me sad that the mikes are coming into play more.

The challenge is less that playgoers hear the actor, and more that they understand him. If an actor doesn't go through text analysis or learn iambs or know what he's talking about when he speaks an archaic phrase, it doesn't matter if he's miked. It's mush. The audience is still not going to understand it, they're still not going to *hear* it. Some actors know what they're saying, and how to deliver it, and some don't. And you can tell even when an actor who does know what he's saying gets to a part that he doesn't feel confident in, because he'll mumble.

A part of me kicks myself that I spent two-and-a-half years of higher education when I could have learned that here at OSF, and better. But I finally did. I was thrown right into it, watching how the veteran actors did it, but it was their generosity as well—someone took the time and taught me. And Libby was good about putting me outdoors a lot, because I really enjoy the space. It's my favorite of our three theaters. To be outdoors on a beautiful night, with twelve hundred people listening to you—there's nothing like it, watching people tell tales as the daylight fades. There's that moment where it gets finally dark and you can see what the picture is supposed to look like. Owls flying through—it's beautiful. But it is a tough space.

After a while you build up that muscle. As long as you know what you're saying, you can tell the story. It becomes a matter of being familiar with the language. What is a caesura, what is a trochee, what is a masculine ending? You learn what these things mean, and it's like training any other muscle. All that time in small parts in *Coriolanus* or *Pericles* paid off, for sure. Laird Williamson, directing *Pericles*, showed me the majesty of make-believe—the play's a fairy tale, it should look and feel like that. There was a moment in *Pericles* rehearsals when Laird said, "Okay, you're all on a ship, you've got these huge oars, you're rowing the ship, and you have to row in time." We're trying to figure it out, trying to follow the two people in the front in order to row together. I remember feeling absolutely ridiculous, standing there in this choral mask and gown, rowing the ship. In tech rehearsal I dropped the oar once so I could actually hop down and see the scene. I stood in the pit and looked up. There were two women snapping the sail in the back, this big old sail, and then the slosh of the water, and you could see the blue of the lights, and—it's a ship! Okay, I believe, I believe—and that was it. In little moments like that, when you say yes, the possibility of "what if" exists, and you can do it. That bolstered me in how I felt about performing Shakespeare, what was possible. People will believe if I believe, if I say it like I believe it, like I know what I'm talking about.

I do have some pre-performance rituals, but the ritual is particular to the show, different for *Romeo and Juliet* than for *Henry IV, Part One*. My vocal warm-ups, too, depend on the show. I'm not a "red leather, yellow leather" or "she sells seashells" person. There's enough of that in the text already. There are passages that I consistently run through for text, things that are tricky to say in terms of vocal support, especially working in the Elizabethan Theatre. When I'm done with my fight call, I'll stand out there, fill my lungs, and say a speech for as long as I have vocal support.

My prep is literally digging into the play. First off, I read all the plays and decide what I find interesting, and I say okay, I'd like to play this. Libby Appel was good about not giving me what I asked for. No, you don't want to play that; you want to play this. Well I don't want to play that, Libby. But it's better for you; you want to play this. So Libby would stretch me, really allow me to grow to a place where I could carry the roles that later on I was asking to get.

But I read the play, and then put it down. Walk around, go drink some coffee, have some cigarettes. Then I come back and read the play. And I continue to read the play. And then when I'm tired of reading the play, I pick it up and I read some more. Seriously, I do that play. Just reading it again and again and again, and talking to myself out loud about it, the lines begin to come. I used to make the mistake of memorizing my lines before rehearsal, but that locks you into choices. In the shower it sounds great like this in my head, but in rehearsal that's hollow, it doesn't fit anything else that's going on in the room. I'm so familiar with the play that by rehearsal, I can say the words without looking at the script, but not so much that I'm committed to one choice. And then I just figure out, okay, the director wants this, my fellow actors want that; what do I want out of the whole thing, and how does it fit? And then I try different choices.

Playing it on my feet, putting it in my body, that sense memory, is the most important way for me to learn lines. But my process is looking at the script: these are the things that everybody says about you, these are the things that you say about yourself. This is how you see the world and these are all the things that are not said about you. Everybody says, look at him, he's got a limp. You have a limp. You have a stutter? And you stutter. You're very fearful. Okay, you're a limping, stuttering, fearful person. So those are the things that are known about you—but it's all the interesting things around that that make your character.

Anybody can limp and stutter and be afraid, but is your limp on your right or your left? How did you get the limp? Fearful of what? How does your fear manifest itself? Does it make you laugh? Some people titter when they're fearful, some people cringe. Building those choices around everything that's not said about you, or isn't obvious, is where your character lives. I try looking for those things—that guy on the bus slobbering, or a friend I met at a party last year who is the model for my Sterling in *Two Trains Running*. He *is* Sterling. I was watching him play cards at my sister's birthday party. We're sitting there, drinking, playing cards, and he looks completely hammered. We're playing these cards, and he says "That's my book." I said, "No, it's not—what are you talking about?" He said, "No, you just got the last book," and he told me what each card was. And he flipped that one over, and he flipped mine over, and lo and behold, it was exactly what he said. Every time he knew exactly what was going on. Loud! Brash! All over the place! And I was like, Oh my God—*you* are my Sterling. I watched him all night. It gave me the biggest inward smile to know "Dude, I'm going to play you. You don't even know, but I'm going to play you." He was so perfect—and he's been married to a woman for twenty-five years who is so quiet and so demure, so like Risa that I thought, "Yeah, that's it. There you are." Going back in your life and finding those people, and being able to give them an *homage*—there's something for you, man, even if you don't know, going back to your factory in Detroit. He won't see the show, but I'm going to take him a nice poster.

I know those guys; I know those characters in an August Wilson play. It's my grandfather, it's my dad, it's my uncles. Watching those people growing up, I have all of that equipment to bring to his work, and I'll think, 'Yeah, I'm going to pull *this* to use." Beautiful language. You can tell what region of the United State someone grew up in, by how they deliver August Wilson texts. J. P. Phillips inherently knows Wilson's language and speaks it well, but there are just little differences, like shifts in tone or inflection, that might make another actor say, "Oh, you must be from the West Coast, because on the East Coast we say it like this." But those tales—it's African-American history, for sure. Generally tragic, as some of our history has been. It felt so good to be able to walk away at the end of *Two Trains Running*, and think, "Thank God, I didn't kill anybody," because *Ma Rainey's Black Bottom* was so hurtful. I had to wade in and kill Abdul Salaam El Razzac (Toledo), to stab him in the back every day. It hurt me. One day—it was a particularly good show, when everybody was moving the pace along—we got to that moment where I turn and flip out the knife, and a woman sitting in the front row started saying "No, no, no!" at every step I took. By the time I stabbed him, she screamed out loud. And that's the feeling that I had every day doing *Ma Rainey*. It gets really, really intense. That's the flavor, the character of that urban environment, when people are desperate and disenfranchised, when people are poor or taken advantage of. Playing Levee in *Ma Rainey*, I almost had to baptize myself every day, walking in there and walking out, because he has no faith in anything but himself, so when that's shaken, his world is destroyed, and he acts rashly. I know that story, deep, deep in me, from having been raised where I did know desperate people, dangerous people, people who ended up in prison or dead because of a need or a loss, not being able to take time to breathe and listen to their elders and their experience (much of it bad experience). "I have talent and you don't understand." To play that was lovely—and painful, painful.

I love August Wilson. *Ma Rainey* is my favorite, a powerful play, and *Joe Turner's Come and Gone* is a beautiful play, too, but I don't think I'm the physical type to play Joe Turner. He's a big, brooding, heavy presence, carrying that child around with him, the weight of the loss of that woman. No one's ever going to cast me as that, it's just not in the cards. You have to be a big six-foot statuesque guy. I loved playing Canewell in Kenny Leon's production of *Seven Guitars* here, another haunting story, especially knowing that he comes back later on as Stool Pigeon in *King Hedley*. I'm looking forward to the day that play pops up. The character I played in *Two Trains*, Sterling, also comes back later on, in *Radio Golf*.

I've just finished doing August Wilson's *Jitney* in Portland, with G. Valmont Thomas directing. The first time I played with G. Val was in *Seven Guitars* at OSF. A few years later, we were together in Suzan-Lori Parks' two-man play, *Topdog/Underdog*, directed by Tim Bond. *Topdog/Underdog* is one of those perspective-changing plays. Are you on the ship or are you swimming beside it? It's only two of us, just G. Val and me, so I gotta be in the boat with him. Early on we were talking with Tim about who our characters are. You've got to go with your own concept—my character's this, my character's that, my character's the other. And Tim just let me go on for fifteen minutes. At the end of it, he said, "Nah—you're character's not any of that. Your character's damaged. But you want him to be liked." I had to really stop and think about what that meant, to want to be liked, because sometimes your character's not likeable, and that's the point. Your character *is* damaged or your character *is* incredibly flawed and that's the interesting thing. No one wants to watch you be likeable; they want to watch you be a person, and sometimes those people are just not likeable. Tim Bond taught me that.

The director had his own very specific perspective on what Booth, my character, should sound like, look like, feel like, but I had to go back through my little mental Rolodex, to find people in my history. I remember being on the bus when I was fourteen, heading to school. I looked up and this obviously homeless man got on the bus. He had maybe three or four teeth in his whole head. He sat and shook his head and talked to himself, and made little gestures. He gnawed on his fingers and he had drool running out of his mouth. He fidgeted the whole time. Yeah, he was damaged. He was damaged. Or the alcoholic—every day, when I was a teenager, I'd walk past an alcoholic heroin addict. Those guys began to boil in my head—what happens when someone abandons you, what happens when you're left to your own devices? Some of these things become obvious to me. Tim was right.

I loved building the show and finding that character with G. Val, who was very generous in his performance, very gentle— the opposite of my damage. The audiences were really small in the beginning because people were scared of the contact. We played to 67 people one day, and the house, I think, sat 276. People would get up and leave, just walk away, because it was vulgar, those first forty-five minutes, completely vulgar. But I think the playwright's point was that these things don't work for the two men. These are the things impeding their progress, impeding their healing. So the tone completely changes in the second act. All that swearing, all that foulness is gone, and you have two people having heart-to-heart conversations with each other about what happened to them and how they'll overcome it. And then it takes that horrible twist, where G. Val is playing Lincoln, sitting there waiting to be shot, but sitting there as a patron of the theater, holding the mirror up to nature—it's just brilliant. I watched it, dying of laughter every time, because G. Val completely committed to every little bit, from the cell phone to the falling asleep. And then all of a sudden it turns, and I shoot him—comedy, up until the point it becomes absolutely tragic, and you stop laughing. It just knocks the breath out of you. It was a privilege to play.

I got a chance to meet the playwright, Suzan-Lori Parks, when she came here to see our production of *Topdog*. Hallelujah for doing these plays! It's one thing to say "Shakespeare was this" or "Shakespeare was that," but it's another thing to meet Suzan-Lori and August Wilson and Naomi Wallace, to get a glimpse of what they're like and why they wrote what they did. We sit in a privileged place, to be able to take advantage of that, to meet some of the best playwrights, directors, designers, dramaturgs (who else even has a dramaturg these days?). That's OSF.

Libby Appel was brave, because she had resisted doing these plays for a long time. But she came to us and said, "Would you all be interested in doing *Topdog/Underdog*? I don't know about it, but if it interests you, we'll do it." She ran with it. It was one of the best theatrical experiences I've ever participated in. It changed my mind about theater. You see what's possible. It's not an old dusty classic, it's not vapid. It's really about the fabric of urban environments in America, desperate people doing desperate things, the people we never see. We read about them in the newspaper or see them on the news, but you never run into these people, not really, not in the environments we live in, but they're there, part of the fabric of American society—the part we don't see.

One day an OSF patron said she was excited to see me in the cast list for a show: "I knew that meant someone was going to die." I had gotten this reputation for playing tragic figures. So I went to Libby and said, "I can't kill anybody this year. I have to have something comedic, something light." So she offered me Algernon in *The Importance of Being Earnest* and Nim in the Shakespeare comedy *The Merry Wives of Windsor*. And it was the hardest thing in the world to do, because it requires a completely different set of tools and skills that I had not been exercising, because I was busy killing everybody, playing these tragic characters. As Algernon in *Earnest*, I didn't get a single laugh, not a single laugh—not from my colleagues, not from people who wandered into our dress rehearsals—not a one, until first preview. I just did the best I could to play it straight. I love language, and as long as you play the language, you should be fine. But I needed those laughs to know what it's supposed to sound like. Once I knew the stops, I knew how to play the show. I trusted Peter Amster, the director, and my cast was so sweet and generous shepherding me, because I just didn't know comedy. I know how to play beats, I know how to play tempo, but comedy requires something different— the ability to laugh at yourself. That was a great lesson to learn. When I went back to doing tragic figures again, I thought, one of the things that makes these characters tragic is that one minute you're laughing, and the next minute you're not. One minute you're completely beguiled or charmed, and the next minute you're not.

Hotspur, in *Henry IV, Part One*, was one of those roles that you always want a chance to play. When Michael Elich played Hotspur and I was his understudy, I kept begging him to let me go on, and he'd say, "You don't want to go on as an understudy. One day you'll play this role." And lo and behold, there I was playing it, a few years later, thanks to Penny Metropulos, the director. Hotspur has all the makings of a great leader—except patience. If he'd had support, who knows what would have happened? He would have been a fine ruler, but for circumstance, as far as I'm concerned. He is intelligent—hot-spirited but definitely intelligent. And people follow him. Men who want glory follow him. I don't know if the story is even Hal's tale. You see Hal becoming the prince, riding on the glory of having killed Hotspur. But then, every play is all about *my* character (*laughs*). Ultimately, you have to play your part. I learned from Penny that you can't stand outside of whatever the vision for the play is, you can't be the odd man out. You're part of the process. It's not for you to fuss and fight and argue. It's for you to have done your homework and to come in with something imaginative and inventive and fit into the grand scheme of these plays.

Penny has cast me in very different roles, but they're always parts I can find some road into, some way to grow from. That has been instrumental in how I think about playing with other people even when as the lead I carry the show—to really open myself up and say, "Okay, I'm a part of this process, and what can I bring to it?" as opposed to "Oh, the director's impeding *my* process." Penny cast me as Orlando in *As You Like It*, where you get to be in love in a way that transcends Romeo's love, more informed and mature—not knowing what Rosalind thinks of you, but responding, after your struggle through life, to her gentleness, her kindness. Penny also cast me as Octavius Caesar in her *Antony and Cleopatra* with Armando Durán and Judith-Marie Bergan and Danforth Comins. That was one of those performances where I was standing outside of the play, doing my own thing in my own head. It was a good production, but I could have contributed more successfully, been more a part of the whole, if I'd taken this little piece of direction from Penny or decided to run with that suggestion from her.

My final speech as Octavius Caesar was trimmed way down. I was sad about that, but it helped get the show in under three hours. Not only have actors changed, in how we play, but audiences and their attention spans have changed, too. Some people don't want to sit there over three hours. The audiences who continuously come to Ashland are trained to the theater, but for newer audience members, shaped by watching TV or movies, it's a long time to sit if they're not engaged. To find a place where they're comfortable, you have to manufacture in them a desire, a need to sit there. If you build it, they will come. If you make it engaging, they will stay with you. The *Coriolanus* I did with Derrick Weeden went well over three hours, and the last *Coriolanus*, with Danforth Comins, was nearly three—but people in the audience were literally leaning in to watch it.

It's easy sometimes to lose focus or lose the pace, so you have to continually drive the show—not so fast that they can't hear it or understand it, but so that it's active and they don't get ahead of you. But I'm cool with cutting Shakespeare. Some of the text I argue for, but there are things you have to lose—lines that are not going to facilitate the story, to help anybody understand anything better. I'd like to think I'm a purist, but no—not really. There are things that traditionally are always cut or trimmed—sometimes the wrong things, like the scene with Mortimer's and Hotspur's wives in *Henry IV, Part One*. You need that balance, to see that Hotspur loves his wife—and it gives her character an arc later on, in *Part Two*, when she talks about how Hotspur has been betrayed. They trimmed that scene way down for Libby's production as well, with Robin Nordli as Lady Percy, but you really need it to see that Hotspur is a husband, not just a killer.

I like directors who have vision as opposed to a concept. I like directors who trust actors. I like directors who know what they want but are willing to listen to you. I like directors who don't know what they want but are willing to listen to you, and are honest about it. Directors who have passion for the work as opposed to "Oh, I've got this gig." It's not just a gig to me. It's my work, my passion. I like telling stories, so I don't want it to be something you just phone in. Take Lou Bellamy—even his remounting of *Two Trains Running* here was based on the fact that the man knew that play. He wasn't just familiar with it, he *knew* that play. And he knew what would work, what all those moments were about. If you didn't do those things, you didn't get the response that he was looking for. And he was absolutely right, 99 percent of the time. He was kind and generous and patient and made you feel as if it was the first time *Two Trains Running* had ever been done.

Intelligence and emotional security and emotional connectedness to the play mean everything to me in a director, and a reliance on actors to do their jobs, not just sets and lights. Because when the lights go out and the set doesn't work, you're still standing naked out there, and you have to do your job. You have to tell that story. No one comes just to see the pretty costumes. They'll sit in the Elizabethan when it's raining and we're wearing slickers, telling the story. If the story's engaging, they'll watch, and they'll be able to say, I remember the day it poured rain, and the show was fantastic.

Ken Albers is an actor who also directs. He could give you an entire education: don't put your hands in your pockets, something as simple as that. Don't cross your arms. Find something else to do. Use the whole of your body. This is the clarity you're looking for in telling a story. And you have to trust him. When I was playing Troilus in love, on the line "I am giddy; expectation whirls me round," Ken said, "You're so happy, turn around! Spin in a circle, you're so happy!" I said, "What are you talking about, Ken?" He said, "Trust me, just spin around." After a while it got into my body and I committed to it, and then lo and behold—Boom!—there it was. Now that moment is a souvenir program cover photo. I never would have thought that was the moment to play. But what else do you do when you're giddy? You jump around, you turn in circles, the world is beautiful—and Ken just went there. It's one of those moments I remember that changed my mind about acting. Ken makes things very clear. If you play these beats, it'll work. If you don't fully commit, it's going to fall flat. Are you in or are you out? So you have to become part of that production, to be a piece in the machine. After a while, it's more than a machine; you're in the body of it. It's a living, breathing thing, and you're doing your part to keep blood flowing through it and keep it alive and moving.

I admire people like Ken Albers who have connectedness to the craft, as actors, but also know how, as directors, to talk to an actor and get the best performance out of him. I'm not big into directors who give me line readings, who want to walk my track for me. Show me, yes. One day Laird Williamson, in a rehearsal for Calderon's *Life Is a Dream*, said, "Okay, you're so delighted that you just want to run in and glide across the stage." I said, "You do it." And he did. He didn't miss a beat, just went "Tssssss!" sliding across the stage—because he's an actor, literally. So I did it, too.

Actors who happen to be directors, who have a vision and know how to communicate, recognize that it's about the craft, that no amount of glitz or glam is going to make that production any better than the actors and the vision. I love Penny Metropulos, Tim Bond, Gale Edwards, Peter Amster. Peter taught me comic timing, teaching me precision, because I'm a slave to consistency. I am. If you come see my performance today, and you come and see it next Sunday, it will be the same, as close to it as I can. There may be slight adjustments of movement or tone, but ultimately those same rhythms are there, because that's what the director built. Peter taught me how important it is to hold— what you're doing when you're not speaking really matters.

Amanda Dehnert, a director who made *Julius Caesar* as much fun as it can be, has a great eye for the theatrical. She's intelligent—not just intellectual IQ, but emotional EQ, the ability to say, "This is what's on the page, what it means to me, and these are the ways that we can go about getting that message across." Lots of directors have a dream of what they'd like a show to be, but a concept is not a vision. Knowing how you get there—that's a vision. You've actually plotted out the path, and it's something we can all walk. Amanda is very clear about that. It's just actors. Simplicity. She knows what the material is, what's interesting about it. Find those things. Play those things. Engage them. Don't make it about pretty costumes or lifts coming up or flying helicopters.

Gale Edwards, my director when I played Macduff in *Macbeth*, really deepened the appreciation that I already had for text. Her focus was on the language; everything is there. It's iambic for these particular reasons. That's why you have a masculine ending here, or a feminine ending to this. You have to think actively; the language is supposed to move. I'm a huge fan, because she *knows* Shakespeare. There are lots of smart, talented directors out there, but it's a huge job. Can you imagine dealing with sixteen actor personalities? We're all "I'm gonna do it my way" until—well, now you have to do it like this, with these other people. It's all part and parcel of belonging to an ensemble.

I had a little trepidation when I first walked into rehearsal for Robert Schenkkan's *All the Way*—we worked our asses off—but it was smooth, because Bill Rauch, the director, had a roomful of people who knew how to do what he asked. It's as simple as that. Not a bunch of new people, not a bunch of freshmen students out doing their first show. Our cast at OSF is made up of veterans who have a shorthand to be able to get to these moments. We're moved by the material and we do it—not a lot of talking, not all of these varying opinions that we're going to try to mish-mash into one thing. This year I'm in the sequel, *The Great Society*. To do it again with actors who know each other's rhythms, who trust the work—how can you beat it?

Having company members who've done five productions of *Romeo and Juliet*, who've done three *Henry VI*s, and can say how the play has been done in the past, makes it so much easier to perform. You have those other artists underneath you—shaping you, educating you in what is relevant and strong about these pieces, what traps to avoid. By the time *A Midsummer Night's Dream* rolls around again, and it's your turn to step in and do it, you know what you're up against, and you've seen some really good actors do what you aspire to do.

It's my argument for a repertory company. People you trust. The ability to chameleon, to play a king in the afternoon and a pauper in the evening. It's exciting, because it's not all about you, it's about the company itself. Sometimes you get a lead or a very important role, and that's about you doing your part, but in a repertory company, everybody's there to catch you and to buoy the production. To watch people grow for five, ten, fifteen years in that environment is very interesting. You get a nice vibe for people's rhythms, their abilities, your rhythms, your inabilities. I remember Nell Geisslinger as a little kid. Now she's playing Kate in *The Taming of the Shrew* and Stella in *A Streetcar Named Desire*. To watch her grow in her craft has been gratifying. Her opportunities to see her dad play in this space, to see us play these spaces, paid off. Longevity in a company—you can't beat it. It's hard to get.

That's the thing—a resident company. OSF is in the process of defining what that means, especially now. The last two or three seasons have brought the question more to the fore because of the breaking of the main support beam in the Bowmer Theatre, and the wildfire smoke drifting into the Elizabethan. What does it mean to have a company that will go to the wall for you, and how do you retain those people, who worked very hard for the continued success of the institution, not just for themselves? Because if it were just about them—a smoky night and they could go home. I think OSF is really starting to re-examine retention, what we really want a company to be. A company is not just a group of people who have tenured themselves to an institution.

It's funny, they always talked about the ghost of Angus in the Bowmer Theatre—the creaking, the footsteps. No, man—those were the beams going snap, snap, snap, over the course of many years. I've been in the Bowmer and I've heard it. What the hell is that? It sounds like somebody walking. No, it was just little cracks in this theater waiting to come down on your head. But they worked it out. OSF is a very well-oiled machine. There was a momentary pause when we had to close the Bowmer, but then we were back playing up in Lithia Park, over at the university, in the music hall, and people came. People still came—that's the thing that impresses me. Some theaters don't sell 50 percent of the seats in their houses, but we fill upwards of 80 percent of the house for classic plays. A good chunk of that is patrons who've been coming for years, sometimes decades. To meet a woman who says, "I've been coming here for 34 years, since I was nineteen"—amazing. Fingers crossed. Because at some point in time these folk will pass, and what work have we done to develop new audiences? I think that's where OSF is starting to turn its gaze, trying to get people to want to come and sit for two hours and forty minutes in a theater and watch a classic play, because we are the Oregon *Shakespeare* Festival. Though we only do three or four shows a year of Shakespeare, that's where we live, and where I hope we will continue to live. Musicals, yeah, probably pay our bills. *My Fair Lady*—great production. But I think that of all our productions, the Shakespeares should be the strongest. Period.

But you also have to have people who trust the material and know how to perform it. How do you get those people to come and spend ten months in little old Ashland? I came in a sweet spot, to an environment that was perfect for my kids, to learn in, to grow in. But how do you find people like me now? How do you find people like Anthony Heald or Dee Maaske who've worked all over and all of a sudden decided to make their homes here? I think Bill Rauch has done it. He's persuaded different folk from places where he's worked to come and start building lives here, and he's retained them.

I keep wondering why they hire me back. You're paying me to enjoy myself? But every year it's, "Oh, you want me to play that? Hmm. Okay, I can do that." That's how I feel about Liverpool Joe, in *The Liquid Plain*. Yeah, I can do that, it'll be fun—something very, very different, and you go out and try to be fearless and you do it. Naomi Wallace gave us a beautifully written play. It's witty, it has a nice pace, Liverpool Joe has an accent—how can you beat that? He comes in, he saves the day, and he's dead. It's a beautifully crafted role, and the fact that Naomi took it upon herself to write about the disenfranchised, to write about black folk suffering as the result of societal oppression, that's very cool.

Even when you don't trust the material or the production, you have to relax. It's not about me, it's about this playwright's vision, and I'm a part of that vision. One of the best things J.P. Phillips ever said to me was "Leave your ego out of it, just get out of your own way." And it's true. I just get out of the way. After a while, shut up, take the direction, and be part of the product. J.P. makes it seem completely effortless, generous of spirit. G. Val Thomas—he's fearless. He doesn't care. Those are the lessons that you learn. Be open. Be fearless. Not that you won't want to look good—but just go there, and you'll look great. So be fearless. That fearlessness allows you to be imaginative, because you don't have any blinders up, you don't have any preconceived notions of what is right or what is playable. Play it all until you find the thing that really works.

Mark Murphey as Ulysses in *Troilus and Cressida*. Photo: Jenny Graham, OSF.

Mark Murphey

In 32 seasons at OSF, Mark Murphey has played, among other roles, Hamlet in *Hamlet*; Romeo in *Romeo and Juliet*; Iago in *Othello*; Atticus Finch in *To Kill a Mockingbird*; Mr. Bennett in *Pride and Prejudice*; Kit Carson in *The Time of Your Life*; Posthumus in *Cymbeline*; Leontes in *The Winter's Tale*; Ulysses in *Troilus and Cressida*; Cassius in *Julius Caesar*; Benedick in *Much Ado About Nothing*; Virgil in *Bus Stop*; Pike in *Paradise Lost*; Pearce in *The Pool of Bethesda*; Robert McNamara in *All the Way*.

I FELL IN LOVE WITH ASHLAND the first time I came here in 1969—as I was coming in on the old Siskiyou Highway. Interstate 5 wasn't finished yet. I remember driving through lots of trees in this beautiful valley, and I loved the first glimpses of the town. There were only three or four motels and restaurants. I liked the Festival, too, but I wasn't getting exciting parts, so I thought I wouldn't return. At a later time, there was a dancer I knew who had been at Baylor, where I went to college—her husband was a lighting designer at OSF. She called me and she said, "I'll bet you haven't even applied again, have you?" I said, "I didn't see any reason to." She said that my name was being passed around the table for some pretty decent roles, so I called OSF, and I got Antipholus in *Comedy of Errors*, and Beralde in

The Imaginary Invalid. That was in 1970.

I think my interest in theater all began when I was in elementary school in Dallas. We had this thing called "auditorium class," which was basically children's theater. We would memorize poems and put on performances like *Jack the Giant Killer.* In junior high, we were taken to the plays at the Dallas Theater Center and we saw *The Tempest, Julius Caesar,* and *Long Day's Journey into Night.* In high school, my brother, who was a debater, encouraged me to take a drama class. Our teacher took us to speech tournaments and we did one-act plays, so these things were all early beginnings.

When I went to college, I decided I was going to be a medical student and chose Baylor University. I think I was more interested in animals than medicine because my uncle was a veterinarian, but I had no aptitude for science or for math either. That lasted one semester. However, I'd seen a campus production of *The Cherry Orchard.* The director made it clear that I would not get cast unless I was a drama major, so I became one. I never looked back. The Baylor Department of Theatre Arts produced each play for a month, and then later, they'd bring back all of them for Spring Rep. I performed in *Imaginary Invalid,* and I played Richard of Gloucester, the lead in *Richard III.*

In my forty years of performing, one of the most outrageous things that happened was in *Richard III* at Baylor. It is a long play, and we were performing it on a small thrust stage in an intimate theater. Onstage was that scene with most of the noblemen sitting around a table and discussing the location of the crowning of the young Prince Edward. I was backstage, ready to go on and to accuse Hastings of the witchcraft that resulted in my withered arm, and then to give the order to cut off his head. My director, a teacher who had been sitting in the audience, had come backstage to tell me, "Mark, now keep it moving along, okay?" And then she continued to bend my ear. There was a trumpet blast and I should have made my entrance. After the fanfare, the actors onstage looked at one another, not know-ing what to do and tried to cover up the silence. Hastings said, "Where is my Lord Gloucester?" and another said, "Yes, where is he?" Then Hastings came off and pushed me onstage—so I thought I had cut off his speech! My first line was, "My noble lords and cousins all, I have been a sleeper." The laughter be-gan. The next line coming at me was, "My lord, had you not come upon your cue, Lord Hastings had pronounced your part," which caused much more reaction from the audience.

When I got offstage, the cast explained this totally absurd thing that had happened. I remember being terribly offended by everyone laughing.

That show had other issues. We had to make our own weap-ons, and they were not very good. Richard and Richmond fought with broadswords and daggers that I had helped to make, con-structed of flimsy steel. You had to be very careful how you used them. Richmond hit my sword on its edge, and it bent into a perfect 45-degree angle. So, I just whacked it on the floor, and it went right back into shape. The audience was loving it at this point. To create the hilt on the swords, the prop department had used rubber balls that were spray-painted gold—one time, the ball fell off and bounced all over the stage. So much for my playing the villain.

Back in my student days, Angus Bowmer and his wife went every year to the University of Texas in Austin, where both Ben Iden Payne and Pat Hines were located, and recruited actors. He also stopped at Baylor, and I auditioned for him. He offered me a season for that summer only, with no pay. I was married so I had to turn it down. Later on, I sent him tape recordings along with my teachers' recommendations, which is how it was done then, and I was set for a summer salary of $500, which it was for everyone unless you were Pat Hines, Hugh Evans, or Ed Brubaker, the top fellows. My first role of any consequence at OSF was Lord Bigot in *King John,* and Ed sat out front smoking a big cigar during the rehearsals.

I graduated in '71 and kept coming back for a few years. My mentors and guides were Angus Bowmer, who founded the Festival, and Jerry Turner, an early and important artistic director, and of course, Jim Edmondson, a director who cast me often. In '75, I played Romeo, seven days a week with no days off. The pay worked out to $170 a week. Being seen in Ashland was providential. Jerry always offered me seasons, casting me in between jobs, recommending me to other companies. He was immensely supportive in keeping my career going. I would rather have always been here, but OSF was not an Equity company until 1984, and being a member of Actors' Equity is essential for actors in the early part of their theater lives.

Jerry warned me that if I was going to be an actor permanently, I would need that union card, so that meant I had to work in Equity theaters to collect Equity points. So Jim Edmondson and I, on a day off, flew from Ashland to the Hollywood Hilton to audition for the Alley Theater, grabbed something to eat, and flew back the same day in time to be in the matinee at OSF. They hired both of us! So then my pregnant wife (with our first child) and I loaded our stuff into a VW bus and drove to Houston's Alley Theater to do a season there and earn points. Then Margaret Booker hired me at the Intiman Theater in Seattle, and I went there to finish qualifying for my card. Next, off to work for director Bill Ball at American Conservatory Theater in San Francisco, who told me to call him before I signed anything, and there I was offered a nine-month contract. What has been fortunate about my career, thanks to Bill and Angus and Jerry, is that from 1969 to the present day, I've had thirty-seven years of good work in two strong repertory companies—seven years at ACT, and the rest mostly at OSF.

Angus and Jerry clearly felt that a group of actors who worked together steadily would generate better work over time than having actors coming in and out of the company constantly. Angus was frustrated in the earlier years because he could not pay good actors enough to keep continuity going. Jerry wanted to build a company, despite the rumor that he said, "As soon as an actor buys a lawnmower, it is time to fire him." I don't really believe he said that—he might have felt that about actors he didn't like very much, but actors he liked, he genuinely wanted to keep.

At OSF, I like the continuity of working with a group of actors you can depend on. Building a company enriches the work, makes it stronger and deeper. You have a lot less re-acquainting to go through initially in getting to know new people. The flip side of that could be—though I've rarely seen it in any repertory company I worked in—that an actor can get dull, do the same thing each time out, and get complacent because he knows he has a job. I think this opinion comes from boards of directors and management. After all, in Sweden, actors were given life-time contracts.

In my early Festival years, there were no text coaches. Once in awhile you could get an actor who had been trained as a vocal coach to do some work with the company. They assumed you'd done voice training in school. Jim Edmondson taught movement, stretching, limbering up.

The director helped you along with Shakespearean dialogue. I never knew much about iambic pentameter when I got here, and in fact as a younger actor, I never studied the text that much. Later on, I realized that it affected what you had to say and I really dug in. First, I learned by doing it, and my techniques developed as I went along, tuning into the rhythm and poetry of it. We did not do a lot of table work, where the actors and the director work on the script and puzzle things out in early readings. There just wasn't much time.

Right when you got to Ashland, we had three nights of auditions. You did a monologue, then an evening of reading from different plays, and finally callbacks. You were cast right away, and you began rehearsals immediately (starting in June and opening in July), with only four or five weeks to get the show up. *Not* eight weeks like we have today. The scripts were rarely cut, depending on each director, but Angus believed in largely uncut productions of Shakespeare with no intermissions. If you can imagine an uncut version of *Hamlet*, you have an idea of what it was like.

The audience wasn't as formal, and it felt more like community theater, and of course, the theater was all outdoors. The locals would show up, bring food with them, and sit down and watch the show. Then they'd get up and wander around and smoke (it was the 70s, so who knew *what*) and buy a cup of coffee. There were also, by necessity, bathroom breaks—you had to scramble out of those long rows of seats.

Angus opened dress and tech rehearsals to the town, everyone out there watching you. He believed that was how you built an audience, by having the community see the process that took place and that would get them excited about buying a ticket. Some people crowded in for those and that was all, so he had to quit that plan.

In an outdoor theater, you had to be heard in the back row. You had to have a voice that carried and to be quite loud, which was easier to do on cool nights. There was only a concrete wall at the back, covered with ivy. All twelve hundred seats were on one level, going back beyond where the booth is in the current Lizzie. The seats were spread from one side to the other, there were no aisles, and they went way back from one side of the wall to the other side of the wall. Where the actual pavilion sits today, the very small original booth was further back, and it was a black house with a flat roof on top of it. The booth was actually sunk underground. The Green Shows were performed on top of that roof. If I were sitting on a stool inside the booth (as a tech person had to be) my head would be just above the heads of the back row of the audience.

For the actors, convincing an audience that you were really "in the moment" and keeping the volume very loud at the same time was difficult. The challenge was—how do you play a realistic, tender, love scene with Juliet when you are shouting in her face? Well, you discovered these tricks over time.

Later on, the only voice coach was a woman who was a trained opera singer, a friend of Jim Edmondson's named Cornelia Clemens. Music coaches can often help an actor because they are experts at finding the correct resonances in the body. She taught this technique of using the nasal bones in order to make sound project to the back of the stage rather than just being loud and shouting. So, it was the use of pitch to a certain degree. You bounced up the voice to a higher pitch rather than using a deep chest sound. The lower you pitched your voice, the harder it was to hear. You also had to have enough breath so that you could sustain actual sound on the line. Texans talk up in their heads all the time, so this quality was natural to me. I think having a voice that carried in the outdoor theater helped me get some good roles over the years.

The Bowmer Theater was built in 1970. As long as you use good diction there, you will be heard. It is a voice and acting style quite different from that in the Lizzie. There is a technique for each theater you are working in, but the actor can learn and understand it and not have to be aware every moment how he is performing technically.

In the old days, we rehearsed in small spaces first, after the Bowmer was built. The Bowmer's stage was occupied with a variety of sets being built on it, so you had to go from those into a larger theater. For the actor to make the transfer happen, he had to bring a smaller level of speaking up to one that could be heard in the back rows of Bowmer. People need to work on vocal levels *before* they get into the theater, because, at that point, there are left only two tech rehearsals, four dress rehearsals, and then playing to the preview audiences. It all happens quickly, with sometimes only three dress rehearsals for the Shakespeares. Now, we have full-time vocal coaches for every show, and they are especially needed in the outdoor theater. Actors need to remember that shouting doesn't cover it, and you have to *find* a voice level for each space you work in.

In the outdoor theater, there is another level of training needed, not just voice but about your placement while you are onstage. Angus was exceptionally good at that. Whenever he had an actor upstaging another, doing something too interesting, he'd simply go downstage and place himself right in front of the culprit. That worked. In the Elizabethan theater, the focus is strongest in the middle and at the front of the stage and not the back or on the sides. Any number of people can be doing things behind you, but they won't be the center of focus.

So many people are onstage in a Shakespeare play. If the actors are not listening to the speaker who has the focus, the audience will not listen either as their attention will be stolen elsewhere. Plays that are cluttered with a lot of action going on around the character that needs to be the center of focus confuse the audience. When people say they don't understand Shakespeare, it is often because there is too much activity taking their attention. An actor does not control focus—directors do, but other actors can help establish focus.

Also, if you are speaking face to face with someone, you will not be heard well from that profile stance. The more you are angled outward, the more you will be heard in both theaters. It's important for *both* actors and directors to know that. Gesture does not need to be larger, but focus counts, using a strong voice, a strong position onstage, and an arrangement of furniture that opens you up to the audience. If you are speaking and moving a lot in the Lizzie—you simply cannot be too active because the audience doesn't take in the language. The more movement, the less interest. It's challenging. If you turn your back to the audience, you have to raise the volume level. Casting is *everything* out there.

I believe in stillness onstage when it's required, but the important thing is that the movement is not more interesting than the words. Everyone gestures when he talks—that is natural in speaking. Gestures should not distract the audience from their important job as listeners.

What you don't want is rhetorical old-school acting. Nor do you want acting for the camera. A lot of theater schools are training their actors that way now because they feel that film is where the money is once they graduate. When you come in cold from that educational background, it's very difficult to learn to reach an audience—which leads to dumbing down the plays and to having to mike the actors. In 2008, I performed in *Romeo and Juliet* in a theater in Salt Lake City. First thing I did was sit in the back of the theater to find out how good the acoustics were in that space, without an audience to absorb the sound. I try to listen to an actor who has a really good voice and gauge by that if I have to use sharper diction and more vocal power. You have to test the theater that way because you can be fooled. Shakespeare repeats information in telling the story, and if the audience doesn't catch those lines, it gets lost in the plot, and everyone is in trouble.

When I was in college, a lot of people did Shakespeare—not so today. Many actors haven't actually performed it, and none can understand it until they do. Some people come here without any experience in speaking Shakespeare's language, and the voice coaches say they cannot train new actors for Shakespeare in six weeks. It's impossible. The problem is the lack of training in the people being hired, and their university and conservatory training is partly to blame—it isn't being taught anymore, not even scansion and other basics. I wanted to work more sessions with the coaches here but was unable to because they had to spend time on the newer people who needed it more.

If I am describing something onstage, I try to see it in my

mind's eye when I say it. I don't really sit down and scan things out unless something feels odd. I've done so much Shakespeare that I can feel when it is scanning well and when it is not. My objective is not to show the audience if a line is prose or poetry but to sound like a real human being, as natural as I can, as if I am just talking and not making a formal speech.

I've had arguments with vocal coaches who say a line "doesn't scan that way." But overly scanning a line is unsuccessful when people are lifting words that could be stressed but those words don't carry the major sense of the line. In a case like that, you try it their way, but you can't please everyone, and the line really can change in both rehearsal and in performance. What works in Shakespeare is using your own common sense about what carries to an audience using the everyday parlance in plain American speech. You also need a good stage manager (who is the present guide after the director is gone) who can tell you that you are drifting away from where the play was, or that the actors are suddenly losing the sense of the scene. It is *in the moment* that the play truly lives.

Acting is a process that you learn slowly over time—it can't be taught in the four or five years you are in training. You can prepare people, but after that, *experience* is the most important thing, being a working actor. The actual profession teaches you a lot through working with different actors and different directors.

In the beginning, you learn the basics. I was brought forward on Stanislavsky-based acting, which in its varieties was what teachers were emphasizing. I think I still do it but not in a text-book way. As you read the play you get a sense of who the character is, and then the detail work after that comes from—what does the character want, how does he get it, and what obstacles are in his way. Those questions help you solve the mechanics of each scene. Anyone can do that part. Also, there has to be a strong sense of belief in the world the actors are trying to create. Belief is a key concept in Stanislavskian acting.

Each actor finds belief in his or her own way. Some actors at ACT would never talk about that in an interview. They'd say, "That's private. The more I keep to myself about how I get there, the more powerful it becomes. If I talk about it to someone, it disappears." Mainly, the audience needs to understand what it is seeing, and if it is believable, they will perceive that right off. They do sense when you are a real person, creating a reality right now. If you are just "putting on," they will turn you off automatically. An actor feels that and knows when he is sounding phony.

Belief is the key. Psychologists try to explain it, but I can't. We all have in us the ability to be someone else. When I am at my best is when I have belief *in the moment it is happening*. When you are acting, what you are trying to find is that part of you that identifies with this character—what parts of you could be that other persona.

I always begin the same way when I prepare a role. At OSF, I have two months off in November and December. I read the play six or seven times, sometimes even when I'm on the treadmill. Next, I focus on what other characters say about the character I am playing. What do they think of him? Are their opinions accurate when they speak of my character? Think about *Othello*—at the beginning of the play, it's "honest Iago," good old Iago.

Then, I want to know the structure of this character—where is he going. I believe in having my lines completely memorized or close to it when I start rehearsal. That is a personal goal and it helps me with my process. I don't memorize inflections or interpretations—I just get them into my head.

First, you have to make sense of what your character is saying. That often takes awhile. Memorizing is about getting ready and is one step out of my way. It informs me about how my character thinks and that tells me how to embody him. I follow the punctuation mostly, but every now and then I will add my own. I don't believe in a lot of pauses in Shakespeare. There are a lot of parenthetical lines in Shakespeare which support the main point—if you focus on all of them, trying to make each one clear, you will never get to the main point which *must* override the others. Take a look at Richard III's "Now is the winter of our discontent" soliloquy. If you stop at all those smaller points along the way, the audience will forget what you are talking about. It's the *throughline* that matters. All the best directors I ever worked with emphasized that—Bill Ball, Edward Hastings, Alan Fletcher, Robert Benedetti, Jim Edmondson and Jerry Turner.

Usually a speech establishes a thought, and getting there can be interesting, but should not be so interesting that you lose the main thought. Often, actors make pauses along the way that do not clarify anything. Those pauses are extremely interesting to the people doing them, but not to the audience. If you waste too much time with the supporting arguments in the middle, the audience will think—"Now what's he talking about? I lost the train of thought here, so I'll just watch those guys playing golf." There is an energy and a power in the language, and if you slow that down, you lose it. Often, a director will take a long speech like Ulysses' famous speech on "degree" and fill it with action because he thinks the audience is bored. But each section builds and leads to a final conclusion, and stage business can obscure the whole point of Shakespeare's creating that character's language in that place.

The process is organic—once I get the lines down, then I sit down and figure out what my character wants and how he is going to get there. This appears to me as I rehearse it. Each scene shows what the character wants in the moment; the ultimate thing at the end of the play is the character's overall goal. When the audience sees that the person got what he was after, there's some fulfillment and satisfaction.

I don't watch famous films of the role I'm cast in because I don't want to be influenced by them. Even when I played Hamlet, I did not watch any. I want to find this character myself, especially if it is a combination of my own traits and the character's. I remember being in a production in 1974 with Ray Birk, and as I performed it in 1983, I heard myself delivering some lines exactly as Ray performed them. Line readings are in our subconscious somewhere. Rather than giving in to the impulse to imitate, I read about the play, because that sparks my imagination. Once I've played the role, I might watch a movie then, and sometimes I see things I've missed. I did watch Jose Ferrer in the film with Orson Welles after I'd played Iago, and I also watched Olivier's Othello.

Once you get into rehearsal, then an entirely different process begins. Because you work with a whole group of people who may interpret things differently from how you might have imagined that character. You have to fit within the director's interpretation and not clash with his point of view. That gets you nowhere. There is always another point of view, and Shakespeare can be done in a number of different ways. I may not always agree with what the director is doing, but I don't fight that battle. Some actors will, and famous actors have, but once the director tells us his concept, the actor has to fit into that. The play is still going to be Shakespeare's story in Shakespeare's words.

Shakespeare's characters are enigmatic and difficult puzzles to solve, and they give you a lot of imaginative fun in trying to. He writes about flawed people, and even his kings feel like real persons with distinct personalities and ways of dealing with others. The thing I love about the *Henry* plays is that these families are at each other all the time—fighting and falling apart, loving and hating, and yet they are still families. The only real hero is Henry V, who is living with the sins of his father being visited on him and all the guilt that accompanies that.

Our 2012 version of *Troilus and Cressida* explored one view of what Shakespeare was after in this play. Was he writing a play that is simply the story of Troilus and Cressida and how their love affair is betrayed, or was he writing an anti-war play? Since the end of the Vietnam war, and forward to the present one in Afghanistan, the play becomes much more the latter. Placing it in Iraq had modern resonances for our audiences. So the focus shifted to where the play takes place rather than the story Shakespeare tells.

However, director Rob Melrose said that we are still Greeks and Trojans, Priam is King of Troy and Agamemnon supreme commander of the Greeks, but the play is merely set in a different place. Shakespeare was talking about the old code of honor. Hector represents that, and Ulysses represents the code of expedience—practicality in war. Shakespeare is saying that as well: wars are not honorable. You can look at any war and dishonorable deeds are done. In our production, Hector was killed with machine guns. Also, the costuming was entirely modern. The lines were heavily cut, including a number of Ulysses' and Hector's, and the show came in at two hours and forty-five minutes. That's a real difference between today's Festival performance and those in the past.

In the 2012 production, the first time you saw the Greek generals was very casual—Ulysses reading a book, Nestor watching the golf game in the background, Menelaus chewing tobacco, and Agamemnon coming in from jogging. Agamemnon was not played as a simpleton (as he is traditionally) but instead had an earnest desire to make everyone happy and to fix the present situation. He says, "Hey, we're winning. What's everyone so depressed about? Jove puts us all through trials and tribulations so we'll get better at what we do." It annoys Ulysses that Agamemnon is blowing smoke and not facing the facts. They've been in Troy for seven years, so Ulysses has been thinking for a long time about winning the war. For him, the problem is Achilles—if we can get him back onto the battlefield, we have a chance

When Nestor speaks, Ulysses respects him, but he favors a more practical solution to the war: he wants strategy, because winning is most important—honor is out the window for

Ulysses. He claims the soldiers are not doing their job, neglecting the orders the commanders give. Two soldiers in the background are playing golf! Ulysses wants to get Achilles back into the game, and the sudden death of Patroclus, his "male varlet" (lover), would be the way to spur the egotistical soldier into action. Ulysses thinks that the ends justify the means. He's a machiavellian to some extent and that comes through in the famous speech on degree—where he describes how the military order has fallen apart: "Take but degree away, untune that string, And hark what discord follows." He asserts that, "Troy in *our* weakness lives, not in her strength."

Later, in the scene where Troilus and he are observing Cressida with her new champion, Diomedes, in the Greek camp, he is quite cruel to Troilus. He's discovered that Cressida is a former lover of Troilus' and Diomedes wants her. An angry Troilus ups the possibility of ending the war with the two sides actively fighting each other. If Achilles is back on the field, victory belongs to the Greeks.

As the actors build the scenes, they slowly and painstakingly discover these things as they work through the text. Sometimes it comes to you in your sleep, so you try things, and it gets a response, and a different scene ensues. Also, scenes evolve as the season wears on. The actors don't always realize that because the changes happen slowly over time. Building scenes is a process. Actors don't sit down with a ground plan or map, and I don't think a director does, either. They have an overall world, theme, or idea about what the playwright intends. Scene by scene, it has to be discovered *by actors.*

Then there is that very odd ending in this play, where Pandarus bequeaths to all of us his diseases, as he has been the go-between for sets of lovers—that is his "role." As if to say, this is the world you live in, and this is all that it is worth. Similar to *1984*—when you have an enemy that is essentially faceless and unreal and hard to find, then you can justify endless war.

I played so many roles. My first roles were Friar John and Mercutio's page in *Romeo and Juliet*, directed by Pat Hines, who played Friar Lawrence, with Rick Russo as Mercutio in 1969. I played Romeo in 1975. I've since played Friar Lawrence twice. It was a real joy to play Benedick in 1980, one of my all time favorites. I played Iago in 1992. The Ulysses I acted in 2012 was not my first—I acted him in a production with Ken Albers in 2001, which was much more traditional. I performed Hamlet in 1984, while I was performing Posthumus in the matinees. I enjoyed every one of the characters I played—Hamlet and Iago the best.

Most of Shakespeare's plays are now familiar to me, not just plot but many of the speeches—I've either heard them often or delivered them, up to the point where I might say to myself, "I could have sworn Shakespeare said something else right there," when I hear one done incompletely. I do not usually look at the folio-quarto research, because that decision is in the hands of the people who are guiding the present play, but playing Hamlet was a different case. Robert Benedetti was the perfect director, and there I looked long and hard at the good and bad quartos, and we talked about them. Jerry Turner did much of that when he directed plays.

When the Gravedigger talks about the day Hamlet was born, it pretty much adds up to age forty, so that's the age at which I played it. Even in the famous "To be or not to be" soliloquy, I performed that speech as if I was speaking to myself. It felt more natural to have him working out the problem in his head.

A difficult scene for me was the one with the Players. Why does Hamlet ask the player to do that particular speech about Priam? Because it returns us to Gertrude, mourning for old Hamlet, which is why Hamlet wants to hear it and watch Gertrude's face at the same time, to discover her guilt. The player even weeps, and that motivates Hamlet right into the "Rogue and peasant slave" soliloquy. Yet he still has more hesitations.

Then he goes, against the Ghost's advice, into his mother's closet to accuse her. When he stabs the intruder, Polonius, behind the curtain, he shouts, "Is it the King?" revealing his *own* guilt.

He still wonders about Gertrude—how much does she give or hold back from Claudius. By the time Hamlet gets back from England, he expresses his conclusions beautifully: ". . . if it be not now, yet it will come: the readiness is all. . . . Let be." He now waits until Providence puts the answer in his lap. He believes the King is guilty, but in the end, circumstances take over and he is forced into action in the duel with Laertes.

I did all kinds of research on Iago. There is one story about Olivier when he began to film the role with Ralph Richardson as Iago. Olivier and the director Stuart Burge went to see Ernest Jones, a twentieth-century critic and psychologist who had written about both Hamlet and Othello with a very Freudian slant. Basically, Jones had said he thought that Iago was subconsciously in love with Othello. When they got back in the car, the director said, "Larry, what do you think?" Olivier said, "I think he's probably right, but don't tell Ralphie." I love that story because it tells you about the kinds of things that inform actors and audiences.

I try to look at a character from all angles, and Iago destroyed Othello, then Desdemona. He used his wife unmercifully—he used the handkerchief to torture Othello. Then he says he murdered Emilia because of a rumor that Othello may have slept with her. The big question is—why does he kill the others? Gleefully, he kills Roderigo and ruins Cassio. He quite simply has a great time destroying people's lives. What kind of a person does that—actually, I began looking at him as if he might have been a serial killer.

Jerry Turner had seen Paul Robeson's Othello live and liked it but felt that Iago was such a moustache-twirling villain that Othello looked like an idiot next to him. You have to address the issue of why Othello does not pick up on Iago's evil side at all. Then you go back to those references to "honest Iago." This character is that smiling, friendly guy next door who slits your throat one night. He has the ability and charm to deceive. So what motivates him subconsciously? He almost wants to *be* Othello. It's not that Othello is greater, better, more famous. It's more "bring down the great" that truly moves Iago to kill. You need to understand the psychology of the person you play—that's important. It informs you about what Iago does, but you cannot play the motivation. The action is all you can play.

Oddly enough, Iago never got stuck in my head after the play was over. I grew up in this tradition where when I walk off the stage, the performance is behind me. I never carry it around with me after the show—not in the sense that if I am roto-tilling in the garden I am thinking about a role.

Whatever part I am cast for, I do the best I know how. Obviously the larger roles have more power and are more central to the plot, and you are going to want to do them the most. In *All the Way*, I played several characters, none of them terribly like-able, certainly not Defense Secretary McNamara and definitely not the Governor of Mississippi. Likeableness is not the draw. However, the ensemble work in that production was essential to making the play work—all those historical characters, each one a known persona, so there was a strong motivating factor for the work. Like a good Shakespeare history play, it condenses some very complicated historical narrative into two and a half hours.

There is one line that sums up the whole play: "Any jackass can kick a barn down, but it takes a carpenter to build one." Much of the play was about Lyndon Johnson's ability to make the compromises needed in order to get the civil rights legisla-tion passed. He was a very Shakespearean character. There are a lot of things about Johnson's past that were really dark. A good playwright focuses on telling the parts that are going to tell the larger story, and those other shadows get hinted at—Robert Schenkkan did a marvelous job.

When former artistic director Libby Appel decided to do a play, she always said her focus was to measure it by a play of Shakespeare's: literarily interesting, character interesting. I love all the clown characters he wrote. They are so very human that you believe that they are who *they* are and not a mouthpiece for the playwright. In fact, you cannot find Shakespeare's mouthpiece.

The better directors know how to make a show work through the actors. Helping them say what they need to say, setting up the circumstances and letting the performance happen. Alan Fletcher at American Conservatory Theater was the best I've worked with—he'd repeat scenes and then he'd nudge them in certain ways until he came up with the specific idea he wanted to highlight. He would tell actors when they acted too much and needed to feel more, or if he thought they could be more specific in delivering the language. That directed the focus to where it belonged. I don't mind a director suggesting things, because a comment can act as inspiration, but I still like to follow my own instincts. A good director fosters discovery but does not treat actors as chattel. Bill Rauch always asks you at the end of a rehearsal to say one of the things that you liked most about this play as you worked on it.

I like doing character exploration in rehearsal even though I work on it outside of rehearsal. I don't like a lot of table talk, but I do like a couple of days of it. Some directors are really good at it and make the exercise fruitful, but some are perfunctory and say, "We're going to work our way through each scene, line by line, until everyone gets to say what they have to say." That can be boring.

I do not demean all the great directors I've worked with anywhere. But. I have seen actors, time after time after time, save plays here that were badly directed, badly thought out, and badly designed. Yet the actors saved it because they knew how to do that. They knew how to get out there and make whatever they have been told to do *work*.

What I do prior to performance depends on the play I am in. There are things I believe in, trying to be as disciplined as possible. I walk into the theater and sign in on the manager's sheet or it sends the staff into a panic. When I forget, that does something to me for a while until I get back to normal. I like immediately starting the preparation. I get my costume on, I put on my makeup, and then I have begun to feel connected to the character. Then I can go to the green room, but I don't chat a lot. Sometimes I just read; sometimes I start focusing on the play if it needs that.

If I have to sing in a show, as in *Bus Stop*, I sit in the quiet, soundproof room in the Thomas Theater forty-five minutes before play time and sing until I go onstage, just to prepare my voice. I am not a trained singer—singing and dancing can make me nervous. I have to feel really confident before I go on to do that, and I need technical preparation. In Hamlet's first scene onstage, he's still, and then his mother and father finally bring him into the dialogue. It takes time for that solitary figure in black that I played, hanging around on the sidelines, near a canon by the vom. He has to have something going on inside him when the scene starts. Before I make an entrance, let's say, in the Ghost scene—I have to know where we are and what I expect when I come in through that door. Creating that biography of a character is important.

One actor I knew used to sit in the dark for half an hour before show time, which is a kind of method-acting way of getting into character. That can make it more real and believable for me. The purpose of preparation is that feeling of confidence. If an audience senses your nervousness, it's a long time before they'll believe you that night. Elementary school kids can turn you off immediately. They sense *phony* and they let you know, especially if you are doing "grand" acting.

I've never had stage fright. I used this notion in college: when we play this play tomorrow night before an audience, it is the one we built and the one we have right now. Let's go out and do it and make this play work the best way we know. I don't re-hash things. If we didn't get it right one night, we'll fix it. That's one thing you have the luxury of saying in Ashland—we will get better at this. Eventually, even with misgivings, something happens and it moves forward.

I have enjoyed very much working with good colleagues, some of whom have gone. Denis Arndt was one of the actors I worked with whom I always wished they would bring back—he left to work in film and television—and now they have cast him for *The Tempest*. He has a lot of power onstage, and he delivers very honest and real moments. Even when he does something unusual, it always catches you off guard in a positive way, not as if he wanted to be noticed but because it fits with the play. It's good to have him back for 2014 playing Prospero.

The majority of the actors here I have really enjoyed working with—Tony DeBruno, Tony Heald, Michael Elich are on that list. They complete the idea of a repertory theater.

I just reread Angus Bowmer's book, and I agree with him. He said that one of the greatest dangers the Festival faced after he left was directors—making the theater about directors and not about actors. If theater becomes about a director trying to put his stamp on the playwright's work, then the playwright's work is diminished. And that is a danger.

Vilma Silva as Queen Katherine in *Henry VIII*. Photo: Jenny Graham, OSF.

Vilma Silva

In 20 seasons at OSF, Vilma Silva has played, among other roles, Goneril in *King Lear*; Sor Rufina in *The Tenth Muse*; Doña Capulet in *Romeo and Juliet*; Julius Caesar in *Julius Caesar*; Portia in *The Merchant of Venice;* Queen Katherine in *Henry VIII;* Emilia in *Othello;* Beatrice in *A View from the Bridge;* Katherina in *The Taming of the Shrew;* Amy in *Gibraltar;* Portia in *Julius Caesar;* Celia in *As You Like It;* Viola in *Twelfth Night;* Thaisa in *Pericles;* Dromio of Ephesus in *The Comedy of Errors;* Isabella and Mistress Overdone in *Measure for Measure;* Lise in *The Magic Fire;* Juliet in *Romeo and Juliet;* and The Bride in *Blood Wedding*.

A S LONG AS I CAN REMEMBER, since fourth or fifth grade, I've liked the idea of acting. I liked watching it, and I liked the idea of putting myself in that place, learning a character's lines, learning a character through the lines. I got involved in theater actively when I went to a girls' Catholic high school in San Francisco. The three boys' schools had a lot of money, so they could do big productions. What they didn't have was girls. So auditions would be posted for their plays, and I went on a dare with a friend and got cast. That was the beginning of thinking I could actually do this. I went to Santa Clara University and got my degree in theater arts, but I had some debt when I got out, so rather than pursue an acting career, I just worked—waiting tables, working sales, being a bank teller. I had been doing that for six or seven years when a friend of mine called and said, "I'm doing a show at LACT [Los Altos Conservatory Theatre]. I'd love for you to step into a role. It'll be easy." I did, and of course it was great. I didn't realize how much I had missed acting.

Once I worked there, I attracted the attention of Timothy Near, the artistic director of the San Jose Repertory Theatre. She was doing a production of a play about Pablo Neruda called *Burning Patience*, which was really unusual back then [1988-89] because nobody was doing Latino plays. So I auditioned—there weren't many of us then—and I got the role. One thing led to another. The director of that production was Tony Curiel, an associate artistic director of El Teatro Campesino, and I went to work for that company for a few years. I continued with San Jose Rep, where I worked with Jack Fletcher, son of Allen Fletcher, one of the main directors of American Conservatory Theatre when Bill Ball was there. So I worked with Jack and with Julia, his sister. Jack took me to the San Francisco Shakespeare Festival, where I met the artistic director Albert Takazauckas, who was directing a production of *Saturday, Sunday, Monday* at ACT, which took me to that theater. I was starting to be known by some of the other Bay Area theaters.

I'd come up to Ashland to visit my college friend Joan Langley [head of OSF's Education Department], and Joan would say "You should audition here." I'd think, "Well, I don't really want to be in southern Oregon"—I was working down in the Bay Area, and it was good. But I auditioned twice, and the second time I was offered a season. I had to turn it down, because I already had other work lined up in Louisville and Dallas, during the beginning of the OSF season. A month later OSF contacted me again about doing just the second of the two shows they had offered, which didn't start until the end of May. That was *Blood Wedding*.

It was the transition year from Henry Woronicz to Libby Appel, so I was hired by Henry. I had been here three days when it was announced that he was leaving. I thought I would just do the one show and that would be that, but the following year Michael Salazar and I were cast in OSF's *Romeo and Juliet*, directed by René Buch, the founding artistic director of Repertorio Español in New York. I hadn't been asked to read for René, so I thought, "I'm going to pack up my car and go home, and I'll be fine." And then René asked me to meet and have coffee. We sat and talked about *Blood Wedding*—I don't think we even mentioned *Romeo and Juliet*. The next thing I know I get the offer to play Juliet.

My first year I was the last company member to join, and I was only doing one show, which was very, very unusual at the time. Now it's more common. What happened next was this: *Pericles* was going to be produced as the last Bowmer show in 1999, and then re-open as the first Bowmer show of the next season. When I was cast in *Pericles*, it was going to be a two-year contract. So my husband David and I found a house a fifteen-minute walk from the Festival. The irony, of course, is *Pericles* ended up being a one-season show. Not to worry—we're still here. *Pericles* came at a time when we were dress-rehearsing *Three Musketeers*. So the company was exhausted, and our first *Pericles* rehearsal was a seven o'clock-to-midnight. And then Laird Williamson, the director, said, "You're all going to sing Gower's lines." Oh no! It was so much work. But Laird had a clear vision of what he wanted, and that made it a joy to perform—one of my all-time top five favorite shows.

Pericles probably isn't on many people's top five list. Neither is *Henry VIII*, but that's one of mine, too, along with *Julius Caesar*. I may have to push it to six because I'm also having a great time with *King Lear*. I had not seen *Lear* many times, although I played Cordelia years ago. When I read Shakespeare scholarship about Goneril and Regan and Cordelia, it's always about the two evil daughters and the good daughter. Reading as an actor, I find that dismissive, simplistic, and boring. It takes all the focus off those *relationships*. And that's a good third of the play, maybe more. I don't want to dismiss as just "evil" two characters who have major scenes and major influence. I want to figure out what makes them tick, what the family dynamic is. It's never as simple as it looks on the outside. There's no mother, and Lear's preference for Cordelia has been clear from the get-go. It's no surprise to Regan or Goneril that Lear says of Cordelia, "I loved her most." What is that like, no matter how old you get? That can sting in a way that takes you right back to being a little kid. The competition over Edmund—the whole thing is set up in that first scene. Lear is constantly comparing his daughters—not a good thing for a parent to do.

I love the fact that Robin Goodrin Nordli (Regan) and I dress differently in the show and are so different physically, too. Regan is the second daughter, the appeaser—the sweet one, the really feminine one. When I went in to talk to Bill Rauch about casting, I said Regan is interesting, but I'd really like to play Goneril because I'm the oldest of three girls in my family, and in many ways my father's son. I also was a bit afraid of having to do Regan's eye-gouging scene 120 times. But I'm fascinated by how that scene is fuelled by my walking out of the room with Edmund, how that throws Regan right over the cliff—that and all the drinking she's been doing. There's just so much that leads to this nightmare where we've thrown our father out into the storm. And I kind of understand them—that's the freaky thing, because it's easy to think these daughters are just wack jobs, Charles Manson people. But when you look at the whole trajectory—all it took was a little alcohol and a little rage and the opportunity, and crazy things start to happen. There's a resonance there that's unexpected, isn't it? The Lear family.

Our show had two Lears, Jack Willis and Mike Winters, alternating in the role, so the relationship was different for us every time. Armando Durán (Kent) and I were talking about this recently. There's a difference in my arguing with one or the other. Mike's Lear was dangerous in his erratic thinking, but Jack's Lear was more menacing, really, really dangerous. So the question I always asked myself in performance, arguing with him, was how far can I push it? I imagined my own father across from me and wondered, "How bold would I be? How believable is it that I could actually say this?" Lear is erratic and unstable and has an armed militia—and he threw out my baby sister, Cordelia, the one he loved most. He threw out his most loyal lord, Kent. The question posed to Regan is, "If he can do that to them, what is he going to do to us?" What is he capable of? That's a real fear, one that I sometimes felt differently with the two different Lears.

When I talk about my top five Shakespeare roles, I'd also throw in Kate in *The Taming of the Shrew*. I'd seen *Shrew* a couple of times, and I always wanted to do it, because I wanted it to not be a big wink at the end. I'd seen that, and I felt cheated. I wanted to believe in that relationship. When I got cast—oh my goodness, the comments! What are you going to do with that speech, that speech, that speech? You're going to get booed. Really? People get booed?

So for me Kate's final speech had to be where I started. Luckily I had a smart, awesome director, Kate Buckley, who is really open to ideas. One afternoon I went over to her apartment and we just talked about it. I wanted to actually mean that speech. I've been married a long time, so I know what that's like. I didn't want to apologize for it, I didn't want it to be out of the side of my mouth, I didn't want to wink. So Kate put us in a world where my character could mean it and not be—in our opinion—subjugated. We kept it in period.

How do I get there? How do I go from rejecting everybody and everything to actually meaning it, and when does that happen in the speech? One day when I was doing dishes at my house, I looked out the window and there was a beautiful doe, eating, in the open field, and with her were these two little fawns—leaping, as they do, straight up in the air, running around, having a fabulous time. As I'm watching and enjoying them, I look up the hill slightly. There was a stag, perfectly, perfectly still—being the lookout, being a protector, being on guard. When I saw the stag and realized what he was doing, taking in the whole picture, it was like "Wow!" There's a kind of natural order that exists. We can deny it, but it exists. It took me to what I saw happen to my brothers-in-law after their children were born—this excitement but also this terror, and taking on the responsibility of all it means to be a father.

So I said to my director, I'll mean what I say, but rather than make this an everywoman speech about every man, it's under these circumstances and to these women—to Bianca and the widow. And they aren't the only ones present for the speech. Lucentio and Petruchio and my father are there, too. Can I find a reason to say what I say to each of these people individually? I can say to Petruchio I'll absolutely do what you ask me to. Your husband is your lord, your king, your governor. I could end the speech right there, turn to him and say, "Is that what you wanted? Awesome—you're happy." But now I have the floor, and I can actually say what I have learned.

So, to the widow: I was bitchy like you. What it leads to is being lonely; nobody wants to be with you. That's what I've learned. And Bianca—don't mistreat your husband. If you want to be happy, treat him well, because he can take care of you and love you. And brother-in-law Lucentio, don't be an idiot and bet against your wife. You have a responsibility to care for her, to honor her, for her to be the center of your life, and where I'm at now, that's my husband. I love him. Whatever he needs done, I'm ready to do.

In this production, when I started to put my hand on the floor, Petruchio stopped me—because he had gotten more of a partner than he thought was possible. That was my approach to the speech. I'm sure there were many out there who did not agree, but I never got booed. There was always dead silence. I don't have to convince them, to make them love what I have to say, but if I can get them to listen—then I've done my job.

We sat down at table work on the first night of rehearsal—everybody in the cast was there—and Danforth Comins, who was playing Lucentio, said, "Okay, I just gotta ask, what's gonna be the deal with that final speech?" And Kate Buckley turned to me and said, "Vilma, tell them what we talked about today." So I told them how I looked out my window, what I was thinking. Interestingly—and I didn't expect this—the guys in the cast who were actual dads were especially moved, a great sign. Everybody was okay—maybe there's some truth in this, we'll see what we can do.

But it had to come from a whole series of steps that Michael Elich (Petruchio) and I luckily were allowed to craft right from the beginning. We used the falcon metaphor in Petruchio's "Thus have I politicly begun my reign" speech, and the wooing scene—which I never hear because it's always so very physical. What if it isn't the usual physical tussle? What if no one has ever spoken to her like that? No one has ever had anything positive to say? Even if at first she thinks it's a bunch of lies that she's going to reject. Is it possible that it's interesting, maybe even kind of nice? Because the next time you see her she's in a wedding dress. She can reject him, she can get angry, but there has to be a moment—the sound of his voice, the ideas that he's expressing—something to give her pause, because you've got to see things changing to allow you to get to that final speech.

Yes, it's controversial! But at least if we can craft it all the way through as a personal journey for both characters, we can get to that speech. Sure, I've said the sun is the moon, but now I have an opportunity to say more. I read about other productions—the one where she has a gun held to her head, or where she kisses his foot at the end. I don't think I can feel good about any of that. There's got to be some other way to do it.

And it was a blast to do, because I could feel from the audience that they liked us together. If you get that, you can get them on board with the journey. We found this great moment in the sun and the moon speech: "I say it's the moon." "OK, it's the moon, whatever." "No, it's not the moon, it's the sun." "Okay, whatever I say, you always say the opposite, we're going home." "Okay—whatever you want me to say, fine, fine, fine." I made sure that some of my old combative Kate came out, and then I stopped, and found it funny. I don't know if you've ever had a moment like that, where in the middle of a raging argument you think, "Oh my God, I sound ridiculous!" I hear it, I actually hear it. Michael and I negotiated that moment. I said, I think I have to be the one to laugh first. I have to be the one to find myself funny—and if I can laugh at myself in front of you, and we share that laugh, then we've got a friendship, then the change is coming from me, the self-awareness and the choice to be happy, rather than feeling forced or threatened or beaten into it. Bless him, Michael really went with it. That was really a wonderful experience of building—and Kate doesn't have the majority of the language in that scene.

I remember reading a Shakespeare actor's account of Kate, "Interpreting the Silences" [in Carol Rutter's *Clamorous Voices*], that was very inspiring. There's that scene with the haberdasher and the dressmaker that ends with a blow-up and tears— Petruchio says you're getting nothing and we're not going to your father's house—and then he says, we'll go, but we're just going to go in the clothes that we're wearing. It doesn't matter what we look like because what's important is what's inside. I'm really unhappy, but I'm listening to what he has to say. We didn't know how to end the scene, because she doesn't say anything. Does he drag her off? Does he leave her alone?

The e-mails were flying between Kate and me and Michael. I

suggested to Michael, "Hey, I have an idea that I'd like to try, just go with me on it. Do you want to tell Kate?" "No, we'll just try it and see what happens." So after he did the speech, I got up like I was going to bite his head off—and stopped. And then I left. I just stopped myself from ranting and left him alone on stage. And then he made his exit. It was just the tiniest change, breaking the habit, breaking the automatic response. He actually said something that made sense, and I didn't want to scream about it. I leave, and he comes after me. Those moments were such fun to play. On opening night, when the rest of the company was taking a bow, before Michael and I had to run back up from the vom for the curtain call, he turned to me and said, "And we only get thirty-three of these!" Oh God, it had been so much work, for just a handful of performances. I'd love to do it again.

My process is a little different each time, depending on the play, the role. There are some things constant, of course. You look to the language, what your character says about herself, what other characters say about her, what the circumstances are, what you want, how you're going to get it. All of these things are the foundation. After that, it might be sitting around the table, looking out your kitchen window, or reading an essay. And sometimes, darn it, those other actors in the scene are terribly inspiring. For twenty years I've been saying, there are some *smart* people here, and I've learned so much from them.

Another role that I would love to do again, maybe for different reasons, is Portia in *The Merchant of Venice*. That one, I discovered in performance more than anything else. For Portia it's about a woman figuring out a relationship *after* the marriage has already happened. It's not an "if" any more, it's a "how"—not "if" you marry Bassanio, but how are you going to be married to him? That was much trickier. I wanted in the very first scene to be sitting at a big dining room table all by myself, surrounded by piles of law books and my father's will, wearing my glasses.

There has got to be a way out of this stupid "three boxes" trick. What the heck? I'm running my own home and I'm going to have to give it up, and I don't even get to choose the guy I want? So the focus of my life is figuring it out, going through these books. "My little body is aweary of this great world." I wanted to be somebody trying to find her own way out of her predicament, legally, in the paperwork.

What was really fun in that first scene was the argument with Nerissa. Why am I so critical of these suitors? Well, this one's an idiot. How about this one? Well, he's an idiot too. Portia is opinionated as all hell, but she's got a great mind. And then Nerissa proves her point: of course all of these guys went into the dustbin, that's exactly what your dad planned. So his system actually works. There's a wonderful argument happening here—not just idle girl talk. It's actually a couple of smart women hashing it out. And these are the women that show up in court.

So you've got a Portia who's already acting like a lawyer. She's also a lawyer with Bassanio at the end. They've just gotten married, they've just met, and there's a lot she doesn't know. Let's test this marriage, let's actually test it, because I'm new to this, and I don't quite get this relationship with Antonio. The characters do interesting things—so how do you fill that out, how do you explain that?

How do you walk into a courtroom where the Christians are crazy, and the Jew is also a little crazy in what he wants? So, Shylock, the Christians have already decided what and who you are, what kind of person you are. But you have the golden opportunity to surprise them. You can actually prove them wrong and put them in your debt. Here's your chance. And he doesn't go for it. It's a very tough part, and a really intriguing one. Tony Heald did a great job humanizing Shylock. But Shylock does demand what he demands. He can't stop himself. It would have been fun to do in the smaller Thomas Theatre, up close and personal, where you can play those shades that are really subtle.

The first small-space Shakespeare I did here was Libby Appel's production of *Measure for Measure* in the Black Swan (1998). I wore my nun's habit over a tattooed body stocking, because I also doubled as Mistress Overdone. Angelo (Richard Howard) played Abhorson, too. There were wonderful double castings—Mariana (Suzanne Irving) was also Escalus, Terri Towns played Juliet and Elbow. One day, for a matinee, we got to half-hour and Terri wasn't there. They called—no answer. Didn't have any idea where she was. They called up her understudy, Carolyn Hitt, and said you'd better get down here and into costume. So she did. We used to do a little energy circle before that show, so we got together and welcomed Carolyn, and off we went. Then I'm onstage for my first scene with Juliet—and it's Terri! My mind is racing—what are you doing here? Where's Carolyn? While I had been onstage earlier, they had gone to Terri's place, brought her back, and got her into costume. She had thought it was an evening show.

The schedule is such a challenging part of working here. How many times I look at my calendar to make sure! When I transfer my calendar to my phone or computer, I'm so careful, and even then, I get it wrong. I can't wait until we can just automatically download it, because it's terrifying. And for people who are new to this company—oh my goodness! Here you just don't have that rhythm where you go to the theater every night to do the show; weekends, weekends—done! So we tell new actors, it's a marathon, not a sprint. Don't wipe yourself out in the first month. But it *is* fun—it's different. Sometimes we laugh about it in the makeup rooms. You're going to go work for another theater and do eight shows a week on a contract? You know what your schedule is, and you have no understudy assignment? That's a paid vacation!

Julius Caesar (2011) was one of those productions that no matter how tired we all were, once we got started, it was a blast to do, so clean and so focused. I loved doing the 2002 production with Laird Williamson, too, when I played Brutus' wife, Portia. Danforth Comins, Gregory Linington, Jonathan Haugen and I were all in Laird's production, and here we all were, doing it again with another terrific director, Amanda Dehnert. But this time I was playing Julius Caesar. Amanda came to me and said, "I'd like to see you as Caesar's ghost in the second part. You have that scene where you appear to Brutus, but I want to see you on stage another time at least. I don't know exactly where or how. So can you just try being there?" I thought, you know what, I absolutely can. Just tell me when you want me more visible, when you don't, when to leave the stage—but I'm going to be there, okay? Sometimes I would do some blocking on my own, sometimes Amanda would give me a bit—it was one of those things that we shaped little by little.

I had done something similar in *The Magic Fire*. I could have sat on a stool on the side, but I was actually woven into the scene. Libby said, "I need you to move when you think it's right, and I'll shape it, but go ahead, just wander around." I had to figure out where I could be, when I could move without pulling focus from someone else, when I could turn to the audience— making it up on the fly.

Rehearsing *Julius Caesar*, Amanda would say, sit here, I need you to recede here, here I need you to be very present. "Maybe I could touch Portia when she dies?" "Yes—in fact, I think you're going to touch everybody when they die, maybe it's clay that comes off your body"—but we couldn't figure out how to do that technically. So I said, "How about that bowl that Brutus and I share wine out of? Could I have some clay in there, and mark everybody with that?" Amanda said okay, let's do that. But I don't mark Brutus with the clay at the end; he marks himself. That final moment with Brutus—that betrayal—was always so painful.

I remember Amanda asking Octavius (Kenajuan Bentley), when Brutus fell, to kneel directly behind my Caesar, but not to see or touch me. She asked me, when Kenajuan started to kneel and take over, to collapse. We were figuring out all the poetry of that in tech rehearsal. It made me think of that wonderful play *Copenhagen*—that ideas and passion and betrayal and friendship and love are so active in these characters that they actually carry into the next life. There's a spirit and an energy, and those are the things that survive. For me, it is Caesar's ghost, who has to walk this earth finding and delivering a kind of justice to those that betrayed her. Finally, to see Brutus take his own life—that felt absolutely right. I'm done, that desire for revenge is done. What is it? It's actually watching one of my dearest friends take his own life. At that point, I have to let it all go.

One day on the bricks, a young girl said to me, "I saw you play Caesar, and that will forever change the way I think about the play." Before the show, when we would chat individually with audience members, and I introduced myself as Julius Caesar, it was the girls that went crazy. There was something so satisfying and sweet in the thought that, as a woman, I have a place at this table. If you get a director with a fabulous mind and great skill—and Amanda is all that—it was not arbitrary, not just a trick.

Months before our first rehearsal, I was asked to do an interview about *Julius Caesar* for a local paper. I said no, what am I going to talk about? They're going to ask me about being a woman playing Julius Caesar, and whether I'm going to be called Julia. I don't want to do that. But I wrote to Amanda—we had barely met—and said, let's talk about why you want me to do this role. And she replied: I think Caesar was a singular personality, and that is what drew people to him, and what scared people about him. He's the other. Being a woman, I can tell you, we make people uncomfortable when we're in positions of power.

Outside the theater were banners, of both historical and contemporary assassinated leaders. The theater artisans weren't sure of what Amanda wanted, so she actually painted some of the banners herself with a big old brush. They should look like they were just thrown together, she said—I don't want anything fancy. For the funeral oration, we came up with the idea of Mark Antony (Danforth Comins) pushing a table onstage, as a kind of a bier, bearing just my bloody, shredded coat to stand for Caesar's body. So for rehearsal the prop shop brought in a beat-up prop table, but said they'd build something nicer and paint it all black for the show. And Amanda said no. This works; don't paint it; don't touch it. Don't repaint the floor. I love that it's a mess of dried clay and chipped parts after the actors leave. That's what I want. I don't want it to be anything other than that.

There are a couple of other Shakespeares I'd love to do. I've never done *A Midsummer Night's Dream*, or *Henry IV, Part One*, or *Henry V*, and those are big plays. But to have done *Pericles*—wow!—and *Henry VIII*. Those are two plays you don't often get a shot at. I have to admit I had never read *Henry VIII*. But that's another play I'd love to do again.

That role—Queen Katherine in *Henry VIII*—came out of the blue. The season (2009) also included *Much Ado About Nothing*, and I had never played Beatrice. But John Sipes, who was directing *Henry VIII*, talked with me about Katherine, so I read the play, and I thought, "This is really a great role." That big courtroom scene is wonderful, but for me the most important scene was her very last one. I've just heard that my enemy Wolsey is dying and I'm anything but gracious—good riddance, and throw the flowers into the grave after him. John said, "Go ahead and be bitter." It was wonderful to start from there and make the journey to forgiving Wolsey at the end of that scene. Only then can the grace of the dream happen, where Katherine receives a heavenly crown.

I hit on the idea that when Howie Seago (Griffith, the Queen's gentleman usher) reports that Wolsey has been reconciled to God, I have to stop being bitter and angry—because there's nothing a Christian would want more than to have a soul reconciled to God. It was hard. It meant actually *being* Christian, not just calling yourself that. To feel the deepest hatred of absolutely the worst person—and then really to forgive him. All kinds of beautiful things happen after that—the dream, and wonderful Eddie Lopez (Capuchius, the Spanish ambassador), who came to me with the idea of speaking in Spanish. What a beautiful idea, that in her last scene she can taste her own language again.

John Sipes was one of those wonderful directors—oh, the best!—who drops ideas into your head and then lets you create with them. Laird Williamson is another, and Bill Rauch on *King Lear*, too. They drop in ideas that can take you on a whole new journey. What a great idea—how do I do that? I don't know—let me figure it out. The director you need depends on the project; it's like process. Not one who tells you *how* to do something, but who gives you something to think about and the space to figure out how to do it.

What happens when you're *given* a line reading is that it's not really yours. You're mimicking. And maybe you can mimic it really well. But then you have a long run—like we have here—and a third of the way through, you wonder, "Why can't I do that anymore?" Because it may not have a foundation that's really yours—even if you can say the line exactly as directed. You need to have the thought, not just the sound, to sustain you however long you're going to be speaking these words. If you take that away from me, you take away energy and specificity and personal ownership. But if I understand what that thing is—really understand it mentally, emotionally, physically—then I can call it up on a dime. I can sustain that when I have to hit the ground running with no brush-up rehearsal after six days off, as we did with *King Lear*, or even longer in the Elizabethan Theatre. Voice and text directors, especially with Shakespeare, are very helpful in determining which words to stress and which to leave unstressed, but as an actor, you'd better figure out how to incorporate that information as more than just a technical solution. If you're clear in your mind about the lines you're saying, the technique will do its work—but you've got to be clear in your mind.

The ideal director is a partner. I think of John Sipes and Amanda Dehnert and Bill Rauch and Laird Williamson, who are really different directors in some ways, but what they all give you is conversations—not just notes and not just direction, but conversations about ideas, about feelings. Those conversations run the gamut but the ones I love most are one-on-one, really looking at your character as a human being, using as much experience as you possibly can draw on, with someone who's willing to throw ideas back and forth—or to say, "You know, I totally get what you're saying, but I'm thinking maybe it's this." Oh! Let's try that. I love those conversations.

How do I judge my favorite roles? They were the ones I couldn't wait to do again. What springs to mind is the Shakespeares: *Romeo and Juliet*, *Taming of the Shrew*, *Pericles*, *As You Like It*. I loved playing a quirky Celia. Penny Metropulos, the director, was wonderful in helping me work Celia out. I was always struck by Celia's wisdom about love and relationships. Where does she get that exactly, growing up in her father's court? She doesn't really know the first thing about it. So my Celia spoke with some unearned authority. I wanted her to be a smartypants, a little bookish.

Of the non-Shakespeare roles, one of my favorites was Beatrice in Arthur Miller's *A View from the Bridge*, a down-to-earth, good person caught in a terrible dilemma—her love for her niece, her love for her husband, her fear of what she feels coming at them. Stephanie Beatriz and Armando Durán and I had a tense scene—an argument about her getting a job and moving out—at the dinner table, eating pasta. Sometimes I would actually make the sauce at home and bring it onstage in my first entrance. Armando and I would eat all of our pasta; we loved it, and it was fun to be able to eat something that I had actually made. I loved everything about my character—the way she looked in her house dresses, those arguments that she couldn't let get out of hand, her deference to her husband, all of that—and I came to love the set, because that was *our* apartment, our home.

Octavio Solis' *Gibraltar* was another favorite, such a poetic journey, so gritty and strange and very personal—because it had been developed from six weeks of improvisation from the very beginning, when there was nothing but ideas, not even a narrative. Octavio just threw out situations and had us improvise, sometimes for twenty or thirty minutes. He would introduce new characters, or new elements, and we would roll with it, see where it went. Once we got over that pressure of producing something, and could just be in the space and speak when we were moved to, it was freeing. I didn't have to make anything happen. Things came naturally out of the situation or what somebody else brought into the scene.

Another wonderful but very different experience was *The Tenth Muse*. It was supposed to be a modern adaptation of Sor Juana Inés de la Cruz's seventeenth-century play *House of Desires*, but at some point Bill Rauch said to the playwright, Tanya Saracho, "You're not locked into this adaptation. If you've got another idea, you should develop that." In March or April, after *King Lear* had opened, we were asked to do a reading of what Tanya had produced—some interesting ideas, but we didn't really know ultimately what the story was. Three days before rehearsal started in May we got a script, and I couldn't put it down. I was compelled by the story of a brilliant woman, an artist, inspiring these girls to take a leap of faith. Her legacy and their empowerment—for someone like me, educated by Dominican nuns, that connection was very moving.

When I read Rufina I thought okay, she's the crabby nun. But then I remember asking why? What's causing this? You could say she's just a crank, but it's not terribly interesting to play that. Could it be twenty years of suppressing her impulses and her great love of Sor Juana's art? I got this take on her as the Mother Superior's second-in-command. That was not really evident in the script when I first read it, but I said, "Can I have glasses? Can I have keys? Can I be *that* one? The one who tries to keep things running smoothly and who takes her responsibilities oh so very seriously?" I kept picturing Rufina as the one that did all the filing, all the cleanup—the teacher's aide. For someone like her who grew up in the convent and had no experience in the outside world, Sor Juana must have been a mindblower.

The physicality of the character was informed by the habit, the wimple, the keys, of course, but even more by her internal pace, the pressure of having to get things done. There's this motor running all the time. She's got to get the embroidery done; she's got to find places for the three new girls that she didn't expect. There's this little bulldog personality in there; it's not graceful, it's not fluid, it's just moving forward—"I've got a lot to do"—and I needed to get that across. Whereas the Mother Superior has a completely different physicality. Everything is done at her command—a wave or a look, and I'm right there to do her bidding.

Costume sometimes defines the physicality of Shakespeare characters. For Katherine in *Henry VIII*, I put on twenty pounds of costume, wig, and crown, and if I didn't move a certain way, the costume could tangle my feet and trip me. If I didn't keep standing up straight, the front of the gown got too long. And with the tremendous amounts of jewelry, I simply couldn't make any fast moves. So the costuming expressed status not only visually, but in how it affected movement.

In the Elizabethan Theatre, we may be working in temperatures of 104 degrees or 34 degrees or in rain. That has to be dealt with in the costuming, and it's a challenge for designers. Sometimes there may be extreme physical demands. At first you think you're fine, and then eight months into it, you're not. In *Julius Caesar*, I would lie dead for twelve minutes after I fell, with my arm behind me. A month after we closed, I couldn't move my shoulder. I had injured it.

I found *The Tenth Muse* even more challenging to learn than *King Lear*. In *The Tenth Muse* a title could shift from "reverend mother" to "holy mother" and then to "fair mother." There is no dramatic reason why; it's simply the way it's written. I had to learn the part by drilling it, simply learning the rhythm of the words and drilling the articulation of the line for many hours. And, of course, I'm working on intention, I'm working on operative words as I go—but especially with the high-speed, overlapping speeches required, it meant saying it over and over, faster and faster.

But *King Lear*—I'd work on that, run it three or four times, get up and do it on my feet. My choices were based on staging, based on the interactions with other characters, and it just came. Shakespeare's language is economical and yet so clear. That doesn't mean that I don't drill Shakespeare, too. I tend to learn lines sitting in my favorite chair. When I get up and walk around, I get distracted. I'll notice things. I don't want to be distracted by stuff. No, what I need is to have that language clear in my mind. So I just sit and read the script and work it out.

This season I'm in *Water by the Spoonful*, playing a woman who is a recovering crack cocaine addict with a tragic past—lots of regret in that play. And then I'm going to be in the all-female *The Two Gentlemen of Verona*, directed by Sarah Rasmussen.

Women make up the whole cast of *Two Gentlemen*, so we'll be playing the male characters as men. I had lunch recently with Lisa Wolpe, who's been playing Hamlet in Los Angeles. I would love to have seen that—and the all-female *Julius Caesar* in New York—but both shows closed before our season ended. I have to say, it was quite the feeling, at the end of *The Tenth Muse*, to go out for the curtain call. It was all of us—all women out there. I didn't expect it, but it's affecting. It makes me proud.

John Tufts as King Henry in *Henry V*. Photo: Jenny Graham, OSF.

John Tufts

In 11 seasons at OSF, John Tufts has played, among other roles, King Henry in *Henry V* and Prince Hal in *1 Henry IV* and *2 Henry IV*; Romeo in *Romeo and Juliet*; King James and Sharpe in *Equivocation*; Puck in *A Midsummer Night's Dream*; Robin Hood in *The Heart of Robin Hood*; Ravelli/Chico in *Animal Crackers*; Chico in *The Cocoanuts*; Dromio of Syracuse in *The Comedy of Errors*; Flutter in *The Belle's Stratagem*; Parolles in *All's Well That Ends Well*; Dumaine in *Love's Labor's Lost*; Yasha in *The Cherry Orchard*; and King of France in *King Lear*.

CHRIS ALBRIGHT-TUFTS AND I were about to have our first baby, Henry James Rutledge Tufts, when my mother gave her my baby book. I never knew it existed. Mom had kept it until I was about four, in monthly progress reports, filling in information about what my interests were. By age two and a half, I was intensely interested in costumes, and my grandmother had given me a trunk full of them that I'd try on. My mom had a giant, red, London-Fog-type overcoat and boots, which were much bigger than mine, and I'd put them on and become the fireman.

We went to a lot of theater when I was a kid, touring musicals that came to town, and children's theater productions,

A Christmas Carol in season—a surprising amount because that was what people did. I loved going. It was so exciting to see a contained environment create a whole world like that. An actor would go into another room, and though we didn't see that other place, in my mind it existed. If they exited the stage, I assumed that here was a real house and they were going into a bedroom. It never occurred to me that these were flats and they weren't real. I finally understood it was illusion and not real life. I remember seeing a production of *Man and Superman* at age twelve. There was a whole scene with a Model T onstage that was being repaired and this just wowed me. I got to go backstage and see it, and up close it was made of bicycle tires and plywood, and I remember being so disappointed and sad that it wasn't a real car.

We'd also go to the ballet, symphony, opera. I love ritual. Even church is theater; it's a five-act play. Seeing all that was hugely influential. You have the opportunity to allow the director or the playwright to coax your imagination into exercising itself. I actually got interested in being *in* theater in seventh grade when I saw a high school production of *Oliver!* with a really good actor named Thomas Shaw. If I were to see a video of that now, despite the youthful tics, I know I'd see him as a solid performer. For me, someone who could transform, be unrecognizable, was the mark of talent.

My grandmother bought me a set of golf clubs, and I took out the putter and used it like a cane and walked around the house, singing, "You've got to pick a pocket or two," as Fagin did in the musical. Thomas Shaw had a slight Humphrey Bogart kind of lisp and a unique way of walking, and I spent a lot of time imitating that. My mother watched me from the dining room table with this look of wonder and curiosity. I was always a shy kid, and I'd transferred to a new school, and expectations were high. I hadn't been fitting in, so it was exciting for her to see this development.

Three Little Pigs was the first play I was ever in, at a four-week summer camp in Georgia, and the play had already been cast. I went to the director and said, "Can I still be in the play?" and suggested a comic bit. He said, "Great. We'll put it in the play." We never rehearsed it, but I walked by the pigs in a huddle and they said, "Who are you?" "I'm John and I'm just looking for the bathroom." I got a big ole laugh from the parents, and I relished the glory of that and had found my peer group. My mother was happy. She was terrified that I was going to be a lonely kid, the youngest with older siblings who never hung out with me. She'd come and spy on me at my new school and saw I was eating lunch at a table all by myself in seventh grade. She was standing by a woman she did not know, and she turned to her and said, "Oh, what the fuck have I done." The woman said, "I'm sorry—I don't know your name." She answered, "I'm Katie Tufts. I'm John Tufts' mother. Who is your kid?" And the woman said, "I'm Jean Smith. The Girls' Dean." My mom was so embarrassed.

My father was very happy that I'd discovered something artistic and could employ that side of myself in a practical way. He was to his core compelled by visual art, woodworking, and poetry in college and then became a businessman.

I took my first acting class in ninth grade, the first time anyone was actually scrutinizing my performance. It was illuminating and powerful because it let me know I could grow and evolve. After my freshman year, I decided to go to summer camp at Interlochen Center for the Arts in Michigan. It was a magical place, and a major transition about how I thought about theater. I discovered there was more about acting than just performance. I'd never considered that there were building blocks to that—didn't you just look at the script and find the character and be emotional? Now, there were tools, like analyzing Shakespeare's words, finding out *what a character wants*, for example. Also, I met so many wonderful people—an actor in my cabin and I got along immediately, Jack Fervor, who was intuitive and kinetic. We were in *Our Town* and *Brighton Beach Memoirs*. I marveled at how a seventeen-year-old could understand how to play a depressed, aging alcoholic. He taught me how one's life experiences could be accessible in a purely natural way, a reservoir to approaching a role.

Interlochen exposed me to avant-garde plays and more abstract theater. We wrote solo performances, one-person shows of ten minutes. These were supposed to be personal, theatricalized, dramatized expressions of some part of each student's life. I wrote a play about a lonely janitor who wants nothing more than a pretty girl, and we saw that through this waltz he does with a mop. As I saw the other pieces, I finally understood. Jack got up and did this whole thing about medications—as a juvenile test subject for anti-depressants on high doses of things like Prozac. He had this wonderful line, "I often wonder if taking this many drugs will replace my actual childhood memories with white picket fences?" An Israeli student was coming up for her two years of national service and was frightened by that. Another wanted to sell tickets in advance to his own funeral— he didn't want it to be depressing but rather a carnival with fireworks and a Ferris wheel. I saw that theater could be wildly expressive, and personal, which could be fascinating if it didn't get indulgent—it could be therapeutic for anxieties and fears.

Jim Edmondson talks about acting being a balance between believing and sharing. There are actors who believe it 100 percent, but if you don't believe it as an audience member, it isn't being shared with you. Then there are actors who share everything with you, acting their subtext to the nth degree, but you don't believe it because they don't. Sometimes being able to experience things on some personal level, relishing life, its silliness, its challenges, its awkwardness and its celebration—being able to enjoy existing in every corner of it can allow one to access the belief part of it. If you have a modicum of performance capability, you hope you can exercise the sharing part.

Finishing high school at Interlochen, I became myopically focused on theater training, not interested in a liberal arts education and hoping to go to a theater conservatory. Interlochen had that built into its education. If you were a visual artist, you wanted to go to Cooper Union; a bassoonist, or a dancer, Juilliard; an actor, either Juilliard or Carnegie Mellon. Interlochen opened those doors. There was precedent.

I was so dumb. My mom and I looked at Princeton, Harvard, Carnegie Mellon, Juilliard, and Yale, which I might have gotten into because of family. I loved Princeton and its theater program, but it was like having a gorgeous Porsche that I'd never be able to drive. I applied to Juilliard, where the audition went well but the callback did not go great; and my Carnegie audition—Tony McKay in acting and Don Wadsworth in voice and text, both liked my work. I didn't hear from them for a long time, so I called them. "Did you not get the packet? We have a place for you." A mailing mix-up! It was a huge relief, and I was pleased to go there because it had a reputation for training people in a traditional way.

Their focus was about pushing people commercially. At the time, I thought that option would work along with skills in classical theater. The longer I was there, the more I thought about what I wanted to do professionally. It would be ideal to recreate my favorite experiences so far in a professional setting. How could I continue to do that? I brainstormed and made that list—it boiled down to *company*, the experiences that had felt like an acting company, a group of people creating theater in a collaborative way.

Carnegie gave me a huge background in training things in the classic sense—those tools were perfectly applicable to theater. Things that influenced me that I continue to utilize: I approach everything through text analysis—how text can be physicalized and vocalized. How we analyzed text in college is not different from how I do it now. Don Wadsworth taught us that you look at a particular speech in Shakespeare for clues. They might be musical, rhythmic, or about breathing.

We'd look at blank verse, then iambic pentameter, then prose. How much of the character's dialogue is cast in each of these styles? Regularly, or more irregularly? What does the irregularity signal? Is it that the character is having a more scattered moment? Are there too many thoughts contained in a single line? Is he thinking more quickly—or even more slowly? Is he in love with the way he is speaking, so he keeps everything very regular and well-paced? Are the sentences ending in the middle of a verse line or at the ending of a verse line? Where does the thought end? Does it end where the punctuation is, or does it end even further down the line?

An example would be someone like Romeo, who speaks in a very regular meter: "But soft, what light through yonder window breaks? / It is the east and Juliet is the sun. / Arise fair sun, and kill the envious moon, / Who is already sick and pale with grief / That thou, her maid were far more fair than she." The stressed and unstressed things fall exactly where they should, in a classical sense.

So, too, with the images—you have antithesis, opposing images, in the sun and the moon. Or "Be not her maid, since she is envious, / Her vestal livery is but sick and green, / And none but fools do wear it, cast it off" and so on. Then, "Two of the fairest stars in all the heaven, / Having some business, do entreat her eyes / To twinkle in their spheres till they return." The language in describing Juliet is so lyrical. Is Romeo in love with his own lyricism? Just now letting loose? The way I thought about it is that he cannot stop himself because of this tumbling, cascading effect of new love.

The Carnegie training allowed me to see that there is a kind of math in Shakespeare's verse and that things add up, in the way things add up in Mozart's musical writing. Things are set up to *pay off*. They reach a conclusion. That is intentional. All of the rhetorical tools employed, like *antithesis*, help set up the main idea and then offer an antithetical idea. Highlighting these devices of language is useful in allowing the character to navigate his own rhetoric. That, in turn, helps the audience to understand the oppositions as well. In *Midsummer Night's Dream*, there is "hot ice and wondrous strange snow," where Theseus is mocking someone else's previous line. He hears Bottom's poor use of the device and then invents his own bad example. In Shakespeare in particular, the characters invent their own language issues, their own rhetorical devices. For example, when you have a slew of repeated consonants, you get the sense that characters are trying to hammer a certain point home. Sometimes they celebrate that gift of invention; sometimes they are just using it as a tool.

There was a revival of rhetoric in the great speeches of Western history with Churchill, Martin Luther King, Kennedy, Reagan to a certain extent. We don't analyze leaders' speeches like we used to. In Shakespeare, since the Renaissance was all about resurrecting classical form, there was a certain gushing celebration of rhetoric. It's the actor's job to discover that. It's not just the playwright creating literary effect—it's the character actually using it for a visceral, active, functional intention. Those tools of language are a means to an active end. I love looking for it and mining it.

I was just thinking of the tennis ball speech in *Henry V:* "We are glad the Dauphin is so pleasant with us. / His present and your pains we thank you for." The "P" sounds act as a dissection of Montjoy and his tennis balls. "When we have matched our rackets to these balls, / We will in France, by God's grace, play a set / Shall strike his father's crown into the hazard." Hal sets up a metaphorical tennis court of the battle he will guide in France, juxtaposing the tennis court with his monarchial court.

The crown on his head, or the physical crown of his head, will be knocked into the hazard. He serves up language and it is hit back to him. It's so spectacular. There is also the sound of the word "mock," which is the noise a tennis ball make makes when it hits the court.

I love the way Shakespeare uses similar images in different forms. Take the sonnet, "Rough winds do shake the darling buds of May"—he also uses a similar image in *Taming of the Shrew*, "Confound thy fame as whirlwinds shake fair buds." *Whirlwind* is a trochee and has a whole new rhythm to it, and the total effect on the line is tremendous. There are great examples in *Richard III* as well, because there is so much manipulation between characters. Richard's language is being used to one end: to ultimately orchestrate a situation, sometimes in a nasty way.

The biggest influence was Don Wadsworth, the voice and text person at Carnegie. He was very good at moving something from the brain to the muscle. I still utilize everything that he taught, all of that analysis of the text in a rhetorical way. With respect to Shakespeare, of course, the two most important teachers have been him and Scott Kaiser. It was a natural progression one to another, and they both have major analytical skills.

The *King Lear* in 2013 was so good—very difficult language in that play, but we didn't worry about whether it was American speech. What came out of Mike Winters' mouth was owned and natural. Mike has such ease with language that we, the audience, are at ease with it. We spend a lot of time trying to figure out how to do Shakespeare in America, because we don't want to sound British, yet if we sound too regional or too colloquial, that can sometimes be jarring for an audience. So, how do we solve this? It doesn't matter how you sound or what your dialect is, in my opinion. It needs to sound as if you have ownership over the language and you are strong enough to be relaxed with it—with those two qualities, it doesn't matter if you are from England or from Georgia. The audience will buy into it.

I started working at OSF right after I graduated from college. I knew that I wanted to work in a place like this, although I didn't know it existed. I met an actor who was with the company and talked about it, so I auditioned in May of my senior year in college with no real expectations. I got cast in three radically different shows with three different directors—a classical American comedy in Kaufman and Ferber's *The Royal Family;* a new experimental take on a classical text with Sophocles and Freud in *Oedipus Complex*, adapted by Frank Galati; and a classical play, Jimmy Edmondson's *King Lear*, played by Ken Albers. It was a wonderful way to start my career, with new sets of actors with differing approaches, and dramaturgically speaking, a great cross section of theater, defining Libby Appel's tenure at OSF.

In 2005, I was in Shaw's *The Philanderer*, then in Hannah Cowley's *Belle's Stratagem*, two rarely produced plays. The first is early Shaw, very whimsical, very *not* like *Man and Superman*—there is a levity to it, big ideas and so funny. *Belle's Stratagem*, which I loved, is a great script, so effervescent and celebratory and unlike other bitter-edged, late Restoration dramas. In two years, five different styles of theater, and the opportunity to get used to all three different performance spaces!

In 2006, I played two teenagers, one in *Up* (I shaved, so it was believable) and one in *Diary of Anne Frank*. I finished the year with *King John*, which had some great moments, and it is an interesting play. Whenever people say subtext does not exist, I say that's bullshit and point them to that scene between Hubert and King John, who speaks first:

KING JOHN: Death.
    HUBERT: My lord?
        KING JOHN: A grave.
            HUBERT: He shall not live.
                KING JOHN: Enough.

During the casting weekend for *Romeo*, I was visiting my father in Lake Tahoe, in a place where there was bad cell phone reception. Libby had called to make the offer, but the phone never rang, and there was no message. I immediately thought I was not cast for the role. When I left the cove later on, there were twelve messages on my phone. One from Libby and the rest from friends calling to ask if I was cast for Romeo. Clearly I was. I called Chris and said, "Are you playing Juliet?" And she was.

Both Romeo and Juliet are brilliant young kids, able to construct their own poetry, totally aware of doing that. It's not just Shakespeare at work—it's them. That was something that I really wanted to explore because that ultimately led to their tragedy. They are so in tune with the sensations they have, they could describe the love they felt, and they each knew they had met their match intellectually and emotionally. They literally finish each others' ideas and sentences. Look at the shared sonnet in "Palm to palm is holy palmer's kiss" and "Let lips do as hands do," created together.

Very few other characters can meet Romeo's level of intelligence. Benvolio cannot meet him at the beginning of the play, because Romeo is on another planet. He has his flaws, but I wanted to explore someone that fiercely intelligent. Those types of people get so frustrated when others do not measure up to their standards.

I don't go for those versions of the play where people say, "Well, he was in love with Rosaline yesterday and now he's in love with Juliet—he'll probably move on to someone else in a couple of years." In fact, he thinks he's in love with Rosaline because he thinks he is supposed to be. *Then* he meets somebody that measures up, and they challenge each other, they argue, they parry, it's Benedick and Beatrice stuff. Not as witty, but as complementary. I'd like to say the play was all good, a mirror of me and my wife, because Juliet is like Chris—although I don't think I've met my intellectual match in Chris because I am so outmatched. She is very bright—even named Albright—it's almost annoying. I mean, I'm smart, but she was the salutatorian. I *salute* the salutatorian.

I loved playing Puck in *A Midsummer Night's Dream*, and I thought it was interesting in that it was so far from our preconception of a traditional production. All that physical activity on that very structural steel and edgy set. If the play is done in a traditional way, it can miss the other messages, which are sensual and sexual and naughty. The late eighteenth and early nineteenth century traditions of *Dream* were locked into a romanticized version of Shakespeare because the Romantic lens in poetry was then the dominant perspective for art forms, but that vision ignored the sexual elements of the play—in the twentieth century, we were reinterpreting many of the classical texts through a Freudian perspective. I don't know what is dominant now. Our version was exciting, even though I did not know at first what director Mark Rucker had in mind.

I wanted to play Puck because he is a dirty boy, he has sex jokes, he spans all four worlds of the play, and he gets things wrong because he wants to get things wrong. When we got into rehearsals, Mark said I want you to think about David Bowie and Iggy Pop and some of the other icons in Pop Culture who are modern day Pucks. So I spent a lot of time watching those people on YouTube. The idea charmed me and made me happy because it had to be so physical and there was leaping and climbing. The costume was spandex pants and platform boots all laced up, a fishnet shirt, and a lot of makeup, a very glam Bowie-like world. I love it when the show takes me outside of my comfort zone and lets me build a new skill set. The concept so matched the play. In the first scene, where the fairy asks Puck who he is, the answer is an image of love—"I am that merry wanderer of the night." He is like a rock star who never sleeps, and his mischief is very wicked. The other fairies are in awe of him, so that was something fun to come up with.

One of the most bizarre experiences I've had onstage was in *Taming of the Shrew* where I played Tranio, this rival wooer to Bianca, in a production that had a Coney Island carnival-like setting. My job in the scene was to convince Brent Hinkley to disguise himself as my father as I courted her. Brent and I have worked together a lot—I was Chico to his Harpo, and we've often been in the comedy trenches together.

There is a moment where I hand him a corn dog (it was a good bit) to distract him, and I suddenly realized that this delicacy was completely inedible. Some crew member forgot, or maybe the backstage microwave broke down, but it was frozen solid, and my every instinct screamed, "DON'T hand it to him." Yet the reflex of having done the show seventy times kicked in, and I extended it. Brent grabbed it and thought he was about to bite into a warm and juicy corndog. He sounded his barbaric chomp, and I watched his face transition from stagey confidence to an accusing look of betrayal. For some reason I'll never understand—maybe I thought it would calm me down— I reached over and grabbed it out of his hand and took a bite. It got lodged in my throat and I actually started to choke. The audience began to thoroughly enjoy this and clearly smelled blood. I pointed to my throat. I summoned a fellow actor, and she proceeded to give me the Heimlich maneuver, no joke! Turns out, Mr. Heimlich knew his maneuvers, and the corn dog shard finally dislodged. I sensed someone in the audience pulling out a cell phone, about to announce my misdemeanor. So I held up my arms and spoke Shakespeare's very famous addition to *The Spanish Tragedy*, "Please, if I could just get out the plot!" Mercifully, amid the laughter, the band started playing and Brent and I ran off the stage.

Notwithstanding this memorable event, I have to say that *Equivocation* was the most intense rehearsal process I've ever done, in terms of collaboration. The playwright Bill Cain was in the room and demanding 100 percent every day. The only way in his mind that he could discover flaws in his text was if we were performing everything at high intensity during every second of every rehearsal. Only when we were rising to the occasion while using his language could he see the flaws in the structure. If ever we took it easy one day, he wouldn't see what needed fixing in his work—instead, he'd see what needed fixing in our performance. There were six of us, three hours of playing time, dense language, lots of switching of characters (doubling and tripling of roles), costume changes, physical *work*. It was demanding intellectually and exhausting at times.

Cain altered text significantly, speeches were cut, scenes were completely rewritten, whole new ideas evolved, some things were cut and added back in, some of the conspirator scenes completely altered, totally changing the structure. For example, in the original draft, a character named Tom Wintour was hanged and drawn and quartered, and his corpse was onstage during intermission. We changed that early on and made it more interesting.

We would get acting notes from both director and playwright. Sometimes those would be contradictory, or I'd get emails from Bill Cain at night. Like what if the character of Sharpe had a cocaine addiction—come into rehearsal with that tomorrow. I was often angry during the rehearsal process. I had this tiny bag of cornstarch in my pocket—I was mad at him yet I was doing what he asked. Finally, I took the pack of it out and threw it at him. He said, "You hate me, don't you." I said, "70 percent of me hates you, but 30 percent of me realizes it was a good idea."

It was a challenging time. King James I loved playing. The script said he had a Scottish brogue. I was obsessed with the idea that he was smarter than people thought he was but also that he loved conflict. There had to be somebody who was annoyingly more powerful than Robert Cecil in the play and who could actually bait him. Piss him off—humiliate him—because

Cecil thrived on being feared. The only one who could laugh in his face was the King, who thought of Cecil as his beagle. That became enormously fun because Jonathan Haugen (who played Cecil) is a terrifying person. So to *act* as if you were someone who was not afraid of him—that served the story. That was fun.

I find that our director, Bill Rauch, is very strong when he is working on new plays, and it was a fantastic experience because of him. He knows what is necessary. My favorite work of his has been new plays. I think about *All the Way, Equivocation, By the Waters of Babylon, Handler*—all very interesting productions. It is exciting to see such power and strength coming from these new works. He's very different in how he works with actors on a new play from what he does with us on a Shakespeare play, especially in the way he communicates with us, a different approach with each.

Before *Henry V* began, Chris and I had this idea to go to England and retrace Henry's route as much as we could do it and knew of it. My brother-in-law is a dealer in rare books in London, so we could meet up with family as well. We got to touch, with bare hands, a Caxton *History of the World*, books from the late fifteenth and early sixteenth centuries, and to see the techniques employed in making them. So our journey blended well. I'd like every trip I do to be that focused, specifically to learn.

We decided to follow his whole journey from youth to kingship, and the trip was done in a roundabout way, seeing places he would have seen. Highlights were going to Shropshire to the Shrewsbury battlefield. There is a town just north of Shrewsbury called Battlefield—with Battlefield Farm and Battlefield Church, which was built on what they thought was the center of the actual battleground. Under that is a mass grave of the soldiers who died, where Henry IV, Hal's father, fought the Percy family's army. The Archbishop of York was the mediator. The two sides negotiated first and then decided that their plans wouldn't work out, so they went to battle instead. Hal was wounded with an arrow. The church, erected seven years later, had descriptions of what is known about the actual skirmish.

At Shrewsbury, they had a replica of the tool that was used to extract the arrow from Hal's left cheek. Really fascinating. This wound was briefly touched on in *Henry IV, Part One*, where Hal claims, "It's just a 'shallow scratch.'" It is rarely featured in productions. Historically, it was gruesome, and the only extant portrait of him is from the right profile. Then when you are standing there, reading about how long it took to remove the arrow with this medieval but sophisticated instrument! Shakespeare references the wound again when he talks about stripping sleeves and showing scars in *Henry V.* The wounds from war we carry with us, both physical and mental, have such an impact on the way we deal with trauma. Henry knew firsthand what the physical cost of war was. I thought it would be interesting to use the wound in all three plays for those reasons.

So, the trip to the battlefield revealed this horrible tool, where you squeezed the handle at one end to activate the claws at the other end. They dislodged the arrow from his face with this over a period of two weeks by inserting a shunt around the arrow, enlarging the wound, and then pulling out the arrow and then the shaft. It was gruesome. Given the surgery of the day, the inventor of the tool was a genius. He extracted the arrow, then used a gauze soaked in honey and herbs as a disinfectant, because that was the biggest concern. You can hold the tool in that museum, and see how it works. The doctor's notes still exist, describing every day of the process in vivid detail.

Also there was a crude manikin-like dummy that had a bodkin-tipped arrow in its face, just below the cheekbone. During the battle of Shrewsbury, Hal had been mounted on his horse and at some point, must have lifted up his visor to wipe off sweat or to get a view of the field. That thin-tipped arrow could find its way through chinks in armor or even through chain mail.

There were snipers nearby, perhaps up in trees, with incredible short-to-medium range accuracy, who would be thrilled to *take out* Henry, the Prince of Wales, which would give the Percys and the Mortimers a much stronger claim to the throne.

There are also his lines with Katherine, "...If thou canst love a fellow of this temper, Kate, whose face is not worth sunburning, that never looks in his glass for love of any thing he sees there..." I felt we should think about that comment both literally and figuratively. He's talking about vanity, that he is not one of these vain Frenchmen and that he's got this mark—no tan is going to fix this ugliness. The whole business with the scar was a link through all three of the *Henry IV* and *Henry V* plays. I got the bloody wound at the end of *Henry IV, Part One.* In *Henry IV, Part Two,* it looked recently stitched up, then in *Henry V,* the stitches had been removed and it had healed slightly. I did my own makeup.

Going back to Agincourt Battlefield was remarkable, even though it was a non-event for the French because they won it back years later. There is a farm there you can wander through. Also a museum that is dedicated to a description of the battle with interesting artifacts—spurs from boots worn by the combatants, rusted swords, saddles. There is an exhibit where you can feel how much strength it took to pull the one-hundred-pound weight of the bowstring, the archery equipment used by the English in the battle. You feel how challenging that was, and you imagine doing it ten times a minute in the heat of battle.

I believe in ghosts, so in going to those battlefields, you think of thousands of soldiers' bodies resting in the earth. Shakespeare's language is so rich in its visual landscape, that when you have something specific and clear to relate to, the rest falls into place when you speak the lines. When I acted Hal talking to the soldiers in the St. Crispin's Day speech, the images I'd seen, smelled, and touched were concrete and not a general wash of poetry.

We drove to Monmouth in Wales and saw the ruins of Monmouth Castle, where he, Henry of Monmouth, was likely born. Next, we went to Southampton, disembarking at Le Havre, which is just north of where Henry arrived. We then went to Harfleur and saw some interesting artifacts of his siege of Harfleur. We crossed the Somme further inland and made our way up to Calais.

Researching the role can only go so far, but I do find that there are certain lines, for example, one to Montjoy regarding ransoming himself, "I pray thee bear my former answer back. / Bid them achieve me and then sell my bones. / Good God! Why should they mock poor fellows thus? . . . / A many of our bodies shall no doubt / Find native graves, upon the which, I trust, / Shall witness live in brass of this day's work . . ." Just to think what he means by "native graves"—he knows from experience what that pit would look like—a giant trench, and they will all be laid there with one single headstone with a brass emblem. He's probably dumped a few bodies himself. To be able to say defiantly to Montjoy as he continues, "And those that leave their valiant bones in France, / Dying like men, though buried in your dunghills, / They shall be famed . . ." He calculates the costs and delivers that brag with a half line of verse, "*They shall be famed.*" This is so muscular and proud on Henry's part. For someone like me to have seen what he's talking about, to know as much as I possibly can know—I've walked on their bodies—I'm thinking about a farmer's field covered in manure—all of this makes the context of that line so much more particular for me.

I did not know when I was cast as Hal in *Henry IV, Part One* that I would be doing all three plays in the trilogy. So I didn't think in terms of one giant journey when I began, nor do I think of these plays as one giant journey, but rather as building very individual pieces. I had three directors: Penny Metropulos directed *Henry IV, Part One*, Lisa Peterson directed *Henry IV, Part Two*, and Joe Haj directed *Henry V.* The language for Hal is so similar in the three plays, with a definite evolution into the third in the sequence, so that I could rely on that were I to be cast for all three shows. The number of times Hal uses "honor" in all three is huge. Also, Hal doesn't use the royal "We" that often—mostly with Montjoy and with the French. By the time he has reached the leadership of the army in *Henry V,* his "We" mostly means himself and the soldiers. The scene at night with his men before the battle made that change in him. These language patterns helped me navigate through all the plays and allowed fresh points of view from three talented directors with unique sensibilities and three different looks for each play.

What I liked was that there were seven actors who were shared among all three productions—Chris Albright-Tufts, Howie Seago, Richard Howard, Brent Hinkley, Jeff King, and Daisuke Tsuji and myself. There was this sense of continuity in terms of the acting company with the audiences recognizing these people carrying through the three seasons of the *Henry IV/V* plays—doubling roles, e.g., Howie Seago playing Poins and then playing Exeter, and so on. If it had been three different groups of actors in three different shows, I would not be excited about that. Nor would I as an audience member, either. The seven shared actors guaranteed a similar presentation. We weren't trying to force it into a trilogy.

When I begin a project of this size, I want to know all my lines. I make a note of every plot and the story of every scene. I circle any words I don't know and define them. I paraphrase passages that are dense in the margins, in a very contemporary and specific way, so that I understand the sense of them. The line to Falstaff, "Fall to thy prayers" might be "Get out of my face," for example, because the latter has such a clear intention and application. The audience can then understand what I am doing if they cannot understand what I am saying. I also make notes of any ideas that I am curious about trying. I do all that before rehearsals start. That way, I am more relaxed in the rehearsal hall because I know the events and I know the words I am saying, and then I can make more important discoveries, like kinetic reactions to what other people in the room are doing. If another actor has an intention behind his lines, knowing how the scene plays out helps me be in a more responsive state to move the scene in the direction that it needs to go. It becomes a more kinetic and less static process.

Everybody has his or her own way of working. How actors do their work is very individual, but it's all directed toward putting on a good show. Nonetheless, if I'm holding my script in rehearsal, I get frustrated. Other people hold script well and manage to be effective. In the cast of sixteen in *Henry V*, maybe three or so were memorized from the start. I really enjoy that point where people are confident with what they are saying because the whole point of acting is communicating, and I do that better without a script in my hand. It's not like you are "instantly good," but you can access more tools and choices earlier on in the process. It's never about *how much* rehearsal you have, it's about how it's *used*. If you find the focus from an early point forward, it flowers into a better production.

I also watched whatever movies about the plays I could get my hands on. There is Kenneth Branagh's production and also Laurence Olivier's of *Henry V*, and an old TV version from the 1960s with Robert Hardy and Judi Dench, the last of an era of doing Shakespeare in that fashion. Hardy has a moment where he is using a kind of medieval French phrasebook in the scene with Katherine—she giggles at his French, and he tosses it behind him. There is the BBC production, which suffers from being done too fast and the budget of time and money too small. Then there is one with Michael Pennington's company, which is quite good. I prefer to watch several versions, because you realize how many choices can be made. If you carry your choices through and connect them, you are okay. You also sometimes get to watch an actor who is very respected make bad choices on occasion, which gives me confidence to do that same thing.

I love Kenneth Branagh's version so much, but there are little things that make me crazy—the music over the great speeches seems so much less honest, and I didn't like the way he handled the speech before Harfleur, where he breathes a sigh of relief when the governor of the city agreed to stop fighting, like he's saying, "Oh thank god, he bought our ruse." I prefer it when Henry says that speech and means it, then he and the audience have to face the fact that this guy they think is a hero actually threatened women being raped and babies killed. They need to really question Henry. The whole point of the play is what leaders have to do, in war or in any difficult time—to make horrible, challenging, brutal decisions.

The genius of Shakespeare in this *Henry* trilogy is showing that what is happening on the large scale of history is also happening in the microcosm of other scenes in the play. We see a major set-up with kings and queens that the fools and servants carry out on a different level. That happens in *Henry IV, Part One,* where the world of joy and celebration is on the verge of collapse. I liked *Henry IV, Part One* because there is such a great spirit of camaraderie in the context of a world on the verge of imploding, the calm within the storm. While they are celebrating and carousing, the country is disintegrating politically. Also, Hal's relationship with his father is rupturing in a similar way. This is the ultimate coming of age for him. A lot is at stake.

I enjoyed the relationships with Falstaff and Poins, as well as Hal's awareness of where he is in the tavern—and then his single-minded determination to ignore that. He has that great speech at the beginning, which can go so many different ways: "I know you all, and will awhile uphold / The unyok'd humor of your idleness. / Yet herein will I imitate the sun, / Who doth permit the base contagious clouds / To smother up his beauty from the world, / That when he please again to be himself, / Being wanted, he may be more wonder'd at / By breaking through the foul and ugly mists / Of vapors that did seem to strangle him." Then my favorite line in Shakespeare: "If all the year were playing holidays, / To sport would be as tedious to work; / But when they seldom come, they wished-for come, / And nothing pleaseth but rare accidents." He is *so* aware of the dilemma of it all, and how much his father hates his behavior, and yet he is determined to continue along this path. He says people are going to like me so much more when I come out from behind this cloud, which is a youthful way to justify himself. Sometimes that speech is interpreted as if we are seeing the beginning of his genius as a kind of Machiavellian prince, although I wasn't interested in that idea. Whereas if he says, "I am in control of this," yet he doesn't realize how much of it is *out* of his control, it's more interesting.

There is also the evolution of Hal's relationship to Falstaff in *Henry IV, Part One,* which is fairly complete. This person that has been a father to him suddenly grows distant from him. We did two things in *Part One*: first was that the "peppered soldiers" that Falstaff speaks of—in the process of his drafting them, he has actually accepted money from people to *not fight*, and then he's enlisted lowlifes and farmers because he had to come up with warm bodies, whom he sees as cannon fodder. We had those characters visually represented onstage, so Hal sees them all and witnesses these sorry draftees and then questions Falstaff about that. Therein is the beginning of their separation.

Then Penny Metropulos had me visible onstage for the first part of Falstaff's "Honor is a mere scutcheon" speech, where he cynically and bitterly rails about it. Well, there is nothing more important to Hal than honor, and even when he is drinking and carousing, if someone accuses him of being dishonorable, he reacts. So Hal witnesses Falstaff's cynicism. At the end, when Falstaff carries Hotspur's body off the stage, announcing that he personally has killed him, Hal *sees* that, and it enrages him even more.

Henry IV, Part Two is occasionally considered a lesser play than the others in the trilogy, but there is incredible language in it. It develops more the changing relationship between father and son, Henry IV and Hal, destined to be Henry V. There is the scene where he thinks his father is dead, and he leaves the prostrate body to mourn. When he returns, his father is alive, and Hal has to plead with him not to be angry. Every ounce of the challenges of their relationship is brought forward in that scene in the speeches between the two of them. They love each other so deeply, but the relationship is so complicated and filled with so much tension because Henry IV carries the stain of his usurpation of the crown from Richard II—he is trying to be kingly and a good decider, yet Hal dreads that a kind of curse might get passed on to his own reign.

When two people are both terrified and yet love each other so much, it creates a tense relationship. What I like about the scene is the floodgate of tears, a beautiful and sensitive and dear scene. Also, the time Hal walks into the Boar's Head Tavern and realizes how different it is from what it used to be. The tavern scene in *Henry IV, Part Two* is a shadow of the same scene in *Henry IV, Part One*—significantly shorter, and in both scenes, someone tells Hal he has to leave because his father is looking for him. In *Henry IV, Part One*, Hal brushes it off. In *Henry IV, Part Two*, he leaves and doesn't even say goodbye to Falstaff. We see so many differences between the two plays. It all culminates in that incredible scene where Hal declares, "I know thee not, old man. Fall to thy prayers." Such a pressure cooker, difficult, and necessary for Hal, and the anger for Falstaff emerges there.

When I began *Henry V*, it was a big deal, and my reaction to that was to go into a hyper-focused state of thinking about what needed to be done. I was cast in July and didn't begin rehearsals until April, so that gave me an enormous amount of time. I decided to pace myself and really work hard on it the rest of the summer, and then take a break from it in January and February, and a total furlough during March and April. I organized it so I could completely absorb it, and then I'd have time for discoveries in rehearsals.

There are great speeches in *Henry IV, Part One,* including the "I know you all" and the "I'm gonna shape up" speeches. In *Henry IV, Part Two*, he has that "I swear I thought you were dead" speech to his father. Then he has his speech, heard by all but delivered directly to Falstaff, "I know thee not, old man." We know Hal has a great facility for rhetoric, to be able to speak truthfully and honestly—to communicate what he's feeling in a clear and decisive way. Sometimes characters in Shakespeare are not good at telling us what is going on inside of them. In King Henry's case, the words match his inner life. "Once more unto the breach" can tell you what is going on. He loves language, but he is not *in love* with it. It's not, "If music be the food of love, play on, / Give me excess of it." He's capable, knows himself, and knows how to use words for persuasive effect.

He has also fantastic orations: "Once more unto the breach," the St. Crispin's Day speech, for example. For the last forty years in acting practice, actors have worked to make those famous pieces *not* seem like formal speeches onstage, but more like dialogue to urge his soldiers to action with persuasive tactics that spur them on—appeals to their manliness, to their sense of history and family. We pushed those speeches actively, using Stanislavskian principles to find the goal and the objective of the scene, applying that to Shakespeare with language at once poetic and still clarifying the story. Joe Haj experimented with having the soldiers come in utterly exhausted, make them think about how close they are to victory yet so far, and allow Hal to lift them up in the scene, soldier by soldier, into battle-ready stance with his words.

There's the other great oration before the Governor at the gates of the city of Harfleur. That one is easier to make active because it's a series of questions he's asking the official directly.

Then it's all those threats—we're going to destroy you, rape your women, kill your men, put your babies on pikes, *if you do not end this now*. Ultimatums. This King Henry has learned from the costs of his campaign, and he acknowledges the building blocks toward his leadership, even though the siege of Harfleur took longer than expected.

I love the checkpoints marked by the entrances of Montjoy, the messenger from the French camp, and how the two relate with such honesty. There is the tennis ball scene where Montjoy was present, and also the visit right after the execution of Bardolph where Montjoy suggests that the young king set a ransom upon himself rather than do battle, and the most telling one, after battle at Agincourt when Montjoy says to him, "The day is yours." Hal has brazenly said "we will kill you" to Montjoy at the opening of the play; later that he will not be ransomed; and he also tells the messenger that a lot of us will die today but with honor. Then he breaks down in front of him when he is told his own English soldiers won the battle and hears how many French have died. Montjoy is his witness throughout these important passages in the young king's life.

The relationship is so moving because Montjoy reflects back to Henry who he is. The other French are idiots, overconfident, foppish, structurally designed by the playwright to be the antithesis of the English soldiers. Montjoy has pleaded with his own countrymen, telling them, "You underestimate this British king. He's much more confident and smarter than you imagine."

Along the way, Henry has acknowledged Montjoy's integrity: "What is thy name? I know thy quality." Henry is straightforward with this man and at the same time makes his own men proud to fight. He will not seek a battle, but he will not shun it, either. This shocks Montjoy, given the odds of the imminent battle. Henry makes the point that we're weakened, but whatever men we have left are better than yours. He loves these fellows and he will never desert them. We're trying to get to Calais, and if you stop us, we will fight to the death. The herald acknowledges Hal's decisions along the way, calling him "Your highness" and "King Harry." There is this respect on both sides.

In the St. Crispin's Day speech, Henry is truthful and honest about the situation, yet helps his men to muster the strength to go forward. One fellow is so ragtag, another's weapon is broken, another is practically dead, yet Henry claims they are ten times stronger than the wimpy French army. At first, as they listen, they wonder—"Whattaya mean?" By the end of the oration, they react and shout and are shored up and ready to go into the fray roaring. This is leadership, and Henry has created it with "a little touch of Harry in the night," visiting the men beforehand, arguing about their situation, defending himself (even though they don't know they are speaking with the King), and all along instilling in them courage, faith, and total trust. His is a truly amazing facility with language, to be uplifting and humble in the same breath.

Every leader, from the beginning of time, successful or not, could be considered a war criminal for choices he made, by any measure of the definition. Lincoln basically approved the burning of the South, Roosevelt interned the Japanese during World War II, and Truman approved the plans to kill millions of Japanese with the A-Bomb. Obama sent the drones, killing American citizens without trial. There is a fine line between the actions of Henry V and Richard III. That Richard was more conscious about it is the difference. It is more about how they make these decisions, how they confront them, and then how they live with them. They grow gray very quickly, and they die very young.

I don't think of Shakespearean heroes in a contemporary sense but more in a classic sense, protagonists on a journey that affects them greatly. Like Oedipus as a hero, Creon as a hero. I don't think of it as too different from playing Tranio or any other character. The question is, "What is the toll the environment takes on this person from the beginning to the end?" In a role like Henry V, the journey is larger because the character is onstage for a longer time. There is so much opportunity for variety and physical expression. Playing a fun small role is like a rollercoaster ride; doing a larger one is two hours and forty minutes of a ride that doesn't stop and just keeps going.

Hamlet has "To be, or not to be," and he has his antic disposition, but he also has, at the end of the play, a huge swordfight to achieve with Laertes. He has his musings on death with the Gravedigger, but he also has the play-within-the-play. There is an ocean of various challenges in these large characters, and to be able to jump in and swim it, to try and navigate it and yet indulge in it, is so much fun. It's something I don't ever want to stop doing.

If there is one thing I've learned about being an actor, it is that you can be very happy making no money. It's better in some sense because you don't have to be burdened by *things*. When you have nothing, you want nothing. To be kind of free of want is the goal in life. If my son can be doing what he wants to do, then he will be happy. The role of father, the biggest thing, is on-the-job training—no amount of experience can train you for this duty. It requires 100 percent devotion when he is awake, and it is fun to see him develop. It's immediate, it's total, and it's hugely rewarding. He might be fussy, but there is that intense moment when he smiles and you just lose it all. It's as though you were dropped into the ocean, like "Find your way, find your way to land."